So You Think You're An Ethical Solicitor

The New SRA Standards And Regulations In Action

Mena Ruparel

Richard Burnham

Published April 2020

ISBN 978-1-9164315-7-7

Text © Mena Ruparel & Richard Burnham

Typography © Bath Publishing

All rights reserved. No part of this publication may be reproduced in any material form (including photocopying or storing it in any medium by electronic means and whether or not transiently or incidentally to some other use of this publication) without the written permission of the copyright holder except in accordance with the provisions of the Copyright, Designs and Patents Act 1988 or under the terms of a licence issued by the Copyright Licensing Agency (www.cla.co.uk). Applications for the copyright owner's written permission to reproduce any part of this publication should be addressed to the publisher.

Mena Ruparel and Richard Burnham assert their rights as set out in ss77 and 78 of the Copyright Designs and Patents Act 1988 to be identified as the authors of this work wherever it is published commercially and whenever any adaptation of this work is published or produced including any sound recordings or films made of or based upon this work.

The information presented in this work is accurate and current as at April 2020 to the best knowledge of the authors. The authors and the publisher, however, make no guarantee as to, and assume no responsibility for, the correctness or sufficiency of such information or recommendation. The contents of this book are not intended as legal advice and should not be treated as such.

Bath Publishing Limited
27 Charmouth Road
Bath
BA1 3LJ
Tel: 01225 577810

email: info@bathpublishing.co.uk

www.bathpublishing.co.uk

Bath Publishing is a company registered in England: 5209173

Registered Office: As above

Contents

Introduction from the authors   xi

Chapter 1: Introduction   1

1.1	The current system	2
1.2	The dawn of the SRA Standards and Regulations	4
1.3	Using this book	5
1.4	What is ethics about?	10
1.5	Is it important?	11
1.6	The relationship between law and ethics	12
1.7	Different ethics for different people	14
1.8	How does "the ethical solicitor" practise?	16
1.9	Ethics v Compliance	17
1.10	Conclusion	18

Chapter 2: Rules-based ethics and regulation   19

2.1	Introduction	19
2.2	Ethics and regulation	19
2.3	Criminal behaviour, ethics and regulation	21
2.4	Outcomes-Focused Regulation (OFR)	24
2.5	A Question of Trust	26
2.6	Practical operation of OFR under the new Standards and Regulations	27
2.7	Ethical decision making in the OFR arena	28
2.8	The Principles	30
2.9	Are ethics and compliance the same?	32
2.10	Considering the Principles and ethical decision-making	32
2.11	Comparing ethics in financial services to the legal profession	42
2.12	Anti-Money Laundering (AML) and Data Protection	43
2.13	Summary	46

Chapter 3: Behaving ethically   47

3.1	Do the right thing, for the right reason	47
3.2	Differences in approach	47
3.3	Ethically minimalist solicitor's motivators	48
3.4	Types of behaviour generally recognised as being unethical	51
3.5	Duty to self-report	52
3.6	Personal virtues	55

3.7	The ethical solicitor	58
3.8	Identify the ethical dilemma	63
3.9	Do <u>you</u> need to learn how to behave ethically?	66
3.10	What is the right thing?	68
3.11	Do the right thing	70
3.12	The firm's influence on the "ethical solicitor"	72
3.13	Is unethical behaviour deeply embedded at your firm?	76
3.14	Do the right thing - for the right reason	81
3.15	Conclusion	82

Chapter 4: The client is king   87

4.1	Introduction	87
4.2	Regulatory issues	88
4.3	The Codes of Conduct – the client's perspective	94
4.4	Corporate/Commercial lawyers	104

Chapter 5: You v The rest of the world   107

5.1	Introduction	107
5.2	The client above all else?	108
5.3	The Principles	109
5.4	Undertakings	115
5.5	Undertakings - Policies, systems and controls	119
5.6	Do solicitors have an obligation to correct mistakes of third parties?	120
5.7	Mistakes where the other side is represented by a solicitor	123
5.8	Mistakes where the other side is a litigant in person	124
5.9	The proper administration of oaths, affirmations or declarations	129
5.10	Fees paid by third parties	130
5.11	Contacting the opposing party or their McKenzie Friend	132
5.12	Stealing clients	134
5.13	An abuse of your position in personal circumstances	139
5.14	Conclusion	140

Chapter 6: Complaints and negligence   141

6.1	Complaints	141
6.2	What is a complaint?	141
6.3	The framework for dealing with complaints	142
6.4	Main areas for client complaints	144
6.5	Client service	145

6.6	Pricing information	148
6.7	Making an informed decision	151
6.8	Complaints handling	151
6.9	Negligence	153
6.10	What are the principles of negligence?	154
6.11	Does the solicitor owe a duty of care?	155
6.12	Duty of care to third parties	155
6.13	Breach of duty of due care and skill	155
6.14	Is a solicitor culpable for lack of knowledge of the law?	156
6.15	Complex cases and specialist lawyers	156
6.16	Can a lawyer be found negligent for not following the instructions of a client?	157
6.17	Can a solicitor be found negligent for advice given in relation to settlements?	158
6.18	Following the advice of a barrister	158
6.19	Wasted costs orders	158
6.20	Summary	160

Chapter 7: Ethics and social media — 161

7.1	Introduction	161
7.2	The rise of social media and online interactions	162
7.3	Social media in the legal profession	162
7.4	The benefits of social media	164
7.5	The risks of social media	166
7.6	The ethics of social media	167
7.7	Why do ethics apply to social media?	167
7.8	The importance of social media in the legal profession	170
7.9	Understanding different social media platforms	171
7.10	Facebook	172
7.11	Twitter	175
7.12	LinkedIn	177
7.13	YouTube	178
7.14	WhatsApp	179
7.15	Online forums and social media sites which encourage discussion	179
7.16	Blogs	182
7.17	Websites	182
7.18	Other social media platforms	183
7.19	Engaging with social media ethically	184
7.20	Understanding privacy settings	186
7.21	Being your client's friend	187
7.22	Social media policies	190

How To Be An Ethical Solicitor

7.23	Dealing with social media backlash	193
7.24	Recent developments and the future	194
7.25	Conclusion	196

Chapter 8: Litigation v ADR 199

8.1	Is litigation ethical?	199
8.2	The purpose of litigation	200
8.3	The adversarial system	201
8.4	The ethics of the cost rules of the CPR	202
8.5	Ethical considerations of the CPR	203
8.6	The ethics of ADR?	206
8.7	ADR processes with no third party	212
8.8	Negotiation	212
8.9	Mediation	217
8.10	Arbitration	221
8.11	Collaborative law	224
8.12	Executive tribunal	225
8.13	Conciliation	225
8.14	Early Neutral Evaluation	226
8.15	Expert determinations	226
8.16	Adjudication/Dispute Review Board	226
8.17	Conclusion	227

Chapter 9: Ethics and the rise of lawtech 231

9.1	Introduction	231
9.2	Ethics and lawtech	232
9.3	So, what is lawtech?	234
9.4	Blockchain, AI, big data, what?	236
9.5	Lawtech in the wild	241
9.6	The benefits of lawtech	245
9.7	The pitfalls of lawtech	246
9.8	Engaging with lawtech ethically	251
9.9	The future	256
9.10	Conclusion	260

Chapter 10: Conclusion 263

Appendix 265

   SRA Principles 265

   SRA Code of Conduct for Solicitors, RELs and RFLs 265

   SRA Code of Conduct for Firms 274

   SRA Assessment of Character and Suitability Rules 280

References 281

Index 283

Introduction from the authors

Mena Ruparel

The aim of this book is to spark debate amongst practitioners about the role of ethics in the legal profession. The SRA's new Standards and Regulations are less rules-based and more flexible to allow practitioners to make their own decisions where issues arise. There is no doubt that the question of ethics will continue to be an area of increasing attention in the coming years.

As my idea for the book developed, I started to look at the reported cases of misconduct in the legal press. The more I read I noticed that some of the reported cases were ethical breaches that the solicitor may not have committed if they had thought about the ethical/regulatory issues. It seemed to me that solicitors needed a practical approach to the issue of ethics rather than a classical education in theories of ethics. This book does not purport to provide all the answers, but it does provide a simple methodology which should assist if an ethical dilemma presents itself.

I originally invited Richard (who was my paralegal many years ago) to write this book with me as I valued his perspective as a (then) trainee solicitor; not yet "in the system" but with a keen eye on the ethical dilemmas we face in practice. When I initially interviewed Richard I set him a number of ethical dilemmas and was impressed by his reasoning. I value his contributions to the book especially with respect to his approach to the ethics of social media.

We both owe Conor Dempsey a vote of thanks (and a drink) for contributing his wisdom regarding the issues faced by practitioners in the financial services world - he contributed greatly to the chapter on rules-based ethics.

I also owe thanks to a number of solicitors and others who were able to assist in reading, suggesting and general support as I tried to put together my thoughts on this subject; my long-time friend Sarah Newens, Roopa Ahluwalia (partner at BDB Pitmans), Lewis Hulatt, Emily Miller (Marshall Walker), The LinkedIn Tutors and Barbara Spoor (MD at CRCS Legal) with her wisdom on the Complaints chapter. I have been truly annoying my colleagues at Chapman Pieri Solicitors with regular ethical dilemma questions (and spot tests) - thanks to them all for their patience. Needless to say, my family have been hugely supportive throughout this process, especially my husband Conor who has read many versions of the book.

Richard Burnham

The 2020 edition of this book has been an interesting one to write, for in the short two years since the publication of its predecessor the profession has been through an exciting set of developments. We have a shiny new rule book from the SRA dubbed the '*SRA Standards and Regulations*' – a title even duller than the '*code of conduct*'. We have a myriad of new cases from the Solicitor's Disciplinary Tribunal dealing with social media, junior lawyers and a debate over what 'dishonesty' actually means. A new would be companion in legal technology called '*lawtech*' has also joined us and brings with it a whole new set of ethical conundrums. As the SRA's regulation becomes increasingly focused on ethics, appreciating the relationship between the law, ethics and regulation is more crucial than ever, and an understanding of their interaction is key from an early stage in every solicitor's career.

To expand briefly on Mena's introduction of the book above, we hope that you will use the book in conjunction with the SRA Standards and Regulations as a "guidebook" to reflect upon moments where you may be faced with an ethical conundrum and the answer is not immediately clear. In light of a great deal of what I shall diplomatically describe as 'disappointing' decisions regarding the careers of junior solicitors (and as one myself) I hope that this book will be of particular assistance to all junior members of the legal profession as they wade through the difficult juggling process that comes with being a junior in the legal profession.

Thanks go to my family, and in particular Margaret Burnham, for always instilling a strong understanding of right and wrong in me; James Burnham for being my partner in (ethical) crime in the lawtech world and Zoe Barnes for the support during the writing process of this book; our publishers David and Helen for the constant support (and answering any stupid questions posed by me). Finally I would like to thank my various supervising solicitors during my legal career (their teachings will no doubt have contributed to this book) namely Victoria Copeman, Daniel Martinez and of course Mena Ruparel who has for the best part of seven years been ensuring that I do the right thing in my career, for the right reason.

April 2020

Chapter 1: Introduction

"Compliance which compromises ethical standards is not helpful at all. We need to properly define and protect the brand of solicitor. The maintenance of professional standards and ethical behaviour is essential."

Andrew Caplen, Former President of The Law Society

The view of The Law Society and that of the Solicitor's Regulation Authority is that there needs to be a greater focus by solicitors on the issues of ethics and ethical behaviour. Compliance with rules is not the same thing as behaving ethically, which is something we will return to time and time again in this book. Compliance with a set of rules in isolation to ethical conduct can compromise ethical standards and produce anti-ethical results.

In the first edition of this book we referred to the fact that the SRA intended to drastically cut the previous Handbook to a mere 10-20 pages, which of course have recently been introduced as the newly published Standards and Regulations. This new horizon of ethical and regulatory requirements is designed to focus on high professional standards and public protection whilst removing the '*red tape*' of the previous handbook and placing more trust in the professional judgement of solicitors. Not only is this smaller set of rules more orientated on an individual's ethical thought process, but it also accounts for the different structures of a solicitor's practice, both in-house and even for those solicitors not working for regulated firms (effectively giving birth to the '*freelance solicitor*').

As was discussed in the first edition of this book the new SRA regime places a much greater understanding and focus on ethics and self-regulation in the context of fewer rules. Given the shorter nature of the handbook, there is undoubtedly a greater expectation that solicitors will be left to make their own decisions about all issues that arise in practice.

The aim of this book is to take a practical look at the ethical challenges that practitioners face in the 21st Century. Whilst we have drawn the material for this book from a variety of sources it is not our intention to set out a detailed history of ethics starting with Socrates and ending with the SRA. This book should be used as a guide to ethical behaviour and more importantly to ethical thinking and decision-making.

We have used abbreviations for a number of common phrases:

New Rules:

- **Standards and Regulations (STaRs)**: 2019 SRA Standards and Regulations

- **Code of Conduct for Solicitors (CCS)**: 2019 Code of Conduct for Solicitors, RELs and RFLs

- **Code of Conduct for Firms (CCF)**: 2019 Code of Conduct for Solicitors' Firms

- **Suitability Rules**: SRA Assessment of Character and Suitability Rules

Terms:

- **COFA**: Compliance Officer for Finance and Administration

- **COLP**: Compliance Officer for Legal Practice

- **LeO**: Legal Ombudsman

- **REL:** Registered European Lawyer

- **RFL:** Registered Foreign Lawyer

- **SDT**: Solicitors' Disciplinary Tribunal

- **SRA**: Solicitors' Regulation Authority

Historic Rules (where applicable):

2011 Principles: Mandatory Principles (2011 SRA Code of Conduct)

2011 Outcomes: 2011 Outcomes (2011 SRA Code of Conduct)

2011 Code of Conduct: 2011 SRA Code of Conduct

IB: Indicative Behaviours (2011 SRA Code of Conduct)

1.1 The current system

Chapter 2 sets out the issues professions face when they are subjected to "rules-based regulation". Solicitors have moved away from rules-based regulation to "Outcomes-Focused Regulation" (OFR) which was originally introduced in 2007. The 2019 introduction of the Standards and Regulations reduced the Code of Conduct and Handbook from its previous tome of pages is in keeping with OFR.

Fig 1: The interaction between rules and ethics under the SRA Standards and Regulations

Lawyers work for the benefit of the public, rather than themselves, their clients, or the courts, and for that reason they must adhere to the seven pervasive ethical Principles and must act:

(1) In a way that upholds the constitutional principle of the rule of law, and the proper administration of justice;

(2) In a way that upholds public trust and confidence in the solicitors' profession and in legal services provided by authorised persons;

(3) With independence;

(4) With honesty;

(5) With integrity;

(6) In a way that encourages equality, diversity and inclusion;

(7) In the best interests of each client.

1.2 The dawn of the SRA Standards and Regulations

In practice the Standards and Regulations are not a substantial change from the previous Code of Conduct. The objectives remain outcome focused, with the logic being that having fewer rules will mean more flexibility for individuals but also increased focus on ethical behaviour and outcomes.

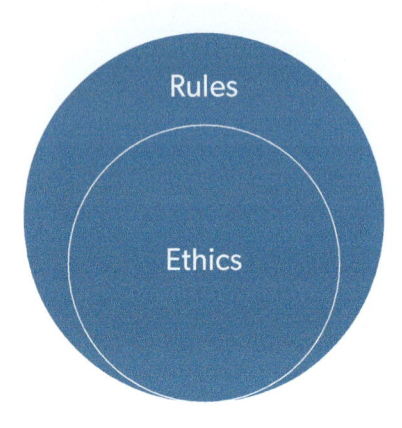

Fig 2: The interaction between rules and ethics under Outcomes-Focused Regulation

Before the announcement of the Standards and Regulations, the SRA opened a consultation called "A Question of Trust" which looked at the ethical behaviour of solicitors and the expectations of the public. The results of the Professional Standards Survey analyses the results of that survey. The survey results make for interesting reading. In conclusion, the authors indicate that:

> *"the SRA have already indicated that they do not see this survey as determining their response to the seriousness of problems; but that it is aimed to help stimulate debate."*

The Standards and Regulations became effective on 25 November 2019 and can be effectively split into four distinct areas:

(1) The Principles;

(2) The Code of Conduct for Solicitors (including those in-house) and the Code of Conduct for Firms;

(3) Regulations surrounding the authorisation of individuals;

(4) The transparency rules.

We reference the SRA, the Solicitors Disciplinary Tribunal and some light comparison to the regulatory framework of different professions. The status that professionals hold in society means that there are value standards that will be common to them all. The comparison between financial services and legal services is interesting as the professions approach regulation quite differently.

We have taken the decision not to name the individuals whose cases we use as examples from the SDT judgments. Whilst we can all learn from the mistakes of others, we did not feel that it was necessary at all to put those individuals through any further anguish. Should you wish to read the judgments in full they are on the SDT website (very few judgments are anonymised by the SDT).

Finally, we recognise that solicitors practise in different fields, for a myriad of firms and each solicitor has their own way to practise law. Whilst this book deals primarily with solicitors in private practice, it also touches on the challenges of in-house practice. In-house practice brings unique challenges and many more solicitors are now opting to work in-house than ever before. We also draw distinctions between the different challenges of working in a "city" corporate culture and High Street practice. The Standards and Regulations have narrowed the differences between the obligations on solicitors who work in-house and those in private practice and aim to ensure that a solicitor's personal obligations are clear cut.

1.3 Using this book

This book can be used as a guidebook for practice or for use where you may require a little help. It can also be used as a way of enhancing your awareness of regulation and ethics in general, and allow you to identify an ethical thought process to respond to a particular situation. We aim to instil ethical thinking in arenas that might challenge you, such as the ethical way in which to use your social media accounts, both personally and as part of your business.

What this book does not do is tell you how you *should* react to a situation in order to achieve regulatory and ethical objectives. The answer to an ethical/regulatory situation is rarely ever clear-cut. The best way to react will depend upon a multitude of subjective considerations. There is never one answer to every ethical dilemma. There is usually a range of options that vary from the best to the worst choices.

Subjective variables that may affect a solicitor's decision-making are;

- the size of the firm;
- the individual solicitor;
- the client.

We aim to instil a method of thinking in an ethical manner, which should result in an ethical outcome.

Ethical scenarios

Throughout this book you will find scenario boxes, many of which have been developed from the decisions of the SDT or real-life practice scenarios. The purpose of these scenario boxes is to encourage you to think about how you would respond to a situation which may not seem, on the face of it, to be an ethical situation. This is what you can expect to see; many of the examples we use are SDT cases.

> **Scenario: An outline of a problem faced by a practitioner**
>
> **SRA rules**: A consideration of the Principles, the Code of Conduct for Solicitors, RELs and RFLs and any applicable regulatory considerations. Chapter 2 on "Rules-based ethics and regulation" might be a good place to start for those unfamiliar with the current regulatory framework.
>
> **Potential ethical issues/professional breaches**: What are the ethical issues that need to be addressed? Being aware of these means that it is more likely that you will take them into account in the decision-making process.
>
> **Possible approaches**: what are the options? These will be suggested approaches, which could all be within the regulatory framework but have different ethical approaches.
>
> **Suggested reaction/steps to avoid**: things to look out for or avoid.

Would it make a difference if...?: subtle changes to the initial scenario that aims to test whether your answer would change depending on additional factors.

For example, consider the entirely fictional and hypothetical example below:

Scenario: Fraudulent practice

Facts

An LLB graduate has a lifelong dream of becoming a solicitor. Unfortunately upon completing their undergraduate degree they are unable to fund the costs of the LPC. Drastically, they hack into the computer of an LPC provider university and enter their name into their database as a student who successfully completed the LPC. A year later they secure a period of recognised training with a High Street firm that solely provides legal aid and qualify upon completion. They practise fraudulently for the next 5 years, demonstrating the same competency as a solicitor and help many vulnerable clients in the process.

Eventually an SRA review of the LPC provider casts suspicion, and eventually the false entry is located. The false solicitor is arrested and spends 2 years in prison for their deception. Upon leaving prison they successfully complete the LPC, having now amassed the funds, and make an application for their character and suitability to be assessed with a view to being legitimised. Imagine you are an SRA admissions officer reviewing this file. Would you approve the application?

SRA Rules: Principles/Suitability Rules

Principles

You act:

Principle 1: in a way that upholds the constitutional principle of the rule of law, and the proper administration of justice;

Principle 2: in a way that upholds public trust and confidence in the solicitors' profession and in legal services provided by authorised persons;

Principle 4: with honesty;

Principle 5: with integrity.

Suitability Rules

Rule 2.1 (Assessment): When considering your character and suitability, the SRA will take into account the overriding need to: (a) protect the public and the public interest; and; (b) maintain public trust and confidence in the solicitors' profession and in legal services provided by authorised persons.

Rule 3.1 (Criminal Conduct): The SRA will consider criminal conduct when assessing your character and suitability.

Rule 4.1 (Other conduct and behaviour): Table 2 sets out non-exhaustive examples of the types of conduct or behaviour that the SRA will take into account when assessing your character and suitability.

[Only the first row of Table 2 is applicable in this scenario].

Type of behaviour	Examples
Integrity and independence	You have behaved in a way: • which is dishonest; • which is violent; • which is threatening or harassing; • where there is evidence of discrimination towards others. You have misused your position to obtain pecuniary advantage. You have misused your position of trust in relation to vulnerable people. The SRA has evidence reflecting on the honesty and integrity of a person you are related to, affiliated with, or act together with where the SRA has reason to believe that the person may have an influence over the way in which you will exercise your authorised role.

Potential ethical issues/professional breaches

Here is an example of where the regulatory and legal situation may conflict with your ethical views. It may be in this scenario that you sympathise with the graduate's situation - maybe you yourself had difficulty funding LPC costs, or you know someone who did. Perhaps you have children experiencing the difficulty of self-funding the LPC. You may be of the opinion that, however wrong the graduate's actions were, they were not acting maliciously by acting as they did.

You may also consider that the graduate demonstrated skills at the same competency as a solicitor and also helped many vulnerable clients who may otherwise not have received the same service. However, the legal and regulatory situation is that the graduate has misled the public, and acted dishonestly and fraudulently for, ultimately, personal gain. In doing so they have also breached many of the Principles, the Code of Conduct for Solicitors and the Suitability Rules.

Possible approaches

In this scenario it is extremely unlikely that there are any exceptional circumstances which justify approving the graduate's character and suitability application. The candidate has also demonstrated that they have breached various Principles and sections of the Code of Conduct for Solicitors. You should reject the application.

Suggested reaction/steps to avoid

Ultimately you should be aware that there will be occasions where ethically you may believe that it is correct to do one thing, where the regulatory and legal position is extremely clear that you should not.

Would it make a difference if...?

The graduate did not act of their own volition. A partner in a firm who knew the graduate could not afford the fees suggested that they hack into the LPC provider's database and that, after doing so, they would give them a period of recognised training to allow them to qualify.

1.4 What is ethics about?

When you ask a lawyer about ethics, the response you get will vary from eye rolling, yawning, or rising guilt. Rarely will solicitors passionately debate legal ethical issues.

Whilst ethics is a subject matter that is difficult to define simply, we all make non-legal ethical choices every day. A simple walk through your day will show that many areas of life are governed by ethical thinking and decision-making. From the time that you wake up you start to make choices. Will your morning coffee be made at home using Fairtrade coffee beans or purchased on the way to the office? If the coffee is purchased at a coffee shop do you choose to go to one that pays few taxes in this jurisdiction or the local independent tax-paying coffee shop? Do you wear ethical clothing? Will you choose your lunch based on how far it has travelled to get to your plate? If it is organic food is this really better for the planet and your health and do you care whether the farmer who provided the eggs gets a fair deal from the supermarket selling them to you? Do you travel on foot, cycle, take a bus or drive? Is this choice based on convenience or because you are trying to minimise your carbon footprint? Do you take ethical holidays or live in a carbon neutral home?

Introduction

Most people are likely to have a view on these everyday choices and the way you make your choices may seem to be an automatic response. If you don't think any of those issues factor into your life it doesn't mean that you are living an "unethical" lifestyle - you are probably an "ethical minimalist". However, the more you think about your everyday choices the more likely you will realise that you have made decisions based on an internal belief system. This may or may not have a religious element, which we do not propose to discuss in this book.

By analogy, the legal and ethical choices you make will also be influenced by your internal belief system. The main difference is that these choices are regularly monitored, controlled and manipulated by third parties in and out of the work environment. This means that sometimes solicitors get caught out doing things that they may not be proud of (hence the references to SDT cases).

"*The ethical solicitor*" keeps their own ethical/moral belief system in the forefront of their mind and learns to cross check those against the regulatory framework. This means that there is often more than one response to an issue.

1.5 Is it important?

> *"The SRA Principles comprise the fundamental tenets of ethical behaviour that we expect all those that we regulate to uphold.*[1]*"*

The requirement for solicitors to behave ethically in modern legal practice is more relevant than ever. We do not intend to go into microscopic detail about the different types of ethical rules that exist but look at the term in a holistic way - this is not a textbook about ethical theories.

Solicitors are still held in fairly high regard, although that has decreased in recent years according to a YouGov poll. Lawyers are less trusted than teachers and doctors but at least we prevail over accountants and bankers. As professionals we hold a position of trust and we must work to hold that position. In this book we draw parallels between different professions as it is of interest to note what they offer the teaching, learning and development of professional ethics, compared with our regulatory bodies.

Focused ethics training for qualified solicitors is not mandatory which surprises other professionals and the public as there is an expectation that this

---

[1] *2019 SRA Standards and Regulations.*

would be the case. During the undergraduate law course ethics is not generally taught as a separate subject and so ethics education generally occurs for those who choose to take the Legal Practice Course (LPC). It is worthwhile noting that this may not be the route many solicitors have taken into the profession. If a solicitor qualified before the introduction of the LPC or took a different route into the profession (the CILEx route for example) they may have been exposed to little or no ethics training. That doesn't mean that they behave unethically.

Contrast this with the focus placed on ethics by the Chartered Institute for Securities & Investment (CISI). 20% of their regulatory unit exam is dedicated to the matter of ethics and integrity. In 2013 CISI became the first professional body to require UK candidates to pass an integrity test. They aim to instil the public with confidence that its members act with integrity at all times, "placing integrity before, and above, profitability." Whether there is any link between more robust ethics in its members by passing this exam we can't say, but putting ethics training at the forefront of their training is a statement of commitment to values that the public expect.

Although solicitors may be aware of their general ethical obligations, they may defer to their firm's nominated compliance officer when faced with an ethical/regulatory conundrum. Many solicitors fail to recognise that daily issues have any ethical element to them and that the problem is theirs to solve. This is why ethical thinking is important as it teaches solicitors to identify issues with an ethical element and think through the best response.

It might be obvious, but if the courts and justice system lack an ethical foundation then society will lose respect for the system of rules. These rules help to provide a civilised order upon which society is dependent. If solicitors, as officers of the court, are seen to act unethically this will undermine the principle of justice. Members of society will take their lead from legal professionals and see little point in following the rules.

1.6 The relationship between law and ethics

Law is the body of rules determined and enforced by the state. The point of legal rules is to channel undesirable behaviour in society and offer remedies to people negatively affected by the breaches of these rules. The law usually forbids an action, whilst imposing a consequence in the event that that action is taken. Murdering someone is against the law - if a person commits murder then there is a penalty imposed.

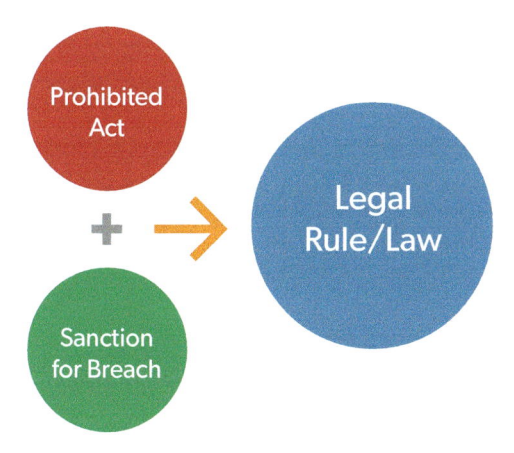

Fig 3: How legal rules are made: prohibit an act and make the breach of it punishable by way of a sanction and you have law

Asking whether something is ethical, and whether that same thing is legal, are two entirely different questions. Ethical principles in law are being increasingly mixed up with regulatory outcomes. The relationship between legal and ethical doctrines is more significant than ever. This is perhaps a natural progression, as both law and ethics serve to moderate our behaviour; law accomplishes this through the threat of sanction.

Ethics utilise other triggers as a control mechanism; when a person performs an act which is considered to be unethical they tend to feel uneasy. If a vegetarian eats a bacon sandwich they will feel that they have done something wrong, even though it is not illegal to eat meat. Their internal moral code has been broken and they will recognise that even if no one sees them doing it. Leading an ethical, moral life means that one monitors oneself - there is no real threat of sanction to moderate our behaviour.

(1) **Where ethical principles alone are best suited to address behaviour**; morality, but not law, will apply more often in the day to day interaction of society. Being rude and dishonest to others is not illegal, but it may be immoral and unethical. The desire to conform, good manners and good upbringing prevent people from being rude and dishonest.

(2) **Where legal rules are best suited to address behaviour**; there are actions that are illegal, but may not be seen to be unethical. The issue of assisted suicide may be a good example. Many believe that

allowing a person who is terminally ill the right to die is an ethical thing to do. Littering is illegal but may not be seen as unethical.

(3) **Where law and ethics should be deployed jointly**; consider for example theft. This is both illegal under s7 Theft Act 1987, but it is also considered highly unethical to deprive a person of their legally owned property.

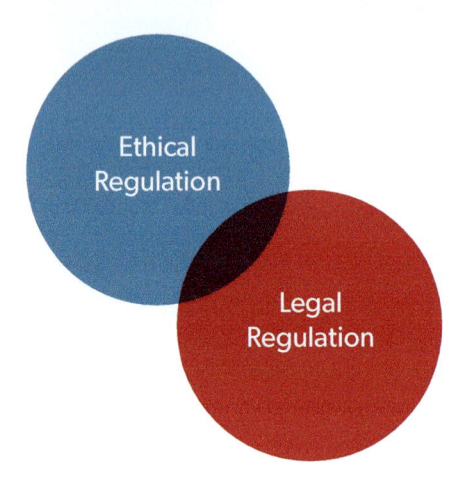

Fig 4: The overlap between ethics and law

Legal rules are considerably more specific than their ethical counterparts - it would be impossible to write down ethical rules as these are contextual and personal. For example, it is unethical to take sweets from a child. However, if the child is diabetic, taking their sweets might be doing them a favour depending on the child's blood sugar levels. It is very difficult to be prescriptive about ethical rules whilst legal rules could not be enforced unless they were written down.

1.7 Different ethics for different people

The question of ethics is a subjective concept. As a result of this the strength of an individual's moral convictions will differ from person to person, and range between a highly ethical person to someone who is unethical or immoral.

An ethical person will consider many ethical principles - in everyday life this person will probably be a vegan who lives in a carbon neutral home. They will only eat organic vegetables and will probably grow their own food. Their negative impact on the world will be minimal; whilst this might apply to a few people most of us cannot possibly live up to these standards.

In theory, we would hope that no solicitor would be amoral as it would be difficult to practise if one lacked any sense of right or wrong. If a person was naturally amoral they would need to be taught how to operate in a legal system that places great emphasis on ethics.

At the bottom of the ladder is an immoral person, who gives little thought to their ethical responsibility to the rest of the world. Solicitors should never be immoral as this would lead to regulatory challenges very quickly.

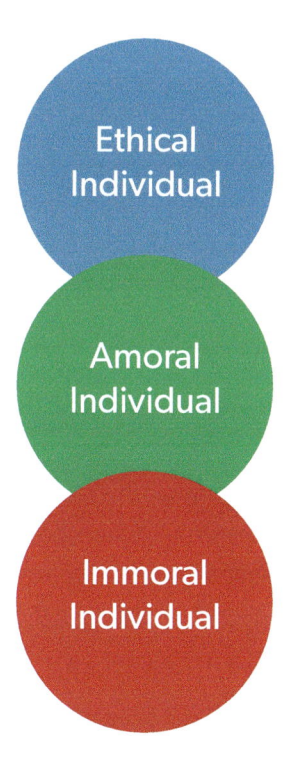

Fig 5: How ethical are you?

1.8 How does "the ethical solicitor" practise?

Whilst many solicitors advocate that ethical codes are merely in place to protect clients from the "bad apples" of the profession, most solicitors appreciate that they must discharge their duties as officers of the court in an ethical manner which goes above the ethical response which would be normally expected from a lay member of society. But why is this?

We will explore further, in Chapter 4, that a solicitor's ability to comprehend, or access the tools to comprehend, is crucial to a correctly functioning legal system. Simply put, individuals in society must be able to understand the law in order to avoid breaching it, or, where they are accused of breaching the law, to formulate a defence in order for justice to be seen to be fair. Solicitors therefore hold positions of privilege within society because of the valuable resource they possess; knowledge of the law. This position of privilege can be described as a monopoly which solicitors could, if they so desired, use to extort members of society who are unable to appreciate the complexity of the law without the assistance of legal counsel.

Ultimately the question of "who is an ethical solicitor" engages Principle 5 (the duty to act with integrity) and 4 (acting honestly) whilst also demonstrating a command of strong moral principles. If you think about it, this is an extremely onerous demand! What is considered to be dishonest and immoral is subjective, not easily defined and wide reaching.

The concept of the standardised "ethical solicitor" is discussed in significantly more detail in Chapter 3. However, an ethical solicitor will generally:

- know what the right thing to do is;
- act to do the right thing; and
- do so for the right reason.

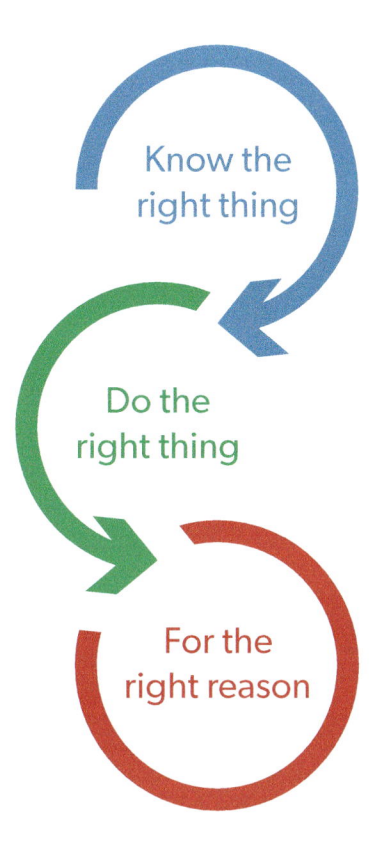

Fig 6: The motto for the ethical solicitor

The ethical solicitor will operate in life, both personally and professionally, with integrity. This is often referred to as "virtue ethics"; how to behave in a virtuous way all the time, not just limited to the practice of law. Virtue ethics is arguably the type of ethics that best applies to solicitors in a system that is increasingly moving away from rules-based ethics.

1.9 Ethics v Compliance

The following questions all operate independently of one another:

(1) Is what I'm doing complying with my regulatory obligations?

(2) Is what I'm doing illegal?

(3) Is what I'm doing unethical?

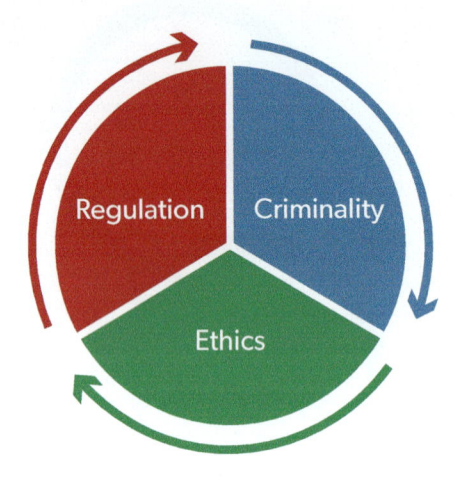

Fig 7: The interaction between behaving ethically, criminally and in a compliant manner

1.10 Conclusion

All lawyers have a general perception of what "acting ethically" actually is. However, after reading this brief introduction to the concept of ethics and its relationship with the law, you will begin to apply a methodology to approach ethical conundrums. Both concepts can operate as independent regulators of undesirable conduct in society, but it is often the case that both streams will intermingle; legal rules often mingle with ethical concepts and ethical concepts can directly influence the creation of the law.

We conclude that solicitors are subject to higher ethical obligations to society than lay people. Ethics for solicitors can therefore be seen as a hybrid of traditional ethical principles and regulatory requirements, and acting in this way can be said to be acting as an "ethical solicitor". However, as we will explore through this guidebook, how to be an "ethical solicitor" will be subject to various external variables which will fluctuate depending upon the situation at hand. This may make it seem like it is an almost impossible task to be an ethical solicitor. It is hoped that, through the assistance of this book, you will be able to anticipate when you are being faced with an ethical scenario and react appropriately in the circumstances.

Chapter 2: Rules-based ethics and regulation

2.1 Introduction

In this chapter, we explore the regulatory matters that every solicitor needs to be aware of. If you happen to be the COLP at your firm then you should already be aware of many of the matters we set out here. For other solicitors not lucky enough to be the COLP this information is very important, by way of background.

We see no need to set out the historic background regarding solicitors' regulation. However, most legal professionals will know that the Legal Services Act 2007 (LSA 2007) has been instrumental in changing regulation for lawyers. This change is ongoing and should be monitored by regulated firms and individual solicitors.

Occasionally in the case studies taken from reported cases we refer to the old rules and regulations but we have tried to keep this to an absolute minimum. Solicitors should know that in recent years there have been four sets of rules and codes that might be relevant. This includes the introduction of the new Standards and Regulations in November 2019.

Rules	Type of regulation
Solicitors Practice Rules 1990 (SPR 1990)	Rules-based
Solicitors Code of Conduct 2007 (SCC 2007)	Rules-based
SRA Code of Conduct 2011 (SRA Code 2011)	Outcomes-focused
November 2019: A new approach - New Standards and Regulations (STaRs) with Codes of Conduct for Solicitors and Firms	Outcomes-focused

2.2 Ethics and regulation

The interaction between ethics and regulation is a tricky one and best outlined as follows:

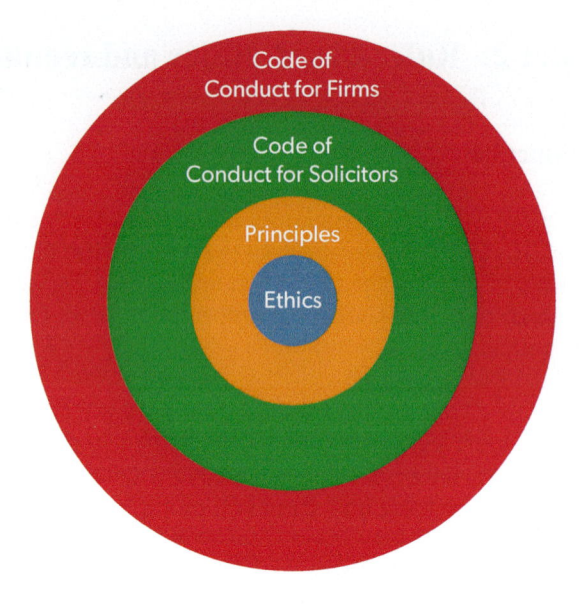

Fig 8: Interaction between ethics and regulation

It is easy to envisage a situation in which a solicitor could have a regulatory problem that has no obvious ethical dimension; however under the 2019 Standards and Regulations ethics are at the heart of the decision-making process. A straightforward conflict of interest might be an example of a case where the ethical element might not be too difficult to address and the rules lead to a clear response.

Scenario: Conflict of interest 1

You currently act for Mrs Patel in employment law matters. Her employer telephones and asks for an appointment. This is a classic conflict of interest issue and is dealt with in a straightforward application of the rules; there is no ethical dilemma at all. The Code of Conduct for Solicitors and the Code of Conduct for Firms are clear about this type of conflict; Paragraph 6.2 (it is not possible for the same firm to deal with employment matters for both the parties as their interests clearly conflict).

If the firm did decide to act for both clients the firm would be in breach of the Code of Conduct for Firms and the solicitors acting in the conflicted cases could also be in breach of the Code of Conduct for Solicitors. The obligations of the firm and the solicitors are the same and each could be in breach of the same rule. Whereas there would also be likely to be a contravention of the Principles, the rules are clear about the way in which firms and solicitors are required to behave.

In a less straightforward conflict matter, the same firm could act for different parties to the same transaction if they are competing for the same objective and they have given informed consent to allow the firm to act. In these cases the dilemma is to ensure that regulatory issues, such as consent and maintaining confidentiality, are properly observed and the "Chinese walls" built to prevent information leaking from one department to another remain robust. The firm would need to ensure when making a decision to accept clients in these situations that they have properly put systems in place to ensure they maintain their professional obligations to each client. Ultimately the firm must make an ethical decision based on the available evidence before it when the possibility of a conflict arises. In this type of transaction there is likely to be a high level of risk that solicitors need to be aware of. This type of transaction needs to be monitored closely throughout with the Principles in mind to ensure that the firm is able to act in the best interests of each client. This is fundamental to the solicitor/client relationship but needs to be monitored as the transaction progresses.

2.3 Criminal behaviour, ethics and regulation

The interaction between criminal behaviour, ethics and regulation is complicated but it is important to note that there is an overlap. An example of this would be in the event that a solicitor takes part in a fraud scheme. Although this seems unlikely, there are reported SDT cases of this happening.

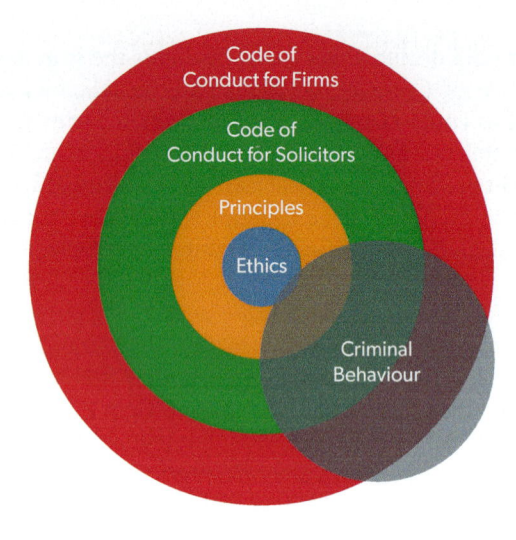

Fig 9: Interaction between regulation, ethics and criminal behaviours

Scenario: Conflict of interest 2

Facts

Solicitor R was involved in an elaborate tax evasion scheme to reduce his client's stamp duty land tax indebtedness to nil on numerous occasions. There were two SDLT "mitigation" schemes that he operated, the success of each which depended on the solicitor failing to disclose information to HMRC about related transactions. In addition, there were Capital Gains Tax "mitigation" schemes that he offered. He wrongly led clients to believe that these schemes had been sanctioned by HMRC when they had not.

Rules

This solicitor had numerous allegations raised against him; he was accused of breaching multiple rules of the Solicitors Code of Conduct, the Solicitors' Accounts Rules, of having conflicts of interest and failing to have a Money Laundering Reporting Officer to name but a few. 161 complaints about the firm had been made to the Legal Complaints Service at the time of the SDT hearing and payments to clients had been made.

Potential ethical issues/professional breaches

The solicitor in question, Mr R, informed the SRA when he was interviewed that he was aware of The Law Society guidelines on property fraud and that he wasn't aware of any instances when he had failed to follow the guidelines. When the SRA wrote to Mr R to ask for details of the schemes he failed to provide this information. The request was repeated, he wrote to the SRA and refused to provide the information to the regulator. He eventually provided some but not all of the information requested.

The Tribunal was satisfied that there had been allegations involving dishonesty against Mr R and this was proved to the higher standard of proof. Mr R was struck off; he offered no mitigation. He was ordered to pay £116,800 in costs to the SRA.

He was pursued by HMRC and criminal matters were brought against him.

Criminal matters

In 2013, he pleaded guilty to seven counts of fraud by false representation and he was sentenced to 2 years imprisonment for each count to run concurrently. These were suspended for two years.

In 2016 Mr R came before the Crown Court under Proceeds of Crime Act offences. He was found guilty and was ordered to pay back £800,000 of the estimated £2m he made from the tax evasion schemes. If he was unable to pay that sum within three months he faced a default jail sentence of up to five and a half months. HMRC said: *"The message is clear: rip off the taxpayer, and we will use the courts to empty your pockets."*

This is a classic example of a solicitor breaching Principles, rules and regulations whilst also being guilty of criminal acts. The regulatory breaches were dealt with first in this case, with criminal matters following a number of years thereafter.

Sometimes a criminal matter will be dealt with which then places on the solicitor an obligation to report. The obligation is to promptly report a criminal charge, conviction or caution to the SRA; Paragraph 7.6 of the Code of Conduct for Solicitors. The solicitor will find that a regulatory sanction will probably follow sometime after the self-report.

Ethical issues are central as there is dishonesty at the centre of any fraud. This is not the behaviour that the public expects to see associated with a solicitor; Principle 2 of the 2019 Standards and Regulations is engaged. A solicitor is expected to uphold the trust and confidence in the profession and legal services offered. This type of fraudulent behaviour is both unethical and criminal.

2.4 Outcomes-Focused Regulation (OFR)

"The more corrupt the state, the more numerous the laws" (Tacitus)

In October 2011, the SRA moved to an "outcomes-focused" system of regulation that moved away from the old "rules-based" approach. The new approach encompassed a high level outcomes-focused style of regulation (OFR). This also marks a shift away from rules-based ethics towards a more "behavioural ethics" style of governance. Your character, reasoning and behaviours are relied upon to self-govern to produce the 'right' outcomes rather than the expectation under the old Codes that you will follow a strict set of rules. The focus is therefore on results through reasoning and ethical decision making rather than adherence to written rules.

New Standards and Regulations (STaRs) – what does it mean?

This OFR system has now been somewhat streamlined under the new Standards and Regulations, which produces separate Codes of Conduct for solicitors and firms. The new system of regulation places increased emphasis on "the fundamental tenets of ethical behaviour" for individual solicitors whether in private practice or in-house. The reason for this is that, since 2011, the way that solicitors offer legal services has changed, with more solicitors practising inside organisations rather than in private practice than ever before. The former system of regulation didn't cater very specifically to those 'in-house' solicitors and so the two Codes were introduced to make it clear what the individual solicitor's obligations are and those that apply solely to firms.

The new Standards and Regulations refers to multiple sets of rules under one banner;

(1) The Principles, which apply to both solicitors and firms;

(2) The new Code of Conduct for Solicitors, which applies to solicitors whoever they work for;

(3) The new Code of Conduct for Firms, which applies to law firms;

(4) The enforcement strategy, which applies to solicitors and firms and underpins the rules;

(5) The new Accounts Rules, which only apply to firms.

The SRA has regularly produced a risk index in order to inform solicitors as to how the SRA views risk and how that can potentially affect firms. They will continue to do so under the new regime to highlight their approach to priority risks. That and their thematic reviews of areas of risk should be of interest to individual solicitors and firms and read in parallel with their enforcement strategy.

It can be seen that a strict adherence to a rules-based system of regulation/ethics can produce perverse "unfair" results for the consumer. The continuation of OFR is intended to ensure that the consumer is protected whether or not there is a specific rule devised for every eventuality or not. In fact, the SRA has repeatedly stated that it trusts the decisions made by solicitors and firms and sees no reason to heavily regulate decision making as it had done under the rules-based regulation system.

The enforcement strategy

The introduction to the SRA enforcement strategy document indicates that the SRA aims to "promote a culture where ethical values and behaviours are embedded". The SRA will enforce the new Principles and Codes of Conduct in a way to ensure that there is a focus on quality and client care and to protect consumers.

The emphasis is on the quality of outcomes for clients - solicitors must be seen to uphold the law and the proper administration of justice and look to the spirit of the Principles and rules. OFR is intended to be a simpler form of regulation and the SRA strives continuously to reduce the number of rules; as it has done with the introduction of the new Codes of Conduct. This in turn means that there is a new emphasis on ethics and on maintaining professional standards.

Ethics and Competence

Both the SRA and The Law Society have publicly increased their focus on ethics as part of the OFR regime and to maintain the brand of the solicitor. Although it can be difficult to teach professional standards, it is very important that solicitors understand that the commitment to OFR in the new Standards and Regulations requires a greater application and understanding of ethics.

This is of course anticipated by the introduction of the Statement of Solicitor Competence in March 2015 which replaced mandatory hours-based continuing professional development (CPD). Although there is no requirement to undertake a specific numbers of hours-based learning, solicitors are expected to maintain their competence over a number of categories.

The statement of competence requires that all solicitors are be able to;

(1) Recognise ethical issues and exercise effective judgement in addressing those issues;

(2) Understand and apply ethical concepts which govern their role and behaviour as a lawyer;

(3) Identify the relevant SRA principles and rules of professional conduct and follow them;

(4) Resist pressure to condone, ignore or commit unethical behaviour.

All solicitors are currently expected to maintain an appropriate level of competency in respect of ethical decision-making. Most solicitors make light of ethics training, claiming that they "know" how to be ethical solicitors and so eschew any formal training or discussion on the issues. It is unlikely that the SRA would accept that these solicitors don't need to demonstrate ethical competence, particularly after the introduction of the Standards and Regulations which has ethics at its core.

Whether or not you believe you are an ethical solicitor, evidencing it to the SRA is quite another matter. It is no different to President Donald Trump repeatedly saying; "Trust me, I'm like a smart person". Most of us would be looking for some evidence to support that claim. I hear solicitors repeatedly saying they 'know' how to be an ethical solicitor, they make this claim in the absence of any evidence in support. They may have avoided criminal or regulatory sanctions over a long career but that doesn't necessarily mean that they have an ethical decision making process in place.

2.5 A Question of Trust

In 2015/2016 the SRA launched its campaign, "A Question of Trust" which invited the profession and public to feed back their views of professional standards. SRA CEO, Paul Philip, said: *"This is a landmark campaign that has really engaged people. Regulation is part of the social contract between the profession and the public and it is important that we calibrate and validate what we do."*

The campaign involved live events with the public and a series of online ethics-based scenarios. The SRA indicated that the campaign secured 2,350 online survey responses in addition to which 3,000 people attended their events around England and Wales. The purpose of the campaign was said to be to develop a reference framework for SRA staff when making regulatory decisions. Both solicitors and the public took part in the campaign to assess the seriousness of offences. This is an important piece of work - the results have been published in part by the SRA in the publication of the solicitor's survey result; *Solicitors' Professional Standards* by Cristina Godinho (UCL) and Richard Moorhead (UCL), which is mentioned elsewhere in this book. The survey results and details of the campaign can be found at https://www.sra.org.uk/sra/how-we-work/reports/question-trust/.

The initial findings from the survey show that criminal activity, dishonesty and misuse of client money rank as the most serious offences with the public. However, solicitors don't rate the issue of their own competence as a serious issue whereas the public do. The public were more likely to rate these issues as being a serious matter whereas solicitors generally saw them as a matter of concern but deserving a lesser punishment.

The results of the survey were said to be inconclusive about the issues that arise in a solicitor's personal life and how or if they should affect their professional life.

Crispin Passmore said of the survey results:

> *"We are considering the findings and are using them to refine our approach to judging the seriousness of offences and what action we might take. We will publish that approach - grounded in the firm evidence of the views of the public and profession - so we can be transparent about our decision-making."*

2.6 Practical operation of OFR under the new Standards and Regulations

In order to assist solicitors to achieve their regulatory objectives, the SRA has now established a framework of 7 Principles, reduced from the previous 10 Principles under the previous Code of Conduct. These are considered

How To Be An Ethical Solicitor

to be "fundamental tenets of ethical behaviour". The Principles apply to firms, their managers and employees. Where Principles conflict with each other, those which safeguard the wider public interest take precedence over that of the individual client.

The Principles are supported by the new Codes of Conduct which are simple statements of the behaviour expected from solicitors and those regulated by the SRA. The Code of Conduct for Firms sets out the standards that firms are expected to provide for the "delivery of competent and ethical legal services to clients".

The broadly drawn Code of Conduct for Solicitors gives them freedom and flexibility to deliver a range of outcomes in any scenario; the solicitor can then decide which is the most suitable outcome in each case. The new Code applies equally to solicitors practicing in-house, in a High Street firm or at a magic circle firm in the city. This remedies a perceived defect in the previous Code of Conduct which didn't always allow for the different ways in which in-house solicitors practiced as compared to those in private practice.

The flexible nature of OFR doesn't really sit very well with many practitioners who have experienced many years of rules-based regulation. When the rules are black and white it is easy to draw the line and to be able to predict the regulator's actions. When the system relies on your personal interpretation of the best outcome, many solicitors feel as though they are being drawn into a trap which is bound to lead them to the door of the SDT.

The new enforcement strategy document should help to put solicitors' minds at ease regarding the intention behind enforcement, the aim of which is to protect clients. We do not propose to look at the enforcement strategy in any detail save where it is directly applicable to ethical decision making.

2.7 Ethical decision making in the OFR arena

When decisions about right or wrong/ethical or unethical/compliant or not compliant are in the hands of the regulated there is no real certainty of outcome. If your interpretation and application of the rules doesn't match that of the regulator then there could be serious consequences. Practitioners are uneasy about this type of regulation because it is unpredictable, or so they believe. The SRA believes that this unpredictability is better seen to be flexibility which is good for a diverse profession where risk is variable.

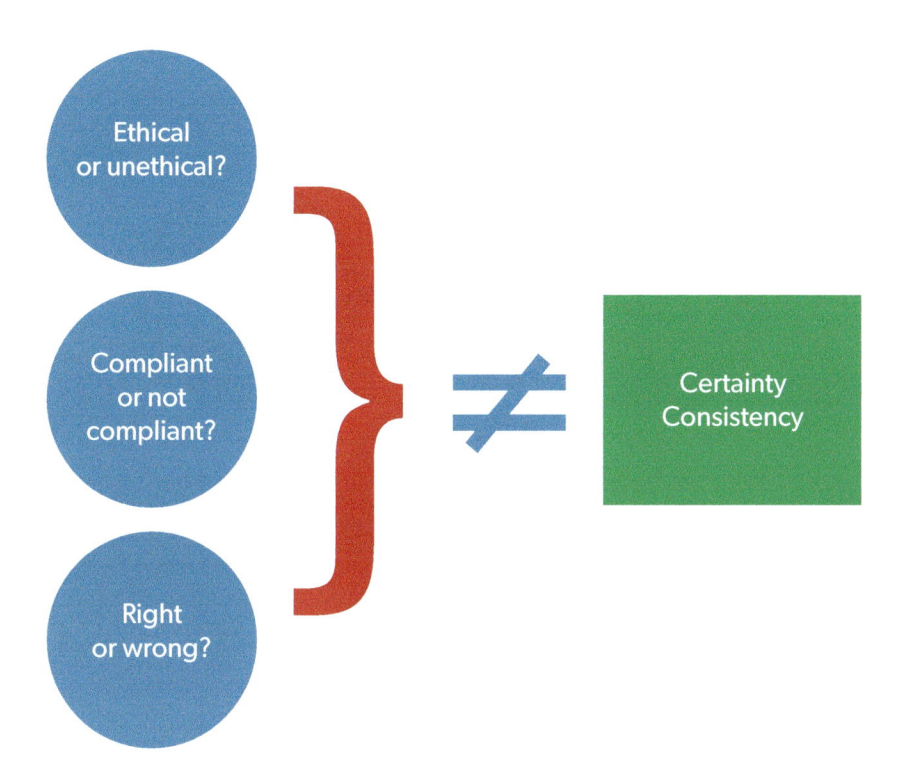

Fig 10: Is an action ethical, compliant or right? Each solicitor needs to be able to make their own decision but this leads to flexibility and not consistency

How To Be An Ethical Solicitor

Ethical decision-making

Fig 11: Resolving a problem from a central ethical base. Ethics is at the heart of decision making. Solicitors do need to take into account the Principles, codes and other rules depending on the ethical decision

2.8 The Principles

You act;

(1) In a way that upholds the constitutional principle of the rule of law, and the proper administration of justice;

(2) In a way that upholds public trust and confidence in the solicitor's profession and in legal services provided by authorised persons;

(3) With independence;

(4) With honesty;

(5) With integrity;

(6) In a way that encourages equality, diversity and inclusion;

(7) In the best interests of each client.

The new Principles are shorter than before and more positive in the message to those regulated by them. Those Principles under the 2011 code that specifically relate to running a business have been relocated to the Code of Conduct for Firms.

When considering ethical issues a solicitor will have their own ethical values - these cannot and should not be erased before approaching a problem, and if these can be acknowledged by the decision maker it helps to balance the weight one places on these. However, in the decision-making process the solicitor should first consider the Principles and the relevant Codes of Conduct as these provide a starting point. It is important to note that more than one Principle may be relevant in any dilemma.

In situations where two or more of the Principles conflict the solicitor is expected to come to the result that promotes the wider public interest over and above the individual client's interests. Ethical considerations, where they are applicable, will be considered in the application of the Principles and Code of Conduct matters.

The Principles apply to everyone working within a regulated entity - this applies to non-solicitor managers and employees. In practice, non-solicitor employees probably know nothing of OFR or their role in the system. This can be problematic as these individuals could easy breach the expected standards expected of them. Students who take work placement opportunities should always be trained on the ethical and regulatory issues so that they don't accidentally breach them. A well-meaning student going to court to meet Counsel and client to take notes can easily breach the client's confidentiality by reading the file of papers on public transport. Training them in the basic standards of expected behaviour is a minimum requirement.

Regulation has moved on to the extent that solicitors can be regulated by the Bar Standards Board, or CILEx regulation instead of the SRA. This is a new innovation and the issues that may be connected to "regulator" shopping are only becoming known now. Individual solicitors are still bound by the SRA's regulatory framework even if the firm is authorised by the BSB. In this book, we are only looking at the SRA regulatory regime which is the most common regulator of choice for solicitors. The new Code of Conduct for solicitors ensures that there is no doubt about the standards expected from solicitors whoever regulates them and wherever they work.

2.9 Are ethics and compliance the same?

It is important to remember that compliance and ethics are not the same. This is a central feature of OFR and of this book. Whilst a solicitor may consider the Principles and the Codes of Conduct, the conclusion he or she draws may be compliant but not entirely ethical. This is one of the major reasons that OFR was introduced in the first place.

In an OFR environment, the regulator creates a regulatory framework which sets out the boundaries for solicitors and regulated entities. Since the current regulatory framework is risk-based there are areas which have an increased emphasis on rules. The *Confidentiality and disclosure* section is particularly rules based with little scope for ethical decision-making. Other parts of the Code of Conduct for solicitors allow for greater ethical reflection - for example rule 71 states: "You keep up to date with and follow the law and regulation governing the way you work". This can mean different things to different solicitors and requires a balance of paying lip service to the rules and deeply embedding learning and development regarding compliance and regulatory issues. It is then for the individual solicitor to make the ethical case for any particular outcome. Chapter 3 that deals with behaving ethically sets out in more detail how that is approached in practice.

The 7 Principles are the first point of reference for a solicitor considering an ethical dilemma bearing in mind that a particular dilemma can involve more than one of the Principles. When a solicitor considers the Principles, they should ensure that client protection and serving the public interest are both important and take priority over the interests of a client where there is a conflict.

2.10 Considering the Principles and ethical decision-making

The first thing a solicitor needs to do on the pathway to ethical decision-making is to identify when an ethical decision needs to be made. This isn't as easy as it appears as solicitors make dozens of decisions every day about a broad spectrum of issues. The solicitor must be alert to the possibility of an ethical problem, to then engage the best decision-making strategy otherwise the problem will not get the attention it deserves.

Every solicitor needs a logical methodology for applying the Principles, considering the priority of conflicting Principles and taking into account the relevant Codes of Conduct before coming to a decision as to which ethical path to follow. Introducing a system to deal with these issues once identified will make it easier to document the decision-making process and explain the framework for reaching the decision to any interested stakeholders including the client, the court, the SRA and possibly the SDT. This style of reflective, considered decision-making is preferable to the more instinctive decision-making that experienced solicitors sometimes resort to and believe to be borne of experience.

The problem with instinctive decision-making is that the result produced is the result of a fast 'automatic' response to a problem which by its nature has not been thought through. The solicitors who depend on this style of decision-making are unlikely to buy (or read) this book as they are convinced that they 'know' how to make ethical decisions. In the worst scenario, the solicitor makes an instinctive decision and doesn't reflect on it any further until or unless questions arise in which case something will have gone awry.

On other occasions, a solicitor's 'gut reaction' to an ethical dilemma is justified by a subsequent cross check against the Rules - this methodology is faulty as it suffers from the user experiencing confirmation bias. Confirmation bias is the tendency to search for, interpret, favour and recall information which affirms one's prior beliefs or decisions. So, although it appears that the solicitor is going through a process of reflecting upon the regulatory framework, the decision has already been made and the solicitor is simply using the rules to justify the decision.

We have introduced the following motto to guide the solicitor through the decision-making process using the reflective style as a foundation;

Know the right thing

Do the right thing

For the right reason

Know the right thing – identify the problem first, and then implement the following practical approach;

- Look at the Principles and weigh them against each other where more than one Principle applies;

- Look at the Code of Conduct for Solicitors;

- Look at the Code of Conduct for Firms (where applicable);

- Look at the other rules of conduct that might apply (Money Laundering/data protection) if relevant;

- Apply ethical reasoning to achieve the "right thing" in this particular situation.

To demonstrate a logical reflective methodology we will go through the Principles outlining ethical situations that a solicitor may face. We will demonstrate those matters that the solicitor will need to take into account and how the decision-making process should be recorded in the event that the SRA subsequently raises questions about the decision and seeks answers from the decision-maker.

Taking each principle in turn, we can see how each affects ethical decision-making within the regulatory context. The Principles set out how a solicitor should act but this is not restricted to their actions whilst conducting a regulated activity, in a regulatory capacity or during work hours. The solicitor is required to adhere to the highest professional standards at all times, whether in an occupational capacity or not.

Principle 1: You act in a way that upholds the constitutional principle of the rule of law and the proper administration of justice

This is not dissimilar to the previous Principle 1 – little has changed regarding this Principle with the introduction of the 2019 Standards and Regulations. Whilst client satisfaction is very important, there is an obligation owed to third parties to uphold the constitutional principle of the rule of law which ranks over and above any individual client's needs. Thus, when considering ethical conflicts, the solicitor's duty isn't only, or even primarily, to their own client. There are wider issues to be contemplated when a dilemma involves the rule of law and proper administration of justice.

In the event that Principle 1 is breached it is possible that there could be a criminal breach as well.

Scenario: Criminal breaches

Solicitor J was fined by the SRA when he self-reported a criminal conviction for assault against his wife. Although the incident took place outside of his duties as a solicitor, the SRA's regulatory function includes the regulation of acts undertaken in a solicitor's personal life.

In another example, the SDT dealt with Solicitor K who deliberately gave false evidence at the trial of a High Court action. In doing so, it was her intention to mislead the court, which would be a clear breach of Principle 1 as it would interfere with the proper administration of justice. Her transgressions weren't limited to potentially breaching Principle 1 but also Principles 2, 4 and 5.

These examples show that a breach of Principle 1 is serious with complex ethical considerations and may enter the sphere of criminal wrongdoing. Whilst it is difficult to consider the ethical issues completely separately from the regulatory and criminal issues they are distinct. It is morally/ethically wrong to assault someone in this context and so this is an ethical issue. There may be a situation in which it isn't ethically wrong to assault someone, for example if the victim is about to commit a crime and the person committing the assault is a law enforcement officer.

Likewise, we could generally agree that it is wrong to lie but even more so to lie in court under oath. Many of the criminal acts extend from simple moral and ethical truths.

Principle 2: You act in a way that upholds the public trust and confidence in the solicitors' profession and in legal services provided by authorised persons

This Principle leads us to the realms of utilitarianism: how to do the best thing for the majority rather than the individual. A solicitor should behave in a trustful way – the stress here is that the public, not just your clients, should trust you.

It is important that all professionals retain a high status in society; professionals hold positions of trust and are held accountable to higher standards than others because of the nature of the work they do. As a result, it would seriously undermine this special status if those behaviours were only required to be displayed "on the job". So solicitors must display their best behaviour at all times in order that the public knows that their trust is well placed. This is a very important Principle as they are held to account for themselves and they are only as trustworthy as their weakest link.

Principle 3: You act with independence

This is framed slightly differently than the previous rule which specified that you do not allow your independence to be compromised. This Principle is stated more clearly in the 2019 Principles.

To act with independence is not to allow your judgement to be affected by another person or an outcome preferred by someone else and imposed on you. Sometimes it can be your client seeking to influence your advice, decisions or behaviour. At other times it could be another legal professional, barrister or solicitor within the firm who seeks to influence you and the advice you give. An example of this could be a situation where the client wishes to nominate a third person for you to communicate with as they are a trusted friend, advisor or another legal professional. This situation could be fraught with problems, particularly if that person wishes to influence your advice in some way.

There is a similar provision in the Bar Standards Board 'Core Duties' which are similar to the Principles. Barristers are required to maintain their independence, which includes maintaining independence from those instructing them. Solicitors are likely to be influenced by a great many voices when representing a client but the solicitor must be able to advise the client without undue pressure or influence from those voices. This doesn't mean that other's opinions can't be sought, but each decision made by the solicitor is made by them alone. This means that a solicitor can't delegate responsibility for decision-making to another person, like the COLP, a senior partner or a supervisor. Unless a dilemma can be simply resolved by following the rules contained in the Codes, each solicitor is responsible for themselves.

You can seek guidance from others, inside and outside the firm (while still maintaining client confidentiality and your contractual obligations to the firm). The SRA ethics helpline is a particularly useful tool which can be used anonymously via their chatbot feature – this usually pops up on the SRA website when a solicitor accesses the Standards and Regulations. The chat feature isn't always available but it is useful to print the discussions with an ethics advisor for the file. Whatever is discussed, the final decision always rests with the solicitor, even if it doesn't always feel that way.

Principle 4: You act with honesty

This is a new addition to the Principles and is different to Principle 5 which requires that you act with integrity. It is likely that this addition to the Principles stems from the result of a regulatory case; *Wingate & Anor v The SRA* [2018] EWCA Civ 366. The Court of Appeal found that there is a difference between honesty and integrity. *"Honesty is a basic moral quality which is expected from all members of society. It involves being truthful about important matters and respecting the property rights of others. Telling lies about things that matter or committing fraud or stealing are generally regarded as dishonest conduct*". A person can act in a way that lacks integrity without also being dishonest; integrity is set at a higher standard and "*involves adherence to the ethical standards of one's own profession*".

Being open and transparent in your dealings with clients and third parties is synonymous with acting honestly. The test for dishonesty in the regulatory framework is objective, taking into account what was in the mind of the person committing the act. At the time of writing, the SDT would expect that any allegation of dishonestly would need to be proven to the criminal standard of proof. This will change in the near future as The Legal Services Board approved an application from the SDT to change the burden of proof from the criminal standard to the civil standard. This change was introduced on 25 November 2019.

An allegation of behaving dishonestly is very serious, thus a finding of dishonesty is highly likely to result in a solicitor being struck off the roll.

Principle 5: You act with integrity

A solicitor must act with integrity at all times – this is behaviour that is expected from all professionals at all times.

The plain language definition of integrity is "the quality of being honest and having strong moral principles".

The ordinary definition leads to another question: is there a difference between ethics and morals? The *Wingate* case makes it clear that the concept of integrity is more than simply acting honestly. The *Wingate* case was joined with that of *Malin*, the solicitor backdated a false letter to be able to claim an ATE insurance fee from an opponent. He was struck off and the Court of Appeal supported this sanction. Lord Justice Jackson said: "*Integrity is a broader concept than honesty. In professional codes of conduct the term "integrity" is a useful shorthand to express the higher standards which society expects from professional persons and which the professions expect from their own members*".

He went on to give an example which is useful to consider: "*To take one example, a solicitor conducting negotiations or a barrister making submissions to a judge or arbitrator will take particular care not to mislead. Such a professional person is expected to be even more scrupulous about accuracy than a member of the public in daily discourse. The duty to act with integrity applies not only to what professional persons say, but to what they do*".

Are morals and ethics the same thing?

Not necessarily. Morals and ethics are often used interchangeably because the meaning and interpretation of both can sometimes overlap. The standard definition for morals is "standards of behaviour, principles of right and wrong". Added to this that most individuals cannot agree the distinctions between the two words and you end up with two terms of flexible meaning.

Within a professional context, specifically for the legal profession, ethical decision-making needs to be defined. This is to ensure that the profession can be judged to be acting ethically (or not) to maintain public confidence in the justice system. However, in general, ethics are deemed to come from a social system and are dependent on a group definition whilst morals are generally an internal, personal compass of what is right or wrong usually based on a personalised belief system and personal experiences.

This leads to potentially three paradoxical scenarios:

(1) a person following a strict ethical code may not have any morals;

(2) a moral person could violate an ethical code to maintain their morals;

(3) a moral person could select an ethical code to fit in with their moral beliefs.

Therefore, a solicitor could easily act according to strong moral principles but not be behaving ethically.

A solicitor who believes that they do not need to buy a train ticket before boarding a train might be committing an ethical breach if they fail to buy a ticket, but they may not be breaching any internal moral code. If their intention is to buy a ticket on the train or before they exit the station then they may believe that there is no lack of integrity on their part and their moral conscience is clear. The regulator is likely to disagree and the train company will have clear rules about when a train ticket must be purchased - these sanctions are inescapable in the event of a breach.

The solicitor may not even be guilty of breaching Principle 4 if they honestly held the view that they could purchase a ticket on the train or didn't know that they should have purchased a ticket for the train before they boarded.

The SRA and potential breaches of integrity

The SRA tends to take a very dim view when solicitors fail to act with integrity. There are many examples of solicitors being sanctioned by the SRA and the SDT for breaches of integrity, for example, failing to buy a train ticket before boarding a train, lying to the police about who was driving a car at the time of an accident, and failing to report a drink driving disqualification to the firm. These are all failures by a solicitor to act honestly in relation to these matters.

Principle 6: You act in a way that encourages equality, diversity and inclusion

Formerly, this Principle was expressed as a requirement only for the firm to consider and not one for the individual solicitor. The previous Principle said that you must *"Run your business or carry out your role in the business in a way that encourages equality of opportunity and respect for diversity"*. This is different now as Principle 6 states that each solicitor must act in a way that encourages equality, diversity and inclusion which is a wider obligation. Firms and solicitors will be bound by a much wider obligation to consider equality, diversity and inclusion (EDI).

It is a legal requirement that one does not discriminate against others on the grounds of their race, sex, gender or sexual orientation. Principle 6 is not a simple restatement of the law on discrimination - it takes matters further than that. The Principle requires that a solicitor should act in a way that encourages equality, diversity and inclusion. This obligation is not limited to actions undertaken whilst working as a solicitor. This is another avenue to showcase the strong argument in favour of virtue ethics - solicitors should behave in a positive and inclusive way in all aspects of their lives. The new mantra is to "encourage equality and diversity" not, "do not discriminate" which is a limited and legalistic approach.

The SRA risk outlook for 2019/2020 makes it clear the risk is that; *"Firms without workplace cultures that promote equality, diversity and inclusion have the highest risk of not treating staff and clients fairly or not making the best decisions for their business or clients."* Behaving in a way that promotes EDI has holistic positive impacts.

There is no real test to see how this is implemented by firms or individuals. Although the SRA requires firms to publish data on equality and diversity there is no way that it can monitor how this can be encouraged or implemented within a firm. It is important that this issue is being addressed by the new Principles targeting every solicitor and not just member organisations. The collection of data itself helps firms to look at the statistics and consider whether there is an issue that they need to address. However, this is the first step along a long road. Diversity training within all firms would achieve so much more to help staff identify issues.

Solicitor membership organisations are required to collect and publish data about the diversity of their workforce every two years. Firms are encouraged to use the 'Law Firm diversity tool' on the SRA website to see how a firm compares against other firms.

How many firms and individual solicitors could say that they actively encourage equality, diversity and inclusion to the best of their ability? This is definitely an area of ethical decision-making that could do with more consideration from all participants.

The Law Society collect and publish data about the gender pay gap, which is defined as the difference between the mean or median hourly pay rate that female and male colleagues receive. This is important information as it looks at the different way in which men and women are treated in the workplace which falls under Principle 6. The pay gap in 2018 is between 9.7% (median) and 12.7% (mean), and broadly reflects the figures collected in 2017. Although the existence of a pay gap is not indicative of equality in the profession, on a positive note the Law Society statistics are much better than the figures published by the Office of National Statistics 2018 which shows a median pay gap of 17.9%.

Principle 7: You act in the best interests of each client

We explore the extent to which the "client is king" in Chapter 4. Individual solicitors can sometimes place the needs and instructions of the client above other ethical considerations which does not accord with the other Principles. It is a difficult balance to strike and one which requires conscious decision-making. It would seem that the new Principles place this obligation at the end of the Principles, perhaps with the hope that solicitors will recognise that this is not the most important goal.

It can be difficult to ensure that you are looking out for the interests of each of your clients, particularly if their interests start to conflict with each other.

The issues that solicitors need to be mindful of are where there are 2 or more clients who are each receiving advice from the same solicitor about the same matter or transaction. The solicitor should ensure that each client's interests are considered individually. For example, in a residential conveyancing transaction where the couple are unmarried the solicitor may notice that Party A is contributing the whole deposit which the solicitor believes should be protected. The solicitor needs to carefully balance the advice to both Party A and the co-purchaser Party B who are both clients. The solicitor may morally believe that Party A should ensure that the money is protected in the event of a future relationship breakdown. The way in which this is done is an ethical choice for the solicitor:

Option A: Telephone Party A and make sure they understand that in the event of a purchase as Joint Tenants their deposit may not be protected. Strongly advise them to purchase as Tenants in Common and advise about the preparation of a Deed of Declaration of Trust.

Option B: Speak to both clients together and explain to both of them the advantages and disadvantages of buying the property as either Joint Tenants or Tenants in Common.

Option C: Send the clients an information sheet about purchasing a property jointly and ask them to sign a form notifying you of their decision.

The choice is for the solicitor to make.

Option A is deficient as there is no corresponding advice given to Party B, and this may be a regulatory breach if a complaint is made by Party B who may never be made aware that the conversation took place.

Options B and C ensure that advice is given to both parties - the advice isn't slanted to benefit either party. By giving oral advice, the solicitor may be able to stress their own view that this is the best way forward for Party A, and, whilst this might not be welcomed by Party B, they are involved in the conversation. Better still, the solicitor may wish to highlight that this is a potential area for conflict between the clients' interests and that they might wish to seek out separate advice about their relationship and financial repercussions in the event that it comes to an end.

These issues are exacerbated in commercial transactions where one firm is acting for more than one party in a transaction. This is the reason why ethical barriers need to be in place to ensure that client information is protected. If Party A's confidential information is leaked to Party B (also a client of the firm) the firm will be in an ethical dilemma when being required to do the best for each client.

COLP and COFA

The roles of the Compliance Officer for Legal Practice (COLP) and Compliance Officer for Financial Administration (COFA) will remain relevant in the new regulatory regime. The scope of these roles is now found in the Code of Conduct for Firms. Paragraph 8.1 states that a person responsible for compliance in the firm is shared with other managers.

Paragraph 9.1(a) to (e) is particularly set out for the benefit of the COLP and Paragraph 9.2(a) to (c) for the COFA.

An interesting matter that the SRA mentions in the consultation paper is that the focus on the COLP role *"may (and does) sometimes allow others to abdicate responsibility (thus placing complete reliance on the compliance officer)."* This may be an example of ethical fading; good solicitors sometimes don't realise they're making an ethical choice at all because it is perceived that the COLP is there to make those choices. Making one person responsible for the entire legal practice seems to have the effect of alleviating all others of responsibility and any ethical decision-making functions. The introduction of separate codes for solicitors and firms should help to ensure that each person is responsible for their own ethical decision-making. Within a firm the COLP has responsibilities to ensure compliance and a reporting obligation of those matters that need to be reported to the SRA, but this is now also an individual requirement for each solicitor too.

2.11 Comparing ethics in financial services to the legal profession

If you pick up a daily newspaper or surf the news pages on the internet with any regularity you can hardly fail to notice the number of scandals or regulatory investigations the financial services sector has been subject to since the financial crisis in the mid noughties. As a result of this, in order to clean up its act, there has been heavy emphasis on ethical behaviours introduced by the Financial Conduct Authority governing the behaviours of senior management down to the lowliest of employees. Whether this has a lasting effect on the ethical behaviours shown by these institutions or the public perception of them remains to be seen.

Most financial services firms attempt to embed ethics into the culture of their firms. It is not uncommon for prospective employees to sign pledges to behave ethically as part of their employment contracts. Upon the commencement of employment each employee undertakes rigorous compliance training which includes behaving ethically.

The emphasis on ethics and integrity in financial services is understandable. The financial regulators want to protect users of the system and to promote confidence in the same system. Is it so different for the legal world? Solicitors have a massive influence over difficult and stressful situations for individuals and companies. Take for example buying a house, making a will, getting divorced, employment law etc. The general public relies on solicitors to guide them through all of these situations placing these crucial life events in the hands of ethical and honest solicitors.

2.12 Anti-Money Laundering (AML) and Data Protection

There are a number of non-legal areas that are central to the work of all solicitors which require a solicitor to do, or refrain from doing, specific acts. For example, solicitors are required to take great care not to unknowingly or unwittingly assist clients to launder money. The AML regulations are therefore in place to ensure that the solicitor knows what to do when taking on a new client to ensure that money laundering isn't taking place. To know one's client is very important and these regulations cross over to other professions such as financial services.

Similar prescriptive rules are in place to ensure that the client's data is protected and that there are no data breaches, and so the Data Protection Act 2018 sets out a system of rules to govern the proper protection of client data.

These are all specifically rules-based systems with little manoeuvre for interpretation or ethical decision-making. We have therefore decided that these areas won't be covered in great detail here as they are more suitable for a book on regulation. However, it should be noted that the National Crime Agency (NCA) have recently levied criticism against lawyers because of the low number of suspicious activity reports filed by solicitors - these reports flag possible money laundering and suspicious activity. It is clear that firms struggle to implement understandable anti-money laundering practices but this isn't because of ethical issues but merely a failure to understand and implement the rules.

Scenario: Anti-money laundering

Facts

Solicitor M practised as a conveyancing solicitor, an area of practice which has a high risk in terms of possible money laundering issues. The solicitor failed to undertake identity checks to keep proper records of his client's identity, this being one of the first steps in combating money laundering (*Know Your Client* is the first mantra).

It transpired that he represented numerous convicted criminals who were laundering cash by purchasing properties, land, plots and other homes. Not only did the solicitor allow himself and his firm to be involved in a series of transactions to assist in money laundering, mortgage fraud was also perpetrated by his criminal clients. There was no evidence of dishonesty on the part of the solicitor but he admitted to deficiencies in his work which allowed the money laundering operation to succeed.

The judge dealing with the criminal allegations against the solicitor stated that: *"this was not however a case of mere inadvertence. There were serious irregularities and deficiencies on the files that in certain respects appear systemic and as I have already said, it is plain to me that you ignored significant and serious legal and statutory duties"*.

The solicitor was convicted of 7 counts of failing to comply with money laundering regulations and one count of failing to disclose his suspicions. He was sentenced to 9 months in prison. Subsequent to his criminal convictions in an agreed outcome with the SRA the solicitor accepted that he would be struck off.

His alternatives in this case were very simple - he should have rigorously checked his clients' identities, kept records of those identity checks and reported any suspicious activities to the NCA as and when they arose. Quite simply, he either overlooked the simple issues or chose to ignore them - the rules are clear.

There are numerous examples in the SDT of solicitors who get caught up in schemes that breach these rules and are punished for doing so. Sometimes the breaches are punished by fines; at other times they are also criminal acts punishable by criminal sanctions.

Scenario: Data protection

Facts

In 2017, Barrister F was the data controller for her business. She was supposed to protect her client's data in accordance with the Data Protection Act 1998 (DPA) and the Bar Standards Code of Conduct which is similar to the SRA Code of Conduct. Both codes require their members to keep their client's information confidential.

Barrister F had created many documents for her clients on her home PC. The report indicates that at least 250 client documents were accidentally uploaded to the internet by her husband who was backing up her computer. He backed up 725 files to an online directory that was not protected and made the documents available via the internet. As soon as this was known to the barrister's husband he removed them from the online directory. The files were visible to the public for a short period but the documents contained sensitive information.

Rules

The reported decision indicates that the data controller was in breach of s4(4) DPA which requires her to keep client data in line with the regulations. She had failed to ensure that she had technical measures in place to prevent third parties accessing the client data - her husband shouldn't have had access to those files at all. She should have encrypted the client files so that even if the data had accidentally been uploaded in the way it was, no one would have been able to view it.

Breaches

In addition to breaching the DPA she was also in breach of her regulator's Code of Conduct, equivalent to Chapter 4 of the Code of Conduct requiring solicitors to keep their client's information secure and confidential.

Outcome

The barrister was fined £1,000 by the Information Commissioner's Office for DPA breaches.

> It is not known whether the barrister was also found to be in breach in respect of her duties owed to the Bar Council under the Bar Standards Code of Conduct.

2.13 Summary

Overall, the interaction between the Principles leaves a huge amount of flexibility for the practitioner to operate within. Ethics and those qualities associated with virtue, behaviour and character are central to this type of regulatory system and will hold more importance under the new regime.

Chapter 3: Behaving ethically

3.1 Do the right thing, for the right reason

Many professionals, not just solicitors, generally aim to behave in such a way that will keep them out of trouble with their regulator. We would suggest that behaving in this way is short-sighted and only requires the individual to meet an end, albeit an important one for professionals. That end goal might be to be "compliant enough" to avoid sanction or just enough to avoid committing a criminal act. To avoid sanction, there is no positive requirement to behave ethically, albeit that this is the general expectation. A solicitor merely needs to avoid the detection of unethical behaviour to avoid sanction - this isn't ethical reasoning (although it may pass as being "good enough").

Behaving ethically means a lot more than just meeting compliance objectives. We will be looking at the positive obligation on professionals to behave in a *positive* ethical way, not only to avoid sanction from the regulator but also to continue to hold the privileged position of being a professional. We suggest that by changing the focus on "positive ethical behaviour", the public will continue to hold solicitors in high regard and perhaps even trust them more.

3.2 Differences in approach

As explained earlier in Chapter 2, prior to October 2011 the Code of Conduct for Solicitors was prescriptive and rules-based. A solicitor merely needed to consult with the Code to understand how they should behave in any given situation. This could lead to situations arising whereby the result is right and governed by the rules but the client is left feeling that the ultimate outcome is wrong.

There is a school of thought suggesting that strict adherence to rules will render unethical situations more likely as it removes the need for solicitors to think about ethics at all.

Post October 2011, the Code of Conduct for Solicitors is in line with Outcomes-Focused Regulation (OFR) and this will continue and expand now that the new Codes have been introduced. The SRA doesn't want to bind solicitors to a set of strict rules but allow individuals and firms to be able to have the flexibility to make the right choice. Essentially, the solicitor and the firm need to be able to think through a problem and find a solution. This introduces a greater capacity for the individual to think ethically and reach a result which is both compliant and fair to the client.

The way that individuals and firms undertake that process of thinking through a problem is influenced by many factors; the ability to behave ethically in these situations is central to that process under the new regime. Whether this is something that is recognised or not during the thinking process, ethics is central to the way that firms navigate everyday situations.

It is said that solicitors behave in "ethically minimalist" ways and we would hope that solicitors would want to change that perception and behaviour if that is accepted to be the case.

3.3 Ethically minimalist solicitor's motivators

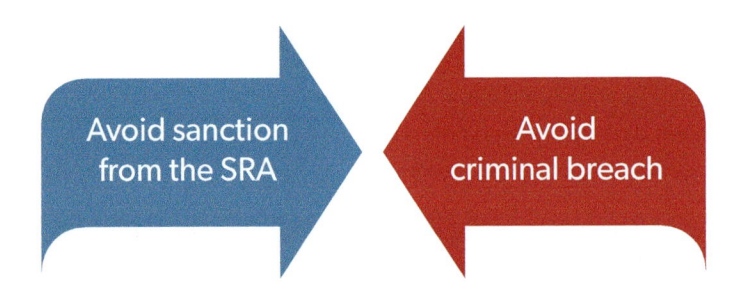

Fig 12: The ethically minimalist solicitor is doing the least that they can to remain compliant and avoid criminal sanctions

We propose that perhaps a better way to deal with issues in practice and any ethical dilemma would be the following three point approach:

Behaving Ethically

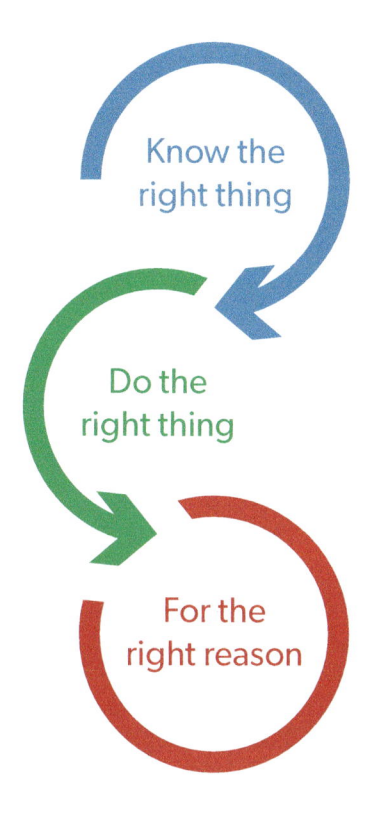

Fig 13: A process motto for the ethical solicitor

Principles 4 and 5: Act with honesty and integrity

We will not cover the regulatory aspects of Principles 4 and 5 in this section - that has already been dealt with in Chapter 2. However, Principles 4 and 5 are possibly the main foundation for a solicitor's ethical behaviour. They are wide ranging as they apply to a solicitor's behaviour in all walks of life, not just in practice. Whilst it may be onerous to act with honesty and integrity in one's professional *and* personal life, that is what is expected of any professional and especially of a solicitor. It is not unheard of for a solicitor to be struck off the roll of solicitors for acts that took place entirely outside of professional life and unrelated to client matters.

Principle 5 is usually taken together with Principle 2, which places an obligation on a solicitor to behave in a way that maintains the trust and confidence the public places in them and in the provision of legal services. These two Principles together ensure that all aspects of a solicitor's behaviour both in work and off the clock are governed by the Codes of Conduct.

Acting with integrity more specifically means that solicitors are expected by the public to behave in a way that is;

- Transparent;

- Honest;

- Open; and

- Fair.

In the context of the financial services profession, integrity has been defined as follows;

> *"In our view, "integrity" connotes moral soundness, rectitude and steady adherence to an ethical code. A person lacks integrity if unable to appreciate the distinction between what is honest or dishonest by ordinary standards."*[1]

Following decisions in recent Court of Appeal cases we now know that in respect of the legal profession, *"Integrity connotes adherence to the ethical standards of one's own profession. That involves more than mere honesty. To take one example, a solicitor conducting negotiations or a barrister making submissions to a judge or arbitrator will take particular care not to mislead. Such a professional person is expected to be even more scrupulous about accuracy than a member of the public in daily discourse. The duty to act with integrity applies not only to what professional persons say, but to what they do."*

In a recent study[2] solicitors indicated that the top six personal virtues that an ideal lawyer should have were:

(1) Judgement;

(2) Honesty;

(3) Perseverance;

(4) Perspective;

---

[1] *Hoodless and Blackwell v FSA (Financial Services & Markets Tribunal)*

[2] *Virtuous Character for the Practice of Law - The Jubilee Centre for Character and Virtues (James Arthur, et al)*

(5) Fairness;

(6) Teamwork.

The top two of these personal virtues help us to understand the central foundation of "the ethical lawyer"; one who is able to respond to dilemmas in an ethically appropriate way, not one who only has an eye on compliance.

As noted in Chapter 2, honesty and integrity have different meanings but are important behaviours to indicate ethical decision making.

3.4 Types of behaviour generally recognised as being unethical

From the list of virtuous characteristics above, we can easily see that there are types of behaviour that we should all agree are unethical;

- Lying/dishonest behaviour to court, client or third party;

- Misleading the court, client or third party;

- Failing to protect the client's assets and wider interests.

However, there are times when it is possible that you have done one or all of the above things. It can be difficult for a solicitor to admit or even recognise their own unethical behaviour.

To illuminate ethical problems that solicitors face we will use examples from the SDT to outline this behaviour, albeit restricted to the regulatory environment. This means that we are limited to looking only at behaviour that has come to the attention of the regulator and which they decided to pursue. Obviously, this means that there are many other behaviours that either haven't been considered serious enough to pursue by the regulator or that haven't come to the regulator's attention at all. We will attempt to look at all aspects of ethical behaviour and not just that which is serious enough to attract attention. If one acts as an "ethical solicitor" it actually means to act with honesty and integrity in all aspects of one's life and not just the professional context.

In the context of regulatory sanction, the worst ethical transgression to accuse a solicitor of is acting without integrity or dishonestly. This goes to the core of the virtues that solicitors are expected to have. Although a dishonest solicitor might be an advantage to some clients, the rule of law would be quickly eroded if this is the norm. The SDT guidance notes on sanction state:

> *"A finding that an allegation of dishonesty has been proved will almost invariably lead to striking off, save in exceptional circumstances."*[3]

The ultimate sanction is to strike a solicitor from the roll; this sanction applies only to the most serious breaches.

The guidance used by the SDT regarding dishonesty is:

> *"a standard which combines an objective and a subjective test, and which requires that before there can be a finding of dishonesty it must be established that the defendant's conduct was dishonest by the ordinary standards of reasonable and honest people and that he himself realised that by those standards his conduct was dishonest."*

Whilst regulatory breaches need to be proven to the criminal standard at the SDT (at the time of writing), the above is good guidance for solicitors to keep in mind in practice.

We will also use examples from different practice areas that have come to our attention and look at the potential ethical issues that arise outside the most obvious and widely accepted examples above.

3.5 Duty to self-report

Every person regulated by the SRA has a duty to promptly self-report behaviour that the SRA would want to be aware of. This duty is now wider under the new Codes of Conduct than before, and prominently applies to all individuals and firms.

Paragraph 7.7 in the Code of Conduct for Solicitors requires that they report promptly to the SRA any facts or matters that they reasonably believe are capable of amounting to a serious breach. This requirement applies to their own behaviour or that of another.

Paragraph 7.8 goes on to widen that obligation to require a solicitor to inform the SRA of any facts or matters that they reasonably believe should be brought to its attention so that it may investigate whether a serious breach has occurred.

---

[3] *Twinsectra Ltd v Yardley & Ors [2002] UKHL 12.*

Paragraph 7.12 states that where a solicitor makes a report to the firm's COLP or COFA then the obligation to the SRA to report the matter will be satisfied on the understanding that they will make the report. This places a reasonable additional duty on those office holders.

These provisions at Paragraphs 7.7 and 7.8 are mirrored in the Code of Conduct for Firms at Paragraphs 3.9 and 3.10.

There are additional reporting obligations for the COLP or COFA considered in Chapter 2 and found in the Code of Conduct for Firms at Paragraphs 9.1 and 9.2.

Each solicitor additionally must meet the Character and Suitability requirements set by the SRA. These are assessed when deciding whether to allow them to practice or continue to practice as a solicitor and the duty to keep the SRA informed about any changes is paramount. The SRA will take into account;

(a) Serious financial difficulty, for example if you register with a credit reference agency;

(b) Action taken against you by another regulator;

(c) Criminal conduct resulting in a conviction or accepting a caution.

Personal virtues or ethics are very important when making these decisions and we can see from decided SDT cases (under the 2011 Handbook) that there are reported cases of solicitors who self-report their own failures. Members of the Bar have the same obligation to self-report, including serious professional misconduct.

Scenario: Professional misconduct

A criminal barrister unintentionally spoke to jurors after a trial in which he was involved. He apparently asked them about the basis for their verdict and disclosed to them that evidence was withheld from them. He received a fine of £300 and a reprimand. The panel took into account as mitigation that he had self-reported the matter and the fact that the conduct was unintentional.

It must have been extremely difficult for the barrister to make the admissions but the fact that he realised his mistake and promptly informed the regulator acted in his favour. His actions show that he was able to use his judgement to report the misconduct to the regulator. It is possible that the conversation would never have come to the attention of the regulator without the self-report. His action to self-report was ethically positive; he understood that he had inadvertently done the wrong thing. The only way to put the matter right was to self-report and accept the consequences of his actions.

Sometimes in the SDT reports, solicitors who do one wrong thing may then attempt to cover up the initial error by doing a series of wrong things. They do so in the hope that they will rectify the original error, without the need for anyone ever finding out about the original mistake. This behaviour can lead to disastrous results, more so than making a difficult admission early on.

In the SDT case below the Tribunal appreciated that it would be difficult for most people to self-report a conviction for a serious offence but that a solicitor should realise that self-reporting is essential, no matter what the consequences.

Scenario: Drink driving

Facts

Solicitor M pleaded guilty to a drink driving offence in 2013. It was her fourth offence and she was convicted of driving a motor vehicle with excess alcohol. She was also convicted of driving whilst disqualified from driving. She was driving without insurance and received a custodial sentence of 4 months which was suspended for 24 months.

She self-reported the conviction within 2 weeks of the sentence; her employer also reported the matter to the SRA.

Unfortunately, she did not self-report a conviction from 2011 but she had reported 2 earlier convictions for driving with excess alcohol in 1997 and 2000 which occurred prior to her admission to the roll.

Rules

It was alleged that she had breached Principles 1, 2 and 6 (2011 Handbook).

Ethical issues/professional breaches

She was aware that the convictions needed to be reported but had failed to self-report the 2011 conviction.

She put forward mitigation regarding her personal circumstances but it was difficult for her to overcome the fact that it took over 2 years to report the 2011 conviction. She only admitted that conviction when asked a direct question by the SRA. In 2011 once her immediate personal difficulties had passed she didn't report.

The reason she gave the Tribunal for failing to report the conviction was the fact that she was convinced she would lose her job. Her decision-making was at that point in time based purely on self-interest. She was not immediately concerned with the Principles or the Code of Conduct.

Outcome

The Tribunal found that she had breached Principle 2 by failing to report the conviction.

The main concern of the Tribunal was to protect the reputation of the profession. In this case, the appropriate way to do so was to strike off the solicitor and order her to pay costs of £2,500.

In contrast to the barrister case above, this solicitor exacerbated her situation by failing to report the conviction in 2011. It should be noted that these incidents all occurred when the solicitor was not working; she was in her own time. None of the incidents involved a client or any detriment to a member of the public, but the number of incidents and the public nature of them were such that they were considered to be very serious.

3.6 Personal virtues

The virtues needed to guide a solicitor to act with integrity go some way towards understanding what it means to act with integrity; judgement, fairness and honesty are central. Additionally, we suggest that openness and transparency are key elements to acting with integrity.

When you are about to embark upon a course of action, whether in the work environment or outside it, it is useful to ask yourself what you would do if your mother/partner/children were watching you. This can sometimes alter the path that you might choose - the additional scrutiny of a close friend or family member can act to shame us out of making potentially unethical decisions.

In a more professional context, would you be able to justify your actions if you were cross-examined? How would you feel in the cold light of a courtroom if a judge scrutinised your decision?

This technique can be revealing about our ethical choices when you shine a light on them; taking a step back and then making a balanced decision can help to maintain integrity.

When are private emails not private?

In the following case, taken from the SDT decisions, 3 solicitors in the same firm sent each other emails that they didn't think would ever be seen by other people. One solicitor indicated that if he had known other people would read the emails he would never have written them and that in fact the content did not represent his views. The emails were sent between the 3 as a joke.

The 3 solicitors didn't stop to think about the content of the emails they were sending - they knew the emails weren't serious. The third respondent in his mitigation told the Tribunal that he *"shuddered to think he had been party to such emails; he was still struggling to understand how it was that he had written this material."*

Scenario: Rude emails

Facts

Solicitors A, B and C were all partners at the same firm. They were using the firm's email accounts to send each other emails that contained comments about co-workers that were described by the SDT as "crass, offensive, puerile and inappropriate." The solicitors did not think that anyone would ever read their emails aside from the recipients; a non-solicitor employee who revealed the content read them. She was the subject of some of the emails between the three partners. It is worth noting that;

- No clients were involved;

- No fraud was involved;

- No malice was intended;

- The solicitors didn't think anyone would ever see the emails.

Rules

Potential breach of Principles 2, 6 and 9 (not proven) using the 2011 Handbook.

Potential ethical issues/professional breaches

The SDT found that the three solicitors had acted in a way that breached Principle 2 and Principle 6 - the requirement to act with integrity and not to behave in a way that diminishes the trust the public places in them or the legal profession.

This was to the criminal standard of proof. Two solicitors were dismissed from the firm when the emails became known; the third had resigned before that time. All three were ashamed of what they had written.

The solicitors hadn't acted with integrity in that they weren't honest and open. They demonstrated a dire lack of judgement when sending the emails.

Solicitor A was fined £5,000 and costs of £2,700; Solicitor B was fined £5,000 and costs of £2,700; Solicitor C was fined £4,000 and costs of £1,800.

3.7 The ethical solicitor

For the purpose of this book, we are using a specific approach to ethical dilemmas and a specific definition of ethics. We therefore propose that a solicitor who behaves ethically is one who does so *even when no one is looking*. Take for example the barrister who self-reported his conversation with the jurors - it is possible that the BSB would never have come to find out about that matter unless he reported it. He reported it anyway because he understood that it was the right thing to do, even though he faced sanctions.

The solicitors who sent each other crass and offensive emails would have benefited from bearing this matter in mind when they sent them. They each believed that their emails were private and that no one would read them. Perhaps they would not have written the emails if they had approached the emails thinking through the prospective ethical issues. They didn't think about these matters as they didn't think anyone else would find out; they thought that no one was looking and so they could do as they pleased. Perhaps the cynical solicitor will say that had they sent the emails from their personal email accounts instead of their firm accounts the outcome would have been different.

The issue of ethics isn't about what you do when you are likely to be scrutinised for your decision-making. It's about all those decisions you make in everyday life which may not be scrutinised but the Principles and Codes require solicitors to contemplate their ethical decision making at all times. It should be second nature to think through the ethical issues, so much so that it becomes conscious ethical decision-making.

The ethical solicitor;

(1) knows what the right thing is;

(2) acts to do the right thing; and

(3) does the right thing for the right reason,

even when no one is looking and no one is likely to find out what he/she has done.

Fig 14: Remember the motto for the ethical solicitor!

All professions are held in high regard in society because *"arguably professions were moral communities based upon shared expertise and occupational membership."*[4] The place of the professions in society is changing in the 21st century and some say that the regulation of these professions is not keeping pace with that change.

Scenario: Undercharged in a restaurant

Facts

You go to a restaurant and aren't charged for a bottle of wine you have ordered and drunk. Do you tell the waiter that there has been a mistake and pay the additional money? Or do you pay the bill and leave without mentioning it?

The process of ethical decision-making

Know the right thing - to pay for the wine you ordered.

---

[4] *In Professions We Trust (Phillip Blond, Elena Antonacopoulou and Adrian Pabst, July 2015).*

How To Be An Ethical Solicitor

Do the right thing - tell the waiter to add the wine to the bill.

For the right reason - Principles 2, 4, and 5; to act with fairness, honesty, morality, integrity and with good judgement.

The best ethical outcome for the solicitor is to pay for the wine. This may not be the best outcome for all parties at the table.

There are various other factors that might impact on the decision-making process:

Other people - your guests might not want to pay anything more than the original bill.

But you all drank the wine so it's only fair that you all pay for it.

Money - you realise that you don't have enough money to pay for the wine. You only have enough to pay for your share of the original bill.

You could ask someone else to cover your share and pay them back at a later date.

Time - the restaurant is very busy and you need to get the last train home. You don't have time to wait for them to correct their mistake. If you wait, you'll have to get a taxi home and this will be very costly.

You could leave to catch your train and ask someone else to wait for the correct bill.

None of these other factors act to change the ethical decision; in fact, all they do is make it more difficult to make the **right** decision.

Many people would use the external factors as a justification not to make the right ethical decision. In fact, the above example shows that there are many ways around the other factors - if you look hard enough you should be able to make the right decision.

In the context of the solicitor's regulatory framework, what is "the right thing"? The SRA outlines that where one or more of the Principles clash: *"Should the Principles come into conflict, those which safeguard the wider public interest (such as the rule of law, and public confidence in a trustworthy solicitors' profession and a safe and effective market for regulated legal services) take precedence over an individual client's interests."* The importance of upholding the rule of law and upholding the public trust is paramount. In this example there is no client interest and so the solicitor's concerns should centre on reputational protection, not only for the individual solicitor but the profession at large.

Solicitors (wrongly) believe that they should act in the best interests of their client at all times. Where the solicitor works in-house or for influential individuals or companies, the temptation to place the interests of the clients above all else can be overwhelming. This can and does lead to unethical decision-making to benefit the client but to the detriment of the solicitor. The solicitor should act with independence and this can be difficult to achieve with clients who are powerful and influential.

As in the examples above, there are times when the solicitor faces a dilemma that does not involve the client's interests at all. Principles 1, 2, 3, 4 and 5 are very important in times where client issues aren't the focus of the dilemma.

Ethics isn't *only* about compliance. We propose that every solicitor approaches every ethical issue from a compliance-based perspective *first*. As and when the Codes of Conduct require further thought, the next approach is from the point of view of the ethical solicitor. Remember the ethical solicitor's motto.

This decision-making process involves two traditional ethical approaches:

(1) The rules-based approach - what does the SRA say we should do?

(2) The virtuous/behavioural approach - what should an ethical solicitor do?

The application of these two approaches will often result in a number of compliant solutions to the ethical dilemma; the individual solicitor then needs to decide which approach to take. The point at which a solicitor finds themselves with a variety of compliant options is when ethical issues can be explored more deeply.

Taking this approach to ethical dilemmas both in and out of practice should help the solicitor when faced with sudden split second decision-making. Getting into the habit of ethical decision-making will make a difference in these situations. Consider the following case:

Scenario: Lying in court

Facts

Solicitor F gave evidence in court proceedings and he was asked in cross-examination whether, during the course of his career as a solicitor, any allegation or breach of the solicitors Code of Conduct had ever been upheld. He had answered no.

In fact he had been suspended from practice for two years from February 1995. His response was an automatic response, which was to tell a lie to end the cross-examination rather than tell the truth and face further questions.

Four months after giving oral evidence, he advised the solicitors for the Claimant that he had given incorrect information. The Claimant's solicitors reported his conduct to the SRA but they took no action at the time. It would be interesting to know why they didn't think that a solicitor lying in court needed further investigation.

Solicitor F self-reported to the SRA more than two years after the date that he gave the evidence. As a result of his self-report the matter was referred to the SDT.

Rules/ethical issues

Technically his answer on cross-examination had been the truth but he knew that the question was a broad question, which wasn't specifically about this conduct under the Code of Conduct 2007 which was in place at that time. The reasons for his previous suspension were in respect of accounts rules breaches and conduct unbefitting of a solicitor.

The Tribunal stated: "*Ordinary members of the public would expect a solicitor to be frank, transparent and complete in the giving of evidence.*" Solicitor F had not been frank and honest with the court.

Under the terms of the new Codes of Conduct, he would have been in difficulties for failing to deal with the matter promptly which is required under Paragraph 7.7 of the Code of Conduct for Solicitors.

Behaving Ethically

Outcome

Solicitor F was fined £10,000 and ordered to pay costs of £6,000.

Had Solicitor F developed the habit of ethical decision-making, he may not have lied in court despite the difficult position he found himself in at that time. Being honest was the difficult choice but in that moment an honest answer should have come easily to the solicitor.

3.8 Identify the ethical dilemma

Real life ethical dilemmas aren't often very straightforward or like exam questions. Many readers will believe that the answers are simple when the questions are laid bare. However, it is worth noting that there are often a number of external factors that the solicitor needs to take into account when reaching a decision in the heat of the moment. It can be a problem for an individual solicitor to identify the fact that the issue at hand is in fact an *ethical* dilemma in the first place. The first step is to identify the problem, recognise the ethical issues and then act accordingly.

Scenario: Tampering with forms

Facts

A solicitor sees a client and asks him to complete and sign a form to send to the Legal Aid Agency. When the client leaves the office, the solicitor realises that the client forgot to complete his address on the form.

What is the right thing to do?

There could be a number of possible options to explore:

Option A: The solicitor completes the address and submits the form - after all no one will ever find out that the form was altered after signature.

Option B: The solicitor completes the address and submits the form with the amendment initialled by the solicitor, thereby ensuring that the recipient knows there has been an amendment not seen by the client.

Option C: The solicitor speaks to the client and asks them if they have the authority to change the form to add in the address. The solicitor keeps an attendance note of the conversation.

Option D: The solicitor asks the client to return to the office to complete the address (and initial the amendment).

What does the solicitor do?

The first consideration should be with reference to the SRA Principles and Codes of Conduct with an eye on the prospect of any sanction. This is more a rules-based approach, but the decision-making process doesn't end there. Once any obviously non-compliant options have been ruled out, the solicitor could choose any of the remaining options. The ethical decision is for the solicitor to make; which of the options sit best with the solicitor?

Many solicitors reading this will know instantly what choice they would make and this is likely to reveal much about the individual's virtues and ethics. Any quick decision made would be an automatic response and wouldn't benefit from the reflective approach we favour.

SRA Principles to consider - the rules-based approach

Principles

You act:

Principle 2: in a way that maintains the trust the public places in you and the provision of legal services.

Principle 4: with honesty.

Principle 5: with integrity.

In addition the solicitor should consider Paragraph 1.4 of the Code of Conduct for Solicitors which says: *You do not mislead or attempt to mislead your clients, the court or others, either by your own acts or omissions or allowing or being complicit in the acts or omissions of others (including your client).*

Act with integrity and honesty

Some solicitors may think that it is perfectly fine to change some- thing as uncontentious as a client's address and opt for Option A above on the basis that "no one will ever know" or "what harm can be done by adding in a simple address?"

Others will think that it is unacceptable to change anything on a form signed by a client and ask the client to return to amend the form (Option D above). If acting honestly, a solicitor wouldn't change any part of any form without knowledge or consent of the client. This would not be honest as sending the form to a third party you would represent it as having been entirely completed by the client, which wouldn't be the case.

Bear in mind the ideal personal characteristics for the ideal lawyer - honesty, fairness, openness and transparency. An act of making a change for the client's benefit wouldn't meet these expected behaviours.

SRA approach

When we presented the SRA ethics team with this scenario they advised us to take Option D.

Documents should never be presented as having been signed by the client unless that is the case. Even minor changes are unacceptable.

However, when pushed, the SRA ethics adviser conceded that Option C may be acceptable as long as the third party is aware of who inserted the details of the address. Options A and B are not likely to keep the regulator happy.

The ethical solicitor

As the regulatory approach discounts Options A and B the ethical solicitor has two remaining choices, Options C or D. This is there- fore a dilemma that has an ethical element, albeit quite subtle.

If you are doing the right thing for the right reason, the focus has to be client-based in the context of the regulatory framework. This is where the solicitor's action needs to be context specific. For example, if there is no major inconvenience to the client to return to sign the document then that is the approach to take.

If the client is unable to return, refuses to return, or suffers a disability that prevents them from returning the solicitor will need to consider whether it is appropriate to take the form to the client to complete the address details.

Only in limited specific circumstances could it possibly be necessary to alter the document on behalf of the client.

Other considerations

The Legal Aid Agency could reject the amended application and require the client to complete the form.

This will then cause delay, which might not be in the best interests of the client.

Different facts - different result?

What if we propose to change the details of a will after it has been signed rather than a legal aid form?

Your answer may change depending on the nature of the document but the ethical answer is likely to be the same no matter what the document is. The issue is whether a document can be changed without the client's knowledge after it has been signed.

By approaching all ethical dilemmas in the above way, you should reach the same ethical result.

Solicitors would agree that it is unacceptable to change any aspect of the will after the client has signed it. The risk of being discovered it much higher than with the legal aid form, although this should have no bearing on the decision making process.

3.9   Do you need to learn how to behave ethically?

Many solicitors think that this is "someone else's problem"; you don't need to read this book or go on a course to learn how to behave ethically. In fact, many people don't think it is possible to teach virtuous or ethical behaviour; this is something innate or learned earlier in life. This follows the automatic response theory considered in Chapter 2.

You may know someone in your office who could do with a "steer" in the right direction. When solicitors talk about ethical breaches, often they are recounting someone else's poor choices - rarely are they admitting to their own transgressions.

It's not you; it's them.

This type of thinking isn't unusual. Older practitioners possibly think that younger solicitors need more ethics grounding because they are "wet behind the ears" or too inexperienced to have sound (automatic) judgement to make the "right decisions". As we will see using our examples, there can often be more than one option which leads to a compliant result; the ethical measure of the response is down to the individual to some extent. A reflective approach is always going to help the solicitor to weigh all the compliant approaches to discover the most ethical result, ot just the first ethical approach the solicitor thinks of.

Younger practitioners may believe that older practitioners need more ethics grounding because they have been practicing law for too long. Rather than this having a positive impact on the ethics of a practitioner it can conversely be seen to be detrimental. Ethical numbness can set in, the old practitioner knows what they can "get away with" and makes decisions based on increasing risky ethical responses. With each minor ethical transgression the solicitor ceases to take future lapses seriously, establishing a "new normal".

The older practitioner can pick up bad habits; the same could be said for older and more experienced drivers. Both pick up bad habits that go undetected until an "impact event", when something goes hideously wrong and then the bad practices have a light shone on them.

In the SDT decisions there is often a distinction made between the older experienced practitioner and the younger "foolish" solicitor. That is not to say that a younger solicitor will not receive the same sanction as an older solicitor for the same breach but it is clear in mitigation that age is a factor that is taken into account. Younger solicitors are possibly more obedient to the rules and regulations and also more likely to be persuaded that an older supervisor/partner/COLP or COFA knows better. The new Codes of Conduct should make it abundantly clear to those who have recently joined the profession that they are responsible for their own decision-making.

The UCL Report of Professional Standards indicates that competence of the solicitor impacted on the level of seriousness perceived by those taking the survey. In one example, a newly qualified solicitor's error is treated more

How To Be An Ethical Solicitor

leniently when compared to a similar problem in which the solicitor was not identified as newly qualified; this may be reflected in SDT decisions although there is no research to support this.

One possible reason that different generations of solicitors could regard each other as being in need of ethics grounding is that they have learned different systems of regulation.

3.10 What is the right thing?

When thinking through a practical/ethical dilemma, there are various parties who are directly or indirectly involved in the solicitor's decision-making process.

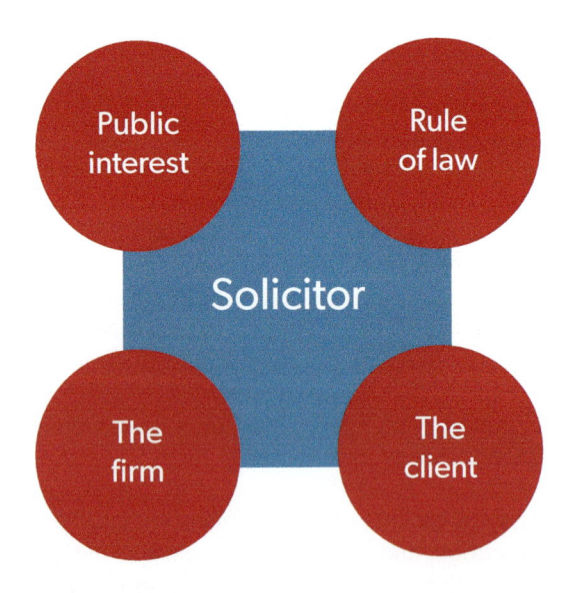

Fig 15: The solicitor isn't making decisions in isolation to other people!

Public interest and the observance to the Rule of Law are at the top of the square because the regulatory Principles and Codes indicate that solicitors should balance their obligations under the Principles and Code to protect the administration of justice for the public interest. This means that no individual's interests rank in priority over this obligation. It is no mistake that the first two Principles reflect the most important matters.

In real life, if a solicitor faces a practical/ethical dilemma, the answer isn't as straightforward as looking it up in the rules. The solicitor needs to keep an eye on the regulatory objectives but also weigh the firm's commercial interests and the public interest too.

Scenario: Double billing

Facts

You travel from London to Leeds to have a meeting with client A at their request. You prepare for the meeting in the office to avoid confidential material being seen in public, charging the client for the preparation time. The journey to Leeds is just over two hours and you decide to work on client B's file during the journey as the work is somewhat administrative and no confidential material will be on display. How do you bill the journey time?

- Do you bill client A for the journey time and client B for the work done during the journey, thus effectively double billing?

- Or do you bill client B for the preparation work but don't charge client A at all?

Clients A and B might not be too happy to be told that they were both charged for the same two hour period, even though you were effectively working for them both during that period.

SRA Principles

You act:

Principle 2: in a way that maintains the trust the public places in you and in the provision of legal services.

Principle 4: with honesty.

Principle 5: with integrity.

Principle 7: in the best interests of each client.

There is no rule that prevents a solicitor from charging twice for the same time. Many firms would think that this is an efficient use of time. The work for Client A couldn't be done on the journey for GDPR and confidentiality reasons which is reasonable.

Potential ethical issues

The public might not think that it is "ethical", honest or fair for both clients A and B to be charged for the same time.

Your firm/department/immediate supervisor may think it is entirely appropriate for you to bill both clients at your full hourly rate for the work done on the train.

This may clash with the individual solicitor's desire to bill only client B for the work as being an individual ethical decision. The firm's influence is usually commercially led and takes priority over the individual solicitor's ethical compass.

The fact that you haven't told either client that you are charging them both for the same time isn't likely to be entirely honest or transparent. Neither does it show a high level of integrity, if integrity is synonymous with transparency and fairness.

There isn't one right answer but a range of answers that could be considered to be acceptable within the current regulatory framework. Openness and transparency are key in dealing with this type of dilemma.

3.11 Do the right thing

This seems to be easy to say but difficult to do. Often the external influences disrupt the solicitor from doing the right thing or can cause the solicitor to do something unethical.

When it comes to doing the right thing, dozens of SDT cases evidence the fact that many solicitors don't manage to do the right thing, even though they usually know what they should have done. When a case comes before the SDT, it means that the individual solicitor has been caught or reported to be doing the wrong thing and that there may even be criminal charges against that individual.

In practice, solicitors make dozens of decisions every day, it is possible we all do something every day that could be considered to be unethical. Even when a solicitor is committing an unethical act, it is highly likely that they know that they are doing the wrong thing. They will have an awareness of the issue and have arrived at an ethical solution but for some reason they don't act in accordance with their intention.

The question has to be that if the "ethical solicitor" knows what the right thing is, why don't they do it? The transgressions of the solicitors reported in the SDT case reports seem quite obviously unethical in the cold light of day; of course, a solicitor shouldn't reveal the identity of their client to anyone else, but it happens more often than most solicitors would care to admit.

Scenario: Confidentiality

Facts

A solicitor leaked information about the true identity of the author Robert Galbraith, thereby breaching the author's confidentiality. The solicitor revealed the information to his wife's best friend during a private conversation to someone in a "trusted capacity". The information then appeared in a national newspaper. The solicitor knew when he was having the conversation that he shouldn't have revealed anything but felt comfortable in doing so, perhaps because he didn't think the third party would tell anyone else. No one would know that he did it until the third party did tell someone else, a journalist, during a conversation on Twitter.

Outcome

The SRA rebuked the solicitor and ordered him to pay a fine of £1,000.

The author brought a legal action against the firm who made an undisclosed donation to a charity in settlement. This no doubt damaged the reputation of the firm. It seemingly didn't affect the solicitor's Legal 500 rankings as he is still at the same firm and listed by the directory.

External influences somehow outweigh the solicitor's correct ethical judgement, for various reasons. Many of you will think that this is just the way of the world and accept this as a risk of being in practice, whether in private practice or in-house. However, if we accept that the ethical solicitor knows

How To Be An Ethical Solicitor

what the right thing is and then acts upon that knowledge, external influences should have no impact on the decision-making process. Many of you will reject this notion entirely as being unrepresentative of your experience in the practice of law. It seems to be totally alien to your direct experiences but the cases from the SDT show that the Tribunal expects all solicitors, including trainees, to do the right thing regardless of external influences.

Potential external influences on the ethical decision-making process

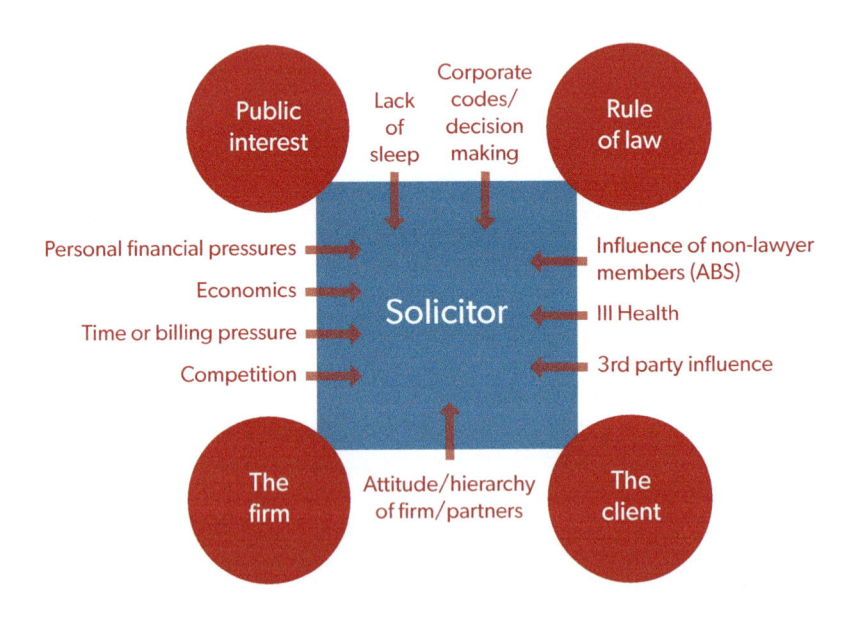

Fig 16: How does the solicitor do the right thing with external issues that need to be balanced?

3.12 The firm's influence on the "ethical solicitor"

Bad apple, bad barrel or bad orchard?

Sometimes the culture of the firm is such that the decision-making processes don't operate the way they should. This could be because one influential person is influencing another's decision-making processes to suit their own needs. In these cases it could be the case of a bad apple - one person who is affecting other solicitors. Or it could be a bad barrel - a certain team or department are operating unethically and because that behaviour is encouraged or accepted the members of that team don't recognise that what they are doing is unethical. In the worst cases, which would be rare, the firm or that particular sector is so competitive that the expectation is that everyone will conduct themselves in the same, unethical, way.

The following phrases aren't uncommon to hear from solicitors regarding ethical decision-making:

- "Solicitor X does whatever s/he wants to do and gets away with it" - *Bad apple?*

- "If it was up to me I would do Y but solicitor X told me to do Z" - *Bad barrel?*

- "If I make the right (ethical) decision, I will lose my job and if people find out what I did I won't get a job in this sector again" - *Bad orchard?*

The individual solicitor may perceive that there is an unethical culture in the firm for some reason and use that belief as a reason for justifying their own unethical decision-making. Crispin Passmore, former executive director of the SRA, says of the new Standards and Regulations: *"If we don't build the right cultures among the profession and law firms then we should not be surprised when solicitors make bad decisions when no one is looking."*

Firm culture is very important to building good practice. Where solicitors are practicing outside a firm structure, they will need to be more aware of ethical issues and how to deal with them on their own.

Remember that "the ethical solicitor" makes ethical choices no matter what external pressure may be applied by third parties for the wrong reasons.

Hierarchy

It is inevitable that the internal hierarchy of a private firm will influence the independence of every solicitor working in that firm. The message being transmitted from the top permeates the decisions made throughout the firm. The same can be said for the personal ethics and decision-making of the COLP and COFA. If it can be seen that the people with power within an organisation have a risky, approach to decision making this sets the scene for everyone else.

For those solicitors working in-house this problem becomes increasingly more difficult as there is only one client and the solicitor will not be able to walk away from that client without losing their job. The issues that face in-house lawyers are explored in the book: *"In-House Lawyers' Ethics"* by Richard Moorhead, Steven Vaughan and Cristina Godinho.

Independence within the firm

Principle 3 states that a solicitor should not allow their independence to be compromised; this is often associated with external influences on a solicitor.

However, the notion of independence is difficult to achieve in the context of power distribution within a firm. It is expected that "the ethical solicitor" won't be influenced by external factors. Arguably, many firms wouldn't want these types of solicitors to be recruited - many firms only recruit from within so that they can build the culture they want within a firm. External hires can upset the apple cart if the culture of the previous firm clashes with that of the new employer. In the case of takeovers and mergers, the problem can be exacerbated with the culture of one firm and its staff clashing with that of the other. The employees of the firm that is taken over could view the culture of the new firm as "bad barrel" or "bad orchard" scenarios causing an ethical ticking time bomb.

Weak → **Strong**

Trained NQ → Salaried partner → Equity partner

Fig 17: The ethical moral compass might be stronger or weaker in different solicitors

It is easy to see from this model that the number of years a solicitor has practised and their standing within the firm will impact on their ability to influence other solicitors and their ethical behaviour. Most fee earners will also be able to influence the other staff to a varying degree; it isn't unheard of for secretaries, paralegals and administrative staff to be asked to do something that would constitute both an ethical and compliance breach for a solicitor. The new Code of Conduct for individuals addresses this issue at Paragraph 3.5: *"Where you supervise or manage others providing legal services: (a) you remain accountable for the work carried out through them; and (b) you effectively supervise work being done for clients."* This ensures that the solicitor can't delegate the responsibility for doing something that could be a breach without the fear of sanction.

Whilst the non-solicitor staff aren't shown on the above model, it is easy to imagine that paralegals, secretaries and other support staff sit at the weak end of the arrow. Likewise non-legal managers of ABSs sit at the strong end and it is known that their non-legal influence on the structure of the firm is very great.

It is difficult to introduce successful ethics training programmes within a firm unless those solicitors (or non-legal managers) with the most influence participate and also act in ethical ways. The approach of the most influential members will impact the daily running of the firm. Any training must start with that of the people who have a strong influence and they must inject ethics training at a grassroots level.

3.13 Is unethical behaviour deeply embedded at your firm?

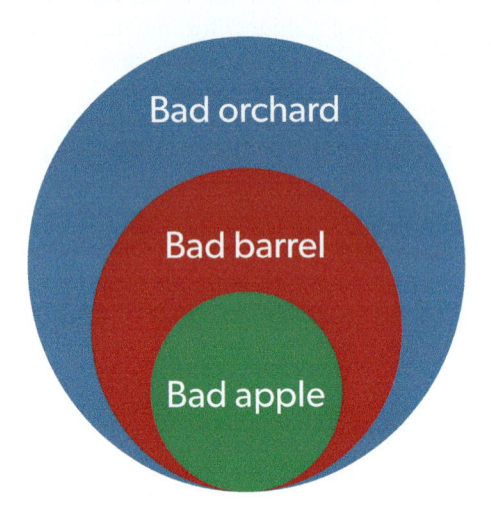

Fig 18: Is there one person causing ethical issues within the firm or is it the firm or sector that is infected with poor ethical decision-making?

Scenario: Pressure on junior solicitor

Facts

Solicitor S is 2 years PQE having trained and qualified with a Tier 1 Legal 500 firm - referred to as a "silver circle" firm.

S/he is told by a Partner to telephone a client to tell the client (in a roundabout way) to find, sign and backdate a vital document.

It seems that the Partner didn't get the vital document signed at the right time during a transaction and this will have a huge tax implication for the client. It is in the client's best interests to have the document in their possession.

Behaving Ethically

Regulatory position

The junior solicitor must observe the following Principles when deciding what action to take:

You act:

Principle 1: in a way that upholds the constitutional principle of the rule of law, and the proper administration of justice.

Principle 2: in a way that upholds public trust and confidence in the solicitors' profession and in legal services provided by authorised persons.

Principle 3: with independence.

Principle 4: with honesty.

Principle 5: with integrity.

The Code of Conduct for Solicitors

Paragraph 1.4: You do not mislead or attempt to mislead your clients, the court or others, either by your own acts or omissions or allowing or being complicit in the acts or omissions of others (including your client).

Paragraph 7.11: You are honest and open with clients if things go wrong, and if a client suffers loss or harm as a result you put matters right (if possible) and explain fully and promptly what has happened and the likely impact. If requested to do so by the SRA you investigate whether anyone may have a claim against you, provide the SRA with a report on the outcome of your investigation, and notify relevant persons that they may have such a claim, accordingly.

Paragraph 7.2: You are able to justify your decisions and actions in order to demonstrate compliance with your obligations under the SRA's regulatory arrangements.

Paragraph 7.7: You report promptly to the SRA or another approved regulator, as appropriate, any facts or matters that you reasonably believe are capable of amounting to a serious breach of their regulatory arrangements by any person regulated by them (including you).

Paragraph 7.12: Any obligation under this section or otherwise to notify, or provide information to, the SRA will be satisfied if you provide information to your firm's COLP or COFA, as and where appropriate, on the understanding that they will do so.

What does the junior solicitor do?

Option A: Do what the Partner says and hope that there is no regulatory fallout.

Option B: Go over the Partner's head and report the problem to the ethics/compliance department at the firm or a more senior person in the hope that they will broker a sensible resolution.

Option C: Report the breach to the COLP at the firm in the hope that s/he will broker a sensible resolution.

Option D: Tell the client that they might have a claim against the firm due to the Partner's error.

Option E: Speak to the Partner about the ethical issues and discuss the difficult position the junior solicitor is in as a result of the Partner's direction.

Potential ethical issues

The junior solicitor is culpable for his/her decision (Paragraph 7.2). The fact that the decision was directed by a more senior solicitor doesn't override the individual's responsibility to the client.

Option A isn't an ethical solution to the problem because it is doing the wrong thing for the wrong reason (protecting the Partner/protecting the firm). This would be an automatic decision made with the hope that no one would find out what happened.

Options B to E are all ethical solutions as they could all lead to the client being informed about the negligent action of the Partner who failed to get a signature on a vital document.

The junior solicitor may not know if the problem is:

- a bad apple - the Partner is acting without the knowledge or consent of the firm;

- a bad barrel - the department or firm condones/encourages this behaviour and internal reporting won't do any good;

- a bad orchard - this type of behaviour is commonplace in this sector/firm (which still doesn't excuse the behaviour).

The junior solicitor therefore doesn't know how to approach the dilemma which could be as follows:

- Bad apple - Choose Option B or E;

- Bad barrel - Choose Option C, D or E;

- Bad orchard - Choose Option D (but more likely to choose Option A if the junior solicitor feels there will be no action if they report further up the line).

A junior solicitor could struggle with Option E whereas a more senior solicitor in that position might always start with that option.

The ethical solicitor

The ethical solicitor knows what the right thing is and does the right thing, for the right reason, even if no-one is watching. Although it is in the client's best interests (Principle 7) to have the document signed, it isn't acting with honesty or integrity to falsify documents to achieve that end. It could be said that by taking option D the solicitor is acting in the best interests of the client in the most ethical way and meeting their personal obligation under Paragraph 7.11 of the Code of Conduct for individuals (the same provision appears at Paragraph 3.5 in the Code of Conduct for firms).

Being transparent about the issue and alerting the client to potential claims that can be made could be seen to be the most ethical solution.

- The right thing to do - don't sign the document.

- Acting on that knowledge - Options B, C, D, E.

- For the right reason - to protect the client's interests (not cover up the Partner's wrongdoing which is the wrong reason).

Additionally, a solicitor, if following Option C, can be satisfied that according to Paragraph 7.12 of the Code of Conduct for solicitors, any report to a COLP on the understanding that they will make the report satisfies their reporting obligation.

The COLP has obligations under the Code of Conduct for firms to ensure compliance (Paragraph 9.1(a)) and ensure a prompt report is made to the SRA of any matters they reasonably believe are capable of amounting to a serious breach. In this case, the document is being backdated to save tax and would therefore be presented to the relevant tax collection agency as a true document when that simply isn't the case.

The new code for firms provides additional whistleblowing protection to the junior solicitor as Paragraph 3.11 states that the firm should not prevent anyone from providing information to the SRA; or Paragraph 3.12 that states that a person isn't subjected to detrimental treatment for making a report or providing information.

In the following case, the SDT dealt with an individual solicitor who outlined a firm where unethical practices were widely practised. Solicitors shared tips with each other to circumvent the firm's file checking systems to ensure that files were active. This seems to be a bad barrel situation.

Scenario: Fabricating documents

Facts

Solicitor L was accused of fabricating documents to cover up inactivity on her files. By doing so she misled the client and the firm about the progress she was making.

Rules (2011 handbook)

Principle 2: Act with integrity.

Principle 4: Act in the best interests of each client.

Principle 5: Provide a proper standard of service to your clients.

Principle 6: Behave in a way that maintains the trust the public places in you and in the provision of legal services.

Ethical issues/professional breaches

Many difficulties for this solicitor came from the fact that she was covering up the actions of the Partner at a branch office. The Partner would often be absent from the office, working from home or a flat in Scotland. He would leave instructions that the other Partners were not to be told he was not there. This type of behaviour creates an unstable work environment and in this case for Solicitor L working unsupervised and under pressure.

The Partner told Solicitor L that she would be made redundant if she didn't meet her targets. He also told her that if she complained to the other Partners the department would be closed.

Another solicitor at the firm showed Solicitor L how to alter time recording to avoid the supervisor from finding out about delay on her files. This practice was widespread amongst the fee earners at the firm. This seems to indicate that the barrel was bad, perhaps as a result of the Partner's leadership and his own deceptions.

Outcome

The solicitor made the wrong choices for which she was suspended indefinitely.

Possible approaches

In hindsight, Solicitor L told the SDT that she wished she had approached another Partner at the other office who she thought would have helped her.

The COLP should have been the first port of call.

3.14 Do the right thing - for the right reason

Solicitors are undoubtedly influenced by third parties and external factors to act with the wrong reason in mind. For example:

(a) The solicitor wants to protect themselves against a complaint;

(b) The solicitor is being asked to cover up a mistake for someone else;

(c) The solicitor is protecting a senior solicitor against a complaint, criminal or civil action;

(d) The solicitor is protecting the reputation of the firm;

(e) The solicitor is maximising profit;

(f) The solicitor is maximising billable hours;

(g) The solicitor is protecting his or her job;

(h) Other financial or managerial concerns.

Any solicitor who acts with these goals in mind isn't acting in an ethical way, although many of you will recognise that it is very easy to put personal or firm interests above those of the individual client or the Principles laid out by the SRA.

In the above example, Solicitor L acted in a way to protect the Partner who was absent from the office without informing the other Partners. She covered up his wrongdoing but by doing so she started to commit her own wrongdoings. There seemed to be no reflection that the choices made by the Partner or the solicitor were likely to be detrimental to the clients. The Partner who caused the solicitor's bad decision-making did so for their own ends.

Occasionally the solicitor believes they are doing the right thing to protect the client but by doing so they breach other codes of conduct. For example, a solicitor who covered up the fact that an Employment Tribunal case had been dismissed thought they were protecting the client by doing this but of course the solicitor lied to the client repeatedly. This is not in keeping with being honest with the client, acting with integrity or acting in the client's best interests. A solicitor who is unable to deliver bad news to a client isn't able to act in their best interests.

3.15 Conclusion

Each solicitor will decide for themselves during the course of their practice which end of the ethical scale they choose to practise. What is certain is that there is no definite ethical line that we can all agree on.

Ethical | Unethical

There are multiple shades of grey and we need to find a shade that we are comfortable with after careful consideration of the regulatory framework.

- The ethical solicitor
- Flexibly ethical
- Ethical minimalist
- Unethical

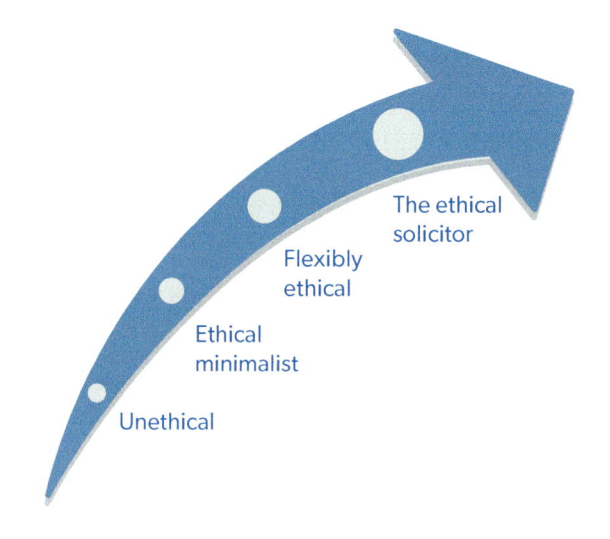

Fig 19: What is your position with regard to risk within the regulatory framework?

Sometimes the choices you make are dictated by the area of law you choose to specialise in; tax law and family law will bring their own unique challenges. The choices you make within your subject area will also be affected by the ethical behaviour of our peers, the Partners and more increasingly the non-lawyers. Whether they are managers in an ABS or corporate leaders in industry, they wield a lot of power. One matter that all solicitors must be aware of is the fact that ultimately you make your own choices. You decide how to act along the ethical scale and only you will be held responsible for those decisions.

It should also be noted that the mental, physical and financial wellbeing of solicitors is important to their ability to make good reflective decisions. A sleep deprived solicitor is more likely to make bad decisions because they simply don't have the capacity to properly reflect on the range of options. Equally, a solicitor who is suffering from financial pressures will make poor decisions in the work arena. In 2018, a young solicitor decided that he wouldn't pay his train fares because of the cost and poor service offered by the rail company. He perceived his personal financial position to be poor and justified his decision-making over a period of time. When he was caught and it was discovered that he regularly and consciously made the decision to travel without paying his fare, he was struck off.

Firms are more aware that the well-being of their solicitors is important - decision-making is much better handled when the external personal influences are recognised and managed.

Hopefully, the SDT cases we use in this chapter highlight that many of the "wrong" choices are made when solicitors aren't thinking about consequences or ethics at all. The example of the solicitors who sent crass emails thinking that no one would ever see them is the perfect case in point. In much the same way that learner drivers are taught to "mirror, signal, manoeuvre" until the repeated action becomes second nature, we propose that solicitors should learn to:

Think twice, act once

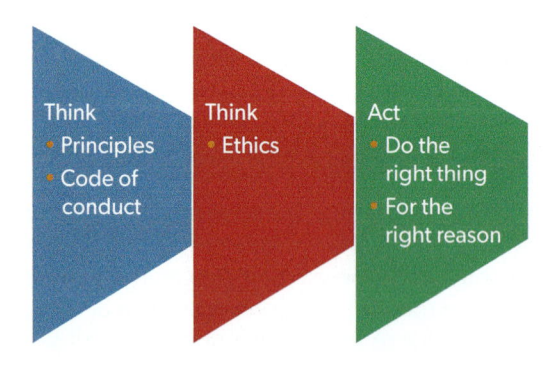

Fig 20: The old carpenter's proverb works here with a little adaptation - rather than "measure twice, cut once" we say that "think twice, act once" will have the same affect!

Many solicitors don't believe that they need to bother with "ethics" - they know the difference between right and wrong and they are relying on their automatic instinctual decision-making. As we have noted elsewhere in the book, the SRA requires solicitors to be able to justify their decisions (Paragraph 7.2 Code of Conduct for Solicitors); this is hard to do if decisions are made instinctively. Many solicitors are able to practise without ever attracting the notice of the SRA, which doesn't mean that they are supremely ethical or ethically minimalist. Solicitors in the 21st century need to ensure that they are familiar with the current system of regulation and how modern practices exert pressure over solicitors that can lead to unethical behaviour.

Behaving unethically can be a bit like 'flu in the sense that it can be catching. What was once a bad apple can infect the whole barrel. A solicitor who implements the "think twice, act once" reflective methodology is not only setting a template for himself or herself but also setting standards for others. What might seem to some as being unnecessary behaviour could impact the culture of the firm in a positive way.

Chapter 4: The client is king

4.1 Introduction

The relationship between the solicitor and their client is very important - the client needs the expertise of the solicitor and often that means that the solicitor is in a position of power and control. The relationship with the client is not the only relationship that needs to be monitored - often it isn't even the most important relationship the solicitor has. In Chapter 3 we explored the different obligations a solicitor has to the public in general as well as to the client. It is important that the client maintains their personal integrity at all times and honours their obligation to uphold the rule of law and the proper administration of justice. The client may not realise how broad the solicitor's obligations are when they retain their services.

The man on the Clapham omnibus may not know that buying a solicitor's time is different to buying a mechanic's time, for example. After all, if you took your car to a mechanic to repair the brakes, you wouldn't expect the mechanic to refuse because they have ethical objections to the way you drive your car. In the same way, the average client wouldn't expect a solicitor to refuse to represent them in a criminal case after telling the solicitor that they are guilty, or refuse to represent any person charged with sexual offences against children. The solicitor isn't able to refuse these instructions that might conflict with their personal ethics. The regulatory and ethical factors that interact with the client relationship are complex.

As expected there is a panoply of obligations set out by the SRA that regulate how solicitors should treat their clients and this applies whether the client is a regular user of legal services or a novice. The new Standards and Regulations which regulate the client relationship are divided into service to the client and further in connection with the deployment of client funds or protection of the client's asset which is outside the scope of this text. The Solicitors' Accounts Rules remain mainly rules-based albeit less prescriptive now. These rules are for the protection of client assets and so the regulatory and ethical obligations are clearly set out.

If a solicitor follows the individual and firm's Codes of Conduct then the client should not have any need to complain about the service received. However, complaints are inevitable - statistics produced by the Legal Ombudsman (LeO) show that commercial clients rarely complain to them about the service they receive. Many more complaints arise from clients requiring personal advice; these clients tend to be irregular users of legal services, whose expectations may not be met by their first interaction with legal service providers. It is useful to understand what is regulated behaviour, why it is regulated and what clients complain about. We deal with the complaints aspects of client service in detail in Chapter 6: Complaints and negligence.

Over the last 5 years the highest number of complaints dealt with by the LeO have been about residential conveyancing - 25% in the year 2018/2019. Contrast this with complaints about commercial conveyancing where complaints have been less than 2%. LeO on average accepts 6,200 cases per annum which means that on average 1,500 of those are about residential conveyancing. This either indicates that commercial clients don't make complaints or that their complaints are resolved by the firm without the need for LeO to get involved.

4.2   Regulatory issues

We looked at the 7 Principles and the ethical elements of each in Chapter 2, so we do not propose to duplicate that commentary here. However, it is worth noting that the best interests of the client is the final principle. Although the Principles are not set out in order of importance, it is no accident that this Principle is last and that Principle 1 and 2 take priority where there is a conflict of Principles that apply to any dilemma. It is instructive to take a close look at the Codes of Conduct to see what the regulatory starting point is.

Issues about client care now set out in Chapter 3 of the Code of Conduct for Solicitors and Chapter 4 of the Code of Conduct for Firms. As set out elsewhere many of the rules are there to ensure that clients are protected and informed about their rights when dealing with a solicitor.

Due to the power imbalance between the solicitor providing personal services and the client, it is important that these safety checks are kept in place. However, commercial clients may not benefit from any additional protections by the existence of these regulations. The new Codes therefore ensure that the right information is given to each client. Paragraph 8.6 (Code of Conduct for Solicitors) and Paragraph 7.1 (Code of Conduct for Firms) ensure that the client understands and can make decisions about the services they need and what options they have. This means that commercial clients may not need as much information to make decisions and individuals may need more information or that it should be presented in a way that is easier for them to understand.

The Client Is King

What it says	Code of Conduct for Solicitors	Code of Conduct for Firms	Rules based	Ethics based
You do not abuse your position by taking unfair advantage of clients or others.	Para 1.2	Para 1.2		✓
You do not mislead or attempt to mislead your clients, the court or others, either by your own acts or omissions or allowing or being complicit in the acts or omissions of others (including your client).	Para 1.4	Para 1.4		✓
You only act for clients on instructions from the client, or from someone properly authorised to provide instructions on their behalf. If you have reason to suspect that the instructions do not represent your client's wishes, you do not act unless you have satisfied yourself that they do. However, in circumstances where you have legal authority to act notwithstanding that it is not possible to obtain or ascertain the instructions of your client, then you are subject to the overriding obligation to protect your client's best interests.	Para 3.1	Para 4.1	✓	✓
You ensure that the service you provide to clients is competent and delivered in a timely manner.	Para 3.2	Para 4.2	✓	✓
You consider and take account of your client's attributes, needs and circumstances.	Para 3.4	Para 4.2		✓

What it says	Code of Conduct for Solicitors	Code of Conduct for Firms	Rules based	Ethics based
You properly account to clients for any financial benefit you receive as a result of their instructions, except where they have agreed otherwise.	Para 4.1	Para 5.1		✓
You safeguard money and assets entrusted to you by clients and others.	Para 4.2	Para 5.2	✓	
You keep the affairs of current and former clients confidential unless disclosure is required or permitted by law or the client consents.	Para 6.3	Para 6.3	✓	
Where you are acting for a client on a matter, you make the client aware of all information material to the matter of which you have knowledge, except when: (a) the disclosure of the information is prohibited by legal restrictions imposed in the interests of national security or the prevention of crime; (b) your client gives informed consent, given or evidenced in writing, to the information not being disclosed to them; (c) you have reason to believe that serious physical or mental injury will be caused to your client or another if the information is disclosed; or (d) the information is contained in a privileged document that you have knowledge of only because it has been mistakenly disclosed.	Para 6.4	Para 6.4 (slightly different wording with same outcomes)	✓	✓

The Client Is King

What it says	Code of Conduct for Solicitors	Code of Conduct for Firms	Rules based	Ethics based
You do not act for a client in a matter where that client has an interest adverse to the interest of another current or former client of you or your business or employer, for whom you or your business or employer holds confidential information which is material to that matter, unless: (a) effective measures have been taken which result in there being no real risk of disclosure of the confidential information; or (b) the current or former client whose information you or your business or employer holds has given informed consent, given or evidenced in writing, to you acting, including to any measures taken to protect their information.	Para 6.5	Para 6.5	✓	
You are honest and open with clients if things go wrong, and if a client suffers loss or harm as a result you put matters right (if possible) and explain fully and promptly what has happened and the likely impact. If requested to do so by the SRA you investigate whether anyone may have a claim against you, provide the SRA with a report on the outcome of your investigation, and notify relevant persons that they may have such a claim, accordingly.	Para 7.1	Para 3.5	✓	✓
You identify who you are acting for in relation to any matter.	Para 8.1	Para 7.1(c)	✓	

91

What it says	Code of Conduct for Solicitors	Code of Conduct for Firms	Rules based	Ethics based
Complaints handling	Section 8			
You give clients information in a way they can understand. You ensure they are in a position to make informed decisions about the services they need, how their matter will be handled and the options available to them.	Para 8.6	Para 7.1(c)	✓	✓
You ensure that clients receive the best possible information about how their matter will be priced and, both at the time of engagement and when appropriate as their matter progresses, about the likely overall cost of the matter and any costs incurred.	Para 8.7	Para 7.1(c)	✓	
You ensure that any publicity in relation to your practice is accurate and not misleading, including that relating to your charges and the circumstances in which interest is payable by or to clients.	Para 8.8	Para 7.1(c)	✓	
You do not make unsolicited approaches to members of the public, with the exception of current or former clients, in order to advertise legal services provided by you, or your business or employer.	Para 8.9	Para 7.1(c)	✓	

What it says	Code of Conduct for Solicitors	Code of Conduct for Firms	Rules based	Ethics based
You ensure that clients understand whether and how the services you provide are regulated. This includes: (a) explaining which activities will be carried out by you, as an authorised person; (b) explaining which services provided by you, your business or employer, and any separate business are regulated by an approved regulator; and (c) ensuring that you do not represent any business or employer which is not authorised by the SRA, including any separate business, as being regulated by the SRA.	Para 8.10	Para 7.1(c)	✓	
You ensure that clients understand the regulatory protections available to them.	Para 8.11	Para 7.1(c)	✓	

How To Be An Ethical Solicitor

4.3 The Codes of Conduct – the client's perspective

The two Codes have similar obligations that individual solicitors and firms owe to their client. The table below compares where these can be found in each Code and whether the obligations are purely rules-based or whether there are ethical dimensions to consider.

We will explore the ethical dimensions of those paragraphs of the New Codes of Conduct identified above. Complaints are dealt with in Chapter 6 so we will not mention them again here.

Code of Conduct for Solicitors and Firms Paragraph 1.2

You do not abuse your position by taking unfair advantage of clients or others.

The focus on fairness has shifted in the new regime; we are now told not to take unfair advantage of the client or others whereas before the Code stated that you would treat your clients fairly.

The concept of fairness is quite subjective even when taken in the context of this regulatory structure. Fairness according to whom? In the context of this regime, you define what is perceived to be taking an unfair advantage and record your decision. If, of course, the regulator feels differently then you could be sanctioned. The likelihood of sanction would be quite high as the enforcement strategy makes it clear that the SRA has a focus on "quality and client care". Suggestions that you might have taken unfair advantage of a client would therefore meet the glare of the regulator. This, of course, would be in the context of proportionate regulation and proportionate sanctions. The SRA say that they "will act fairly and proportionately".

Fairness is defined as follows:

(1) The ability to make judgements free from discrimination or dishonesty; this would be a "value ethics" definition. Using your personal values can you treat this client "fairly"? Likewise can you avoid treating the client unfairly?

(2) The conformity with rules or standards. This is a "rules-based" approach to problem solving - what do the rules and regulations say about the matter? Once you can answer that question you have your answer - there are few grey areas with this type of regulation.

This provision operates in conjunction with Principle 7 that requires the solicitor and firms to act in the best interests of each client. The client is entitled to expect that you will act with honesty and integrity towards them and to do what is in their best interests. However, this is not a carte blanche to disregard the instructions of the client. Many complaints to LeO are that the solicitor failed to act on the instructions of the client; some measure of balance needs to be sought.

There can often be a strain between what you believe to be in the best interests of your client and what they believe to be in their best interests. We look at this further in Chapter 8 which explores the use of litigation and ADR.

Code of Conduct for Solicitors and Firms Paragraph 1.4

You do not mislead or attempt to mislead your clients, the court or others, either by your own acts or omissions or allowing or being complicit in the acts or omissions of others (including your client).

Naturally, Principles 1, 2 4 and 5 are engaged when looking at this provision. Being honest and transparent with the client means that you should not mislead them, even if you believe that you are acting in their best interest.

There are numerous reported decisions of the SRA and SDT that indicate that solicitors can sometimes fail to be honest with their clients about matters. Sometimes this is to cover up mistakes made by the solicitor, which lacks integrity. Other times this is to spare the client anxiety, whilst this might seem noble it lacks transparency and good judgement.

Code of Conduct for Solicitors Paragraph 3.1, and Code of Conduct for Firms Paragraph 4.1

You only act for clients on instructions from the client, or from someone properly authorised to provide instructions on their behalf. If you have reason to suspect that the instructions do not represent your client's wishes, you do not act unless you have satisfied yourself that they do. However, in circumstances where you have legal authority to act notwithstanding that it is not possible to obtain or ascertain the instructions of your client, then you are subject to the overriding obligation to protect your client's best interests.

This provision seems to be mixed; rules and ethics-based. It starts off in a very straightforward rules led manner - you should only act on instructions from a client or someone authorised by them.

There are then shades of grey; if you suspect that the instructions are not your client's wishes you do not act unless you know that they are. This could apply where there could be an opportunity for a third party to be pressurising the client, for example a vulnerable client making a will, or even a client is being pressured into entering into a contract. In these cases you would have to exercise caution when taking instructions.

Finally, you have an obligation to remember Principle 7 where you have legal authority to act but you can't get your client's unequivocal instructions; you must act in their best interests. This is clearly not about following rules and ensuring you have the authority to act but whether it is the best thing for the client to do so.

Scenario: Helping someone to avoid arrest

Facts

A criminal solicitor informed a client that the police were looking to arrest him and gave him some advice on how to leave the country. He suggested to the client that there were a couple of routes that he could take, one of which was via Dublin. The police wrongly believed that the client was already in prison on other offences when in fact he had been released on home detention which is how he had avoided arrest to that point.

Rules (2011 rules and outcomes)

Principle 1: Whilst this might satisfy the requirement to protect a client's interest it certainly doesn't uphold the rule of law and the administration of justice.

Principle 2: Act with integrity. Many would agree that the solicitor wasn't acting with integrity when he alerted his client about his po- tential arrest. The local press reported that he was the "go-to-guy" for some of the area's most notorious criminals. Perhaps not the reputation that most solicitors would seek to foster.

Principle 3: Do not allow your independence to be compromised. Arguably the solicitor hasn't acted in an independent way - he has acted favourably towards the client for some reason.

Principle 6: Behave in a way that maintains the trust the public places in him. The public would not expect solicitors to aid a criminal in his escape from arrest.

Breaches

The solicitor in question was heard on a listening device monitored by the police giving the advice to the client who almost managed to escape the country. He was imprisoned for two years for perverting the course of justice and struck off by the SRA.

All the regulatory breaches were made out against him in his absence. It is interesting to note that the solicitor had not accepted that he had perverted the course of justice by warning his client to flee.

The remarks of the sentencing judge assisted the Tribunal in the absence of the solicitor who failed to engage with the process;

> "...it is abundantly clear to me that by last year you had completely lost your moral compass and instead of seeking to uphold the course of justice you were doing what you could to assist to pervert it.
>
> ...There is no higher degree of trust than [sic] can be placed upon anybody than as being an officer of the court and the system of jus- tice places that highest degree of trust in you as a solicitor."

The solicitor was ordered to pay costs of £3,350.

Code of Conduct for Solicitors Paragraphs 3.2 and 3.4, and Code of Conduct for Firms Paragraph 4.2

You ensure that the service you provide to clients is competent and delivered in a timely manner. You consider and take account of your client's attributes, needs and circumstances.

Code of Conduct for Solicitors Paragraph 8.6, and Code of Conduct for Firms Paragraph 7.1 (c)

You give clients information in a way they can understand. You ensure they are in a position to make informed decisions about the services they need, how their matter will be handled and the options available to them.

Parts of these separate but similar provisions depend on adherence to rules - for example delivering service in a timely manner will not have an ethical element, *per se*. Clients' complaints (section 8 and considered in a separate chapter) that a matter took too long to complete, when there was no specified period within which completion was required to take place, are common.

The issue of competence of the service isn't strictly rules-based, particularly as the issue of solicitor competence is self-regulating insofar as the issue of overall competence is for the solicitor to assess and certify when applying annually for the practising certificate. With no mandatory Continuing Professional Development requirements foisted on the profession we are trusted to keep ourselves updated on the tools needed to do our job competently.

This provision requires the solicitor to take into account the client's needs and circumstances. This can be difficult when dealing with vulnerable clients and those with fluid capacity. In these instances, the solicitor has to engage additional protection for the client to ensure that the client understands the advice that is being given and that their circumstances are assessed regularly.

This can be tricky where the client doesn't disclose any special needs but it becomes clear during the course of the retainer that there might be issues that the solicitor needs to work with. For example, some clients may not admit that they can't read, are dyslexic, deaf, etc. Where the client has suffered a bereavement or is in the process of getting divorced, client service needs to be adjusted to take these factors into account.

The Law Society issued a practice note in 2015 giving guidance on how to meet the needs of vulnerable clients. The Law Society highlights the difficulty for vulnerable clients to access legal services. Solicitors should adapt their practices to identify those clients and adapt their practice to meet their client's needs. Three categories of vulnerable client are identified;

- Clients who have capacity to give instructions but due to a range of physical or mental disabilities need enhanced support from the solicitor to give instructions;

- Clients who lack mental capacity to make decisions;

- Clients who are vulnerable to undue influence or duress who may or may not have mental capacity to make decisions and give instructions.

All solicitors should understand these differences and assess clients who may be vulnerable so that they can adapt their practice to meet the needs of that client.

In addition, the SRA has a note on providing services to people who are vulnerable dated 9 March 2016 which should be read and considered. These are clients who need additional levels of service and so their vulnerabilities must be assessed early and adaptations made to ensure that the client is dealt with fairly and provided a service appropriate to their needs.

The client needs to understand what options are available, what the positive and negative outcomes of each option could be, the costs implications of each option and how each option will be delivered. Only then can they make a decision about the way forward. This will require particular thought and flexibility from the solicitor where the client has different needs.

Scenario: Inappropriate dealings with the client

Facts

A married family solicitor was acting for a vulnerable victim of domestic abuse. During this difficult time he sent her inappropriate text messages which were characterised as "flirtatious". He was representing the woman in a domestic violence application.

During the period of 9 days he referred to her ex-boyfriend as a "cheeky tw*t" and sent multiple messages telling her that she was "lovely" and a "right glamour puss". He invited her out to lunch which she believed to be an invitation to a date. She had responded to the text messages at the time in a similar way.

Rules (2011 rules and outcomes)

Principle 4: Act in the best interests of each client.

Principle 6: Behave in a way that maintains the trust the public places in him.

Breaches

He was dismissed by his firm when his messages came to light and he had not been able to find work in the profession afterwards.

The client told the SDT that the messages made her sick and she felt that she had no choice but to respond to the messages because she did not want to jeopardise her case. This is a classic example of the power imbalance between a solicitor and client, which is highlighted when the client is vulnerable. There were many text and WhatsApp messages between the solicitor and the client and many of them referred to her physical appearance. She had also complained that her solicitor had hugged her and held her hands at least once.

Some allegations regarding the text messages were proven to the required standard; he was found to be in breach of Principles 4 and 6 and Outcome (1.1) - to treat clients fairly.

Only one of the numerous allegations had been proven against the solicitor and he was fined £5,000, which was more than just a nominal order to register the Tribunal's disapproval of the solicitor's conduct. Costs were ordered against him of £3,500.

Suggested course of action

The Tribunal recommended that the majority of allegations were not proven to the required standard, and some sound advice was given for other solicitors to bear in mind:

> *"This case demonstrated the need for solicitors to avoid any dealings with clients which were or could be viewed as inappropriate.*
>
> *Solicitors ought generally to avoid the use of bad language unless it was clearly necessary.... Solicitors should also beware of patronising clients by suggesting there was any need to "go down" to their level. Whilst many clients might benefit from being treated in a friendly and informal way others, including victims of domestic violence, might benefit more from being treated respectfully."*

Code of Conduct for Solicitors and Firms Paragraph 6.2

Where you are acting for a client on a matter, you make the client aware of all information material to the matter of which you have knowledge, except when:

(a) the disclosure of the information is prohibited by legal restrictions imposed in the interests of national security or the prevention of crime;

(b) your client gives informed consent, given or evidenced in writing, to the information not being disclosed to them;

(c) you have reason to believe that serious physical or mental injury will be caused to your client or another if the information is disclosed; or

(d) the information is contained in a privileged document that you have knowledge of only because it has been mistakenly disclosed.

This provision is both rules-based, in that you can't disclose matters to the client if such a disclosure is prohibited (subsection (a)), and has ethical dimensions. An example might be that a report has been made to the National Crime Agency with regards to suspected money laundering.

Subsection (b) refers to the possibility that your client has given informed consent not to be updated; this might refer to a case in which there could be a possible conflict arising and the client has agreed that the solicitor can act. That client wouldn't be in a position to know everything if it pertained to part of the transaction where the possibility of conflict would arise. These are tricky areas and high risk. Occasionally clients might want to control the method and timing of communication of information; for example, in contentious litigation proceedings, clients can sometimes request that they don't receive emotionally distressing information just before the weekend, or by email. However, withholding this information wouldn't be appropriate but managing the delivery of information is responsible.

Subsection (c) requires a good level of interaction and knowledge of your client, their vulnerabilities and how they would receive information. These are tricky cases and any reflective decision-making would need to be carefully recorded for the future so as to be able to recall and justify the circumstances that lead to withholding or giving such information that might cause injury. This type of decision could rarely be made automatically as the seriousness of making the wrong decision would be grave.

Subsection (d) is another situation where the client would struggle to understand that Principle 7, to act in their best interests, could be overreached by other considerations; in this case, a privileged document being mistakenly disclosed. This can easily happen if such a document is emailed to the wrong recipient (the opposing solicitor rather than the client) or even accidentally placed in a bundle of documents made available to the court. In these circumstances, the solicitor would not be able to disclose that information and by a wider interpretation of the provision would not be able to act on information seen in that document. If the solicitor is acting in adherence to Principles 1, 2 and 4 the solicitor will be honest and make the breach known to the other solicitors who may then need to self-report an issue to the SRA, depending on the sensitivity of the breach of confidentiality. Problems can arise when one solicitor appears to be acting in an ethical way to an issue arising but the other solicitor does not.

For example, solicitor A tells solicitor B that they have seen a letter of advice to their client in which their best offer is clear; that offer is better than any made so far. Solicitor A has not shared the letter or information with their client and has been acting in a way that is honest and transparent. Solicitor B, upon discovering the issue, doesn't self-report the mistaken disclosure to the SRA, indicating that they do not consider the matter one that needs to be reported, particularly because solicitor A has been so honest and their client doesn't know anything. This can cause ill feeling between the solicitors, particularly as one client is effectively in the dark about the existence of the issue. If solicitor A's client discovered that their solicitor had information which could have been used to their benefit, they might not feel that their solicitor was acting in their best interests. It would be easy enough to imagine that solicitor A could accidentally disclose the information without anyone knowing; the ethical solicitor of course, does the right thing even if no one is looking.

Code of Conduct for Solicitors Paragraph 7.1, and Code of Conduct for Firms Paragraph 3.5

You are honest and open with clients if things go wrong, and if a client suffers loss or harm as a result you put matters right (if possible) and explain fully and promptly what has happened and the likely impact. If requested to do so by the SRA you investigate whether anyone may have a claim against you, provide the SRA with a report on the outcome of your investigation, and notify relevant persons that they may have such a claim, accordingly.

It is interesting to note that this provision is wider than the previous Outcome (1.16) which said: "You inform current clients if you discover any act or omission which could give rise to a claim by them against you".

The new provision isn't just about legal claims that could be made by the client against the solicitor. It is about things going wrong and the ability to own up to the client and attempt to put things right if possible.

It seems to be the essence of what virtue ethics is about. The "ethical solicitor" is honest enough to recognise when they have done something which could lead to loss or harm or a claim being made. The ethical solicitor will recognise that they have a duty to "do the right thing" and either attempt to put the matter right or, if not, report the error or oversight to the client. It is difficult to say how many solicitors are able to recognise such a failing on their own part. There are instances in the SDT cases of solicitors self-reporting issues which are not proceeded with by the SRA only for the matter to be treated quite seriously by the Tribunal.

There is an identical regulatory requirement for firms to self-report major compliance breaches and the SRA believes that since its introduction under OFR this has led to greater compliance within firms. This is similar to the way in which the financial services sector approaches regulation, nominating a compliance officer to ensure adherence to the FCA regulations.

Since the introduction of compliance officers in firms, self-reporting incidents to the SRA have rocketed. Many of these reports involve the misappropriation of funds either by partners or bookkeepers.

The SRA has a number of case studies on its website which demonstrate some reports received from compliance officers - they can be summarised as follows:

(1) A secretary in the wills and probate department approached a client who had received an inheritance with an investment opportunity. The client was not sophisticated, and also vulnerable with the recent bereavement. The secretary was dismissed. The SRA is investigating.

(2) A COLP reported to the SRA that the firm had not registered with the Information Commissioner. There was no evidence of detriment to clients during the short period that the firm was not registered. The breach was not material and did not need to be made.

(3) During the administration of an estate, the solicitor had on six occasions transferred money from office to client account for the payment of costs totalling £36,956. No invoices were raised and the beneficiaries were not notified of the costs. These are material breaches but the matter had been rectified.

The SRA doesn't seem to have any statistics available on their website that indicates how many self-reports are made under this requirement.

4.4 Corporate/Commercial lawyers

Corporate/commercial lawyers have a reputation for doing what it takes to satisfy their clients. The application of ethics may not come high on the list of personality traits to make a good corporate lawyer for the firm hiring them or for the client wanting to engage their services. Clients in this sector have a huge influence on the firms they engage and the terms on which they are willing to engage their services. The balance of power could be said to be in the hands of the powerful corporate client rather than the law firm or solicitor. This approach to over zealous lawyering with perhaps under zealous ethics application has come into the spotlight in a few cases over the last five years.

This may be changing with increasing numbers of corporate clients only hiring solicitors if ethics testing has taken place. This is particularly relevant with regards to diversity issues. The client holds the key to the importance of ethics in the corporate world it would seem. It is certainly true to say that the regulator doesn't seem to be regularly involved in controlling zealousness on the part of corporate lawyers.

The Law Society Gazette published an article in which they reported that MPs have criticised the SRA for failing to get involved in issues concerning a magic circle firm. There is a general view that the SRA takes a "light touch" approach when dealing with big firms and lately its approach to the possibly improper use of Non Disclosure Agreements (NDAs).

Scenario: Disbursements

Facts

A city solicitor allowed taxi bills and secretarial overtime to be billed to clients as disbursements; this is usually taken to mean photocopying or scanning charges. No clients had complained about the solicitor's bills and they did not seek reimbursement from the firm.

Rules (the 2007 Solicitors' Code of Conduct applied in this case)

Principle 2: Act with integrity (these allegations were withdrawn by the SRA by agreement).

Principle 4: Failing to act in the best interests of his clients.

Principle 6: Behaving in a manner that was likely to diminish the trust placed in him and the legal profession.

Breaches

It is interesting to note that the solicitor was represented by Queen's Counsel at the preliminary hearings - the spending power of the solicitor is clearly contrasted against other ordinary solicitors, some of whom are not represented at all. All the remaining allegations were admitted by the solicitor who was fined £20,000 with a costs order of £38,000. The SDT said that it was unfortunate that the SRA had decided to deal with the case the way it had:

> *"This was particularly so where the impression may be given to the profession and to the public that the applicant was willing to discontinue serious allegations against a City lawyer when it was not often willing to do so against solicitors from smaller firms."*

Chapter 5: You v The rest of the world

5.1 Introduction

What is the nature of the duty that solicitors owe to third parties? The SRA has dedicated Part 7 of the Code of Conduct for Solicitors and Part 3 of the Code of Conduct for Firms to the nature of a solicitor's relations with the SRA. In addition the Codes require firms and solicitors to act in specific ways with third parties which is very important. The sometimes competing nature of the Principles and the Codes means that the solicitor can face any number of dilemmas on a daily basis.

In this chapter, we examine the solicitor's duties to others whilst acting for their client. Solicitors rarely act in isolation to third parties and so there are numerous people and organisations you can expect to deal with, including;

(1) The court (Part 2 Code of Conduct for Solicitors and Paragraph 7.1(a) Code of Conduct for Firms)

(2) Other solicitors

(3) The Land Registry

(4) Estate agents

(5) HMRC

(6) Companies House

(7) Litigants in Person

(8) McKenzie Friends

(9) Members of the Board if an ABS

(10) Managers (non-lawyer)

(11) Non-lawyer owners

(12) Police

(13) Social Services

(14) Teachers

This list highlights the daily interactions a solicitor has with people and organisations other than their client. It is unlikely that a solicitor operates without any interaction with third parties.

Being a professional means that others should be able to interact with you reassured in the knowledge that your conduct is regulated to the highest standards. We previously explored the ethical behaviour of solicitors in Chapter 3 and so in this chapter we intend to highlight the fine balance of a solicitor's duties to third parties and the numerous ethical dimensions to be considered.

Fig 21: Your client is at the centre of decision-making but other issues surround your client and can't be ignored

5.2 The client above all else?

One of the principle ethical dilemmas faced by solicitors is the extent to which they owe a duty to their clients. As a solicitor, ask yourself these questions:

- Do you owe the client a duty to the **detriment** of everyone else?

- Do you **only** owe the client a duty to inform them about the law and then let them make ethical decisions going forward?

- Should the client be the first amongst equals with an **equal duty** to third parties after considering the client's position?

Solicitors in private practice may answer those questions very differently to solicitors who work in-house. In private practice, you will have exposure to numerous clients and the clients may change quickly within a year whereas if you work in-house, you have only one client. This means that the way you approach your client and the way they proceed when in possession of your advice will be very different. As we consider the regulatory and ethical issues the answers to these questions may change.

5.3 The Principles

Solicitors, by the very nature of their profession, have duties that extend beyond the client, even if that person is paying their fee. Whilst some would argue that the solicitor's main or only duty is to advance the interest of their client, the overarching SRA Principles counteract that view. This is sometimes difficult for the solicitor to grasp, given the complexities surrounding the nature of client relationships and the inevitable commercial pressures every solicitor faces.

The foundations

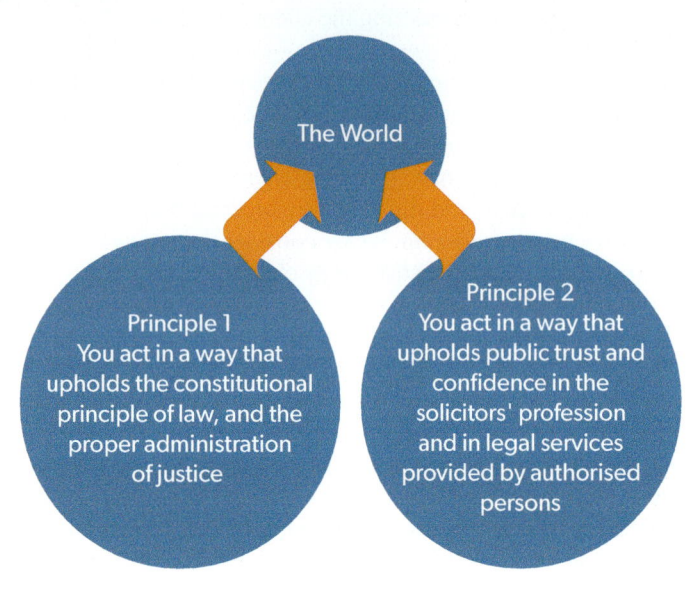

```
                    ┌─────────────┐
                    │  The World  │
                    └─────────────┘
                       ↑       ↑
    ┌──────────────────┘       └──────────────────┐
    │   Principle 1            │   Principle 2    │
    │ You act in a way that    │ You act in a way that
    │ upholds the constitutional│ upholds public trust and
    │ principle of law, and the │ confidence in the
    │ proper administration     │ solicitors' profession
    │ of justice                │ and in legal services
    │                           │ provided by authorised
    │                           │ persons
```

Fig 22: Two of the Principles operate against the world in general as opposed to the client individually

Naturally these are also combined with Principles 4 and 5 - solicitors **must** act with honesty and integrity. This matter is fully explored in Chapter 3. The combination of these Principles means that a solicitor needs to think carefully when interacting with third parties on behalf of a client.

Code of Conduct for Solicitors and Code of Conduct for Firms Paragraph 1.2

You do not abuse your position by taking unfair advantage of clients or others.

Having read Chapter 3 you will be aware that it is expected that a solicitor will act with honesty and integrity at all times. This paragraph of the Codes has been considered in Chapter 4 as it combines obligations to the client and those to third parties.

Solicitors should not take *unfair advantage* of their client or third parties. After all, the professional capacity in which you act places you in a position that is thought of as being trustworthy to all and not just to your clients. The expected level of knowledge that the solicitor has puts them at a distinct advantage, which is why such knowledge should be used wisely.

There is no definition for the term "unfair advantage"; each case will turn on its own facts and solicitors need to be increasingly aware that they could be using their position of trust in a way that will not be interpreted as being ethical.

Scenario: Partnership agreement

Note that this isn't a regulatory case that was before the SRA or the Tribunal. This case was decided in the Court of Appeal.

Facts

Two solicitors had agreed to enter into partnership but didn't enter into a partnership agreement. Mr B thought he was owed money on his retirement and Ms H didn't agree. The Judge indicated that *"Mr B bears the greater responsibility for the failure of the parties to document their agreement and he may to a degree have taken advantage of Ms H's comparative lack of experience"*.

Plainly the fact that one had more experience than the other was a notable issue.

Solicitors are widely accepted as the face of the legal system and they have traditionally been situated on high streets across the country. Widely accessible to both paying and pro bono clients, they are at the coalface. Traditionally barristers have not been so easily accessible and although these roles are changing, the public perception of a solicitor and a barrister is likely to be different.

This client-facing role places a high ethical expectation on solicitors, more so than upon the ordinary non-professional employee. This is because solicitors are expected to show due care and skill and be seen to be upholding the rule of law generally. In fact, all qualified members of the legal profession carry similar ethical obligations, whether they are regulated by the SRA, the BSB or CILEx.

It is possible that the ethical expectations placed upon the shoulders of solicitors is higher than that expected from other types of professionals. If this is correct then the reason for the higher expectation could be that solicitors' skills have a higher impact/harm than perhaps the actions of an accountant. A recent survey holds lawyers in the top three of professionals trusted by the public; GPs came out on top with teachers coming second. Unsurprisingly, lawyers come out much better than politicians, bankers and journalists[1].

Every person whom a solicitor meets in the course of their life is entitled to hold them to account to exercise due care and skill, to adhere to the SRA Principles and to act within the ethical boundaries expected of them. This means that the solicitor must behave ethically at all times and not just between the hours of 9am and 5pm.

If, in your capacity as a solicitor, you send a document to a third party they are entitled to rely on the content and truth of that document. They should not question the veracity of the document - they are entitled to believe that you haven't tampered with the document in any way because you bear the title of "solicitor" and that means that you can be trusted. In recent years this has been tested by a number of banks who were sending letters to their clients that purported to be from separate solicitor's firms when in fact the letters were coming from the banks. It was reported in 2014 that in-house solicitors had been sending debt chasing letters to their clients, which purported to be in the name of firms that were in-house firms. When this practice was discovered it was felt that this could be a breach of the Principle to act in a way that upholds the public trust. In any event it didn't seem to be fully transparent behaviour and certainly wouldn't be considered to be acting honesty in compliance with new Principle 4.

An example of solicitors behaving in a way that is designed to help clients whilst balancing commercial realities is shown below.

---

[1] *In Professions We Trust - Fostering virtuous practitioners in teaching, law and medicine.*

Scenario: Criminal legal aid applications

Facts

It appears that there is a practice within some criminal practices to ask a client to sign a legal aid application form *before* the client has been charged with an offence. This practice has arisen recently as criminal solicitors now receive a fixed fee payment for attendance at a police station with the client. This means that they often won't be with the client at the point of charge - the form therefore needs to be signed by the client in advance.

Arguably the action is carried out for the right reason - it is in the client's best interests as it ensures that they are represented at the first hearing.

Potential ethical/professional breaches

By dating the form on a date after charge, which will be different to the date that the client signed the form, the solicitor is representing to the Legal Aid Agency that the form was signed by the client on that day, which is clearly not the case.

The conveyancing solicitor will hold a signed transfer deed to be dated on the day of transfer. Does this differ from the criminal solicitor holding a signed legal aid form waiting for the client to be charged?

The solicitor's duty to the third party (Legal Aid Agency) is to ensure that the proper administration of justice is done. The solicitor's duty to the client is to ensure that they are able to represent the client at the court hearing and that legal aid is arranged for that purpose.

Suggested action

Arguably, the client's interests could be met by asking the client to attend the office to sign the forms after charge and before the hearing. There are practical issues with this course of action as it can be difficult to get clients to take an interest in the paperwork. The duty to the client is equal to that of the duty to the third party.

In the alternative, the solicitor could re-attend the client at the point of charge, but of course there are fee implications of doing this.

How To Be An Ethical Solicitor

Compare this to the conveyancer who holds the signed transfer deed or contract; all parties in that transaction know that the documents have been signed pending exchange of contracts and completion. Does the Legal Aid Agency know that the forms are being signed in advance and kept on the file? If so, does the LAA regulate against such action?

There are both ethical and regulatory considerations when taking on board Principles 2 and 4 in the above scenario; it is possible that the duty to the third party is greater than the standalone duty to act in the best interests of the client.

There are many of you who could not conceive of such actions happening regularly, but we imagine there are at least an equal number who would not see this as an ethical or regulatory matter.

There are numerous examples from the SDT judgments of solicitors who have "tampered" with documents.

Scenario: Declaration of Trust

Facts

Solicitor N created a Declaration of Trust, which he submitted to the Land Registry. The document purported to be created in 2004 when in fact it had been created in 2007. In addition, he submitted to his lender clients incorrect or incomplete information about transaction values for a series of related transactions for the same clients. There were allegations of dishonesty levied against Solicitor N.

Regulatory matters

The solicitor admitted all breaches of the Rules and Regulations, which were brought under the Solicitors' Code of Conduct 2007. He denied the allegation of dishonesty.

In creating the Deed of Declaration of Trust and sending it to the Land Registry as though it had been created on the earlier date Solicitor N plainly intended to mislead. Solicitor N explained his reasoning to the investigating officer as follows:

"Well, as I said, I perceived the whole titling circumstances to be a mess, they needed to be tidied up, quickly and at a minimum of cost and that wrongly was to save stamp duty and in fact didn't, I mean, what's crazy about it is that it didn't have to, we didn't have to put that in to do that because there was a common shareholding, it was exempt stamp duty, but it was wrong and I put my hands up."

Outcome

In respect of this allegation the Tribunal found that the motivation was financial gain for the client. The conduct was not capable of being anything but dishonest. For this and the four other breaches and a further finding of dishonesty Solicitor N was struck off. He was ordered to pay costs of £22,424.55.

Steps to avoid

Solicitor N made no additional money over his firm's fees as a result of his involvement in these property transactions. His actions were undertaken purely to assist his clients. He said when interviewed that he probably backdated the Deed of Declaration to save

his clients stamp duty. He did not need to take this step, as the transaction was stamp duty exempt.

The solicitor shouldn't have been so accommodating to a big property developer generating fairly substantial fees for the firm.

On the facts of this case, the solicitor was as accommodating as possible, probably to keep the client happy to keep the work. He seemed not to realise at the time he did it that he had stepped over the line between ethical and unethical.

5.4   Undertakings

Regulatory matters

An undertaking is a binding promise to do something, which allows the smooth running of legal processes. An undertaking is usually given to other solicitors or legal professionals or to the court. Undertakings have a high status of reliance placed upon them and are equally valid whether stated orally or in writing. Much of the work of conveyancers would be unfeasible if not for undertakings given to banks and the other side's solicitors.

Paragraph 1.3 of the Code of Conduct for Solicitors states that a solicitor must:

> *"perform all undertakings given by you, and do so within an agreed timescale or if no timescale has been agreed then within a reasonable amount of time".*

Because undertakings can be given and accepted orally, there is wide scope for misinterpretation as to the exact terms of the undertaking. This can extend to situations when parties wonder whether a conversation resulted in an undertaking being given at all. It should be clear whether an undertaking is being offered and if so, that the undertaking is made clearly. It is also important to check that the person giving the undertaking has sufficient authority to do so.

Solicitors will only give undertakings that they can fulfil as they remain personally liable; however the undertaking also binds the firm and is regulated by the Code of Conduct for Firms Paragraph 1.3 which is identical. It is both unethical and impractical to give undertakings knowing that they are not capable of being fulfilled. This would not be viewed as a solicitor upholding the proper administration of justice.

A request for an undertaking to ensure that your client will do something or perform an act shouldn't be given by a solicitor as they aren't able to ensure that the client can fulfil the undertaking. If the solicitor is minded to give the undertaking it should be carefully worded.

You v The Rest Of The World

From who	How	To who
Given by the solicitor OR The client	Orally OR In writing	Other solicitors OR Other legal professionals OR The other party OR The court

Fig 23: How undertakings work

A solicitor should only ever give an undertaking that is possible to perform personally, or on behalf of the firm if authorised to do so - for example to send documents to the court or the other side within a specified timescale.

The solicitor enjoys a privileged position as to the reliance third parties can place on their undertakings. The undertaking of a solicitor is their bond and the giving of an undertaking is an important and actionable matter. Bear in mind that when giving a third party an undertaking the solicitor must be seen to be administering the proper application of the legal system. The solicitor also needs to bear in the mind the potential for third party damages.

When things go wrong

Prima facie, a breach of an undertaking given by a solicitor is interpreted as professional misconduct and there is usually only one exception to this rule. This is if the undertaking is given to the court as only the court has the power to enforce sanctions for the breach. Usually no other action would be taken save for the action of the court. See for example, CCR Order 29 Rule 2(1) which states that; "***An undertaking given by a solicitor in relation to any proceeding in a county court may be enforced, by order of the judge of that court, by committal order against the solicitor***".

Although another party to the proceedings can apply to have the order enforced by committal an application needs to be submitted with an affidavit attached.

117

Where the undertaking is given to the court the proper sanction should be imposed by the court and not by the regulator. Naturally the breach of an undertaking is also taken as a serious reputational matter. As there is no obligation on a firm to give or accept undertakings it is perfectly possible that a firm that doesn't fulfil an undertaking will find in the future that their undertakings are refused.

The court, the SRA, Law Society and SDT will take a dim view of a solicitor breaching an undertaking. Even where circumstances have changed from the time that the undertaking was given, the giver of the undertaking would be expected to fulfil the promise. Enforcing an undertaking is seen as upholding the proper administration of justice and trust in the legal system.

Scenario: Undertaking

Facts

In a family law matter, solicitors undertook not to release the passport to their client, the father in the proceedings. On the strength of that undertaking he was granted an order to see his children.

Rules (2011 Code of Conduct)

Principle 1: Uphold the rule of law and the proper administration of justice.

Principle 6: Act in a way which maintains the trust the public places in the profession.

Outcome (11.2): Perform all undertakings given by you within an agreed timescale or within a reasonable amount of time.

Breach

The solicitors wrongly released their client's passport to him in breach of their undertaking. Father absconded out of the country, with the children.

Outcome

The wife successfully sued the firm in negligence - they owed her and the children a duty of care when they gave the undertaking.

5.5 Undertakings - Policies, systems and controls

In the above example, the failure to comply with the undertaking was an administrative error which caused great upheaval to the parties and the children. Due to the serious nature of undertakings and the potential regulatory and reputational damage that may be caused by failing to fulfil them, firms should devise systems and policies to control risk. These systems and policies are designed to both record any undertakings and also the time and method applied to discharge those undertakings.

Whilst this might seem purely a regulatory matter, the interpretation of an undertaking can include ethical considerations. For example, if a solicitor gave the following undertaking: "*we undertake not to release our client's passport to him*", there are a number of possible interpretations.

This is where the ethical solicitor will interpret the undertaking to their highest obligation, meaning: "*we should never release this passport to this client*".

An ethically minimalist solicitor might release the client's passport to him in the event that he no longer retains the services of the firm. After all, the undertaking says "our client's passport". Therefore, if he is no longer a client, then the firm can't be held responsible. It is splitting hairs to make that distinction but there are solicitors who would do this if their client wanted his passport to be returned to him. In the above example, there was a simple administrative error that should have been avoided when looking at the outcome for the children.

The firm should be able to demonstrate to the SRA that they have assessed the risk and made provision to mitigate the potential risks. The Code of Conduct for Firms has a dedicated section devoted to compliance and business systems (Section 2). However, these systems are also important to ensure that solicitors behave ethically and not just in a regulatory manner. It would be wrong to believe that the giving of an undertaking is merely just an administrative matter. Where there are any issues about the wording of the undertaking, it should be interpreted in the strictest manner possible, from the perspective of "the ethical solicitor". Solicitors who give undertakings should be certain about what they mean in letter and in spirit and ensure that the wording of the undertaking is as specific as it should be.

When giving an undertaking you may wish to make provision for what would happen if the person who gave the undertaking isn't around when the act needs to be completed (e.g. due to resignation or illness). A suitably robust recording system should be developed so the firm knows exactly what undertakings were taken, what tasks the firm or solicitor must undertake and when they have to be completed in order to reduce their risk. Paragraph 2.2 requires firms to keep and maintain records to demonstrate compliance with the firm's obligations under the SRA's regulatory arrangements.

Firms need policies and procedures to ensure that undertakings are properly recorded but this does not replace the need for good training with regard to proper conduct relating to undertakings. The placement of a good policy does not act as a "get out of jail free" card with regard to third parties. Like many things, the policy aspects are there to ensure compliance to the spirit of the rule and not just the letter.

5.6 Do solicitors have an obligation to correct mistakes of third parties?

Most solicitors would view their primary responsibility to be to serve the best interests of their client as discussed above. The firm will want to make profits and maintain a commercial view about the "business of law". These two tensions and the impact they have on ethical behaviour are examined in more detail in other chapters.

Consider this by Lord Phillips of Sudbury:

> "In a country awash with evermore law and regulation of baffling complexity, lawyers are commensurately indispensable as the gatekeepers of justice. Yet the truth is that we are increasingly obsessed with our own profit. The idea of lawyering being a vocation, or a profession, seems out of date to many solicitors who consider themselves just business people."

It is therefore important to keep in mind that solicitors hold a special place in society. To regard the legal professional merely as a collection of businesses with the disadvantage of compliance and ethical handcuffs is entirely at odds with the ethos and behaviours expected of them.

What happens if the other side has made an error of law and the litigation or transaction is likely to be resolved based on an error? We consider the ethical considerations on the solicitor in these circumstances. The manner in which a solicitor behaves might be different if the other side is unrepresented or not.

The main Principles that the solicitor has to consider are indicated below:

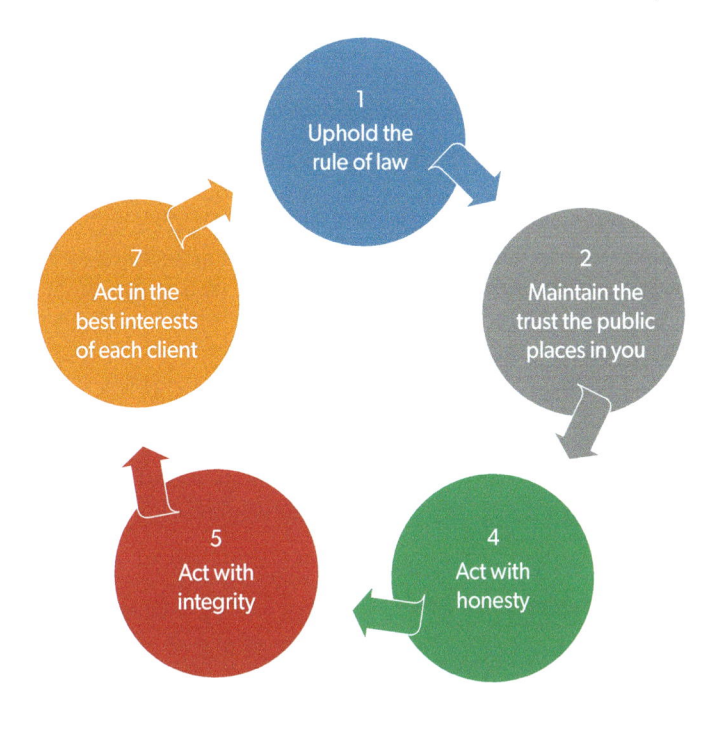

Fig 24: The 5 main Principles a solicitor needs to consider

In addition to the above mandatory principles, the Code of Conduct for Solicitors and Firms states at Paragraph 1.4 that you shouldn't mislead or attempt to mislead your clients, the court or others, either by your own acts or omissions or allowing or being complicit in the acts or omissions of others (including your own client).

Scenario: Conveyancing

Facts

The buyer's solicitor discovers a defective deed which the seller signed when they purchased the property. It requires the seller to pay an additional annual service charge for the maintenance of land near the property. The seller's solicitor doesn't ask the buyer to take over responsibility for the payment by entering into a deed.

Should the buyer's solicitor highlight the issue to the seller's solicitor? If so, this will result in an annual charge to the buyer.

Rules

As per diagram above.

Potential ethical issues/professional breaches

If the buyer's solicitor highlights the matter to them together with the obligation to uphold the proper administration of justice, the clients might not be too happy to proceed forward.

If the solicitor doesn't notify the seller's solicitor about the matter then the seller will remain responsible for the charges which will relate to a property that they have sold. They are not likely to believe that the buyer's solicitor has acted with honesty and/or integrity if they find out that he knew about the defect. It is highly unlikely they would ever discover this fact.

There could be negligence issues that they will take up with their solicitors.

Possible approaches

- The buyer's solicitor can raise the issue with the buyers and let them decide how they want to proceed (Principle 7 prevails - act in the client's best interests).

- The buyer's solicitor raises the matter with the other side without asking the buyers (Principles 1, 2, 4 and 5). [Is this the path of the ethical solicitor?]

- The buyer's solicitor doesn't mention the matter to either the buyers or to the seller's solicitor. [Ethically minimalist?]

Suggested reaction/steps to avoid

Communicating the issue to the clients means that the clients are able to make a fully informed decision about the way forward.

If they decide that they don't want the matter raised then this is a decision for them.

However, the solicitor may take the view that they should bring the matter to the attention to the sellers' solicitor as there may be an action in negligence against the original solicitors who didn't notice that the deed was defective.

5.7 Mistakes where the other side is represented by a solicitor

Most solicitors would say that it is up to the opposing solicitor to be both up to date with the law and have the proper skill set to both interpret and apply the law to a professional standard. After all, Part 3 of the Code of Conduct for Solicitors makes this clear - you ensure that the service you provide to clients is competent and delivered in a timely manner. From 1 November 2016, this, in combination with the Statement of Legal Knowledge, means that you need to demonstrate an appropriate level of competence to practise law. (Code of Conduct for Solicitors Paragraph 3.3: You maintain your competence to carry out your role and keep your professional knowledge and skills up to date).

Each solicitor is required to ensure that he or she can demonstrate competence against a Statement of Competence written by the SRA. Each solicitor needs to assess if they meet the correct standard against the "threshold criteria", also published by the SRA.

If the opposing solicitor makes a mistake, their client can sue them in negligence. Many of you will think that is just bad luck - it is up to each solicitor to get the best result for their client. If you make a mistake which is picked up, you have a positive duty to disclose it to your client (Code of Conduct for Solicitors Paragraph 7.11).

Failing to draw attention to the other side's mistake could lead to an awful lot of stress and expense for the other solicitor's client who may need to apply to rectify the mistake or seek redress. Is it ethical for the solicitor to "keep quiet"? Or is it more important to keep your client happy? Is it possible to keep everyone happy (including the regulator)?

Your response to this particular kind of problem will rest on the specific error:

- Is it a simple "typo" style of mistake? Has the other side put 56% instead of 65%?

- Is there a misunderstanding about the law? The other side thinks A

How To Be An Ethical Solicitor

when actually B is the case.

- Has the other side overlooked something? In the conveyancing example above the other side has overlooked the existence of the poorly drafted deed and continuing liability of the sellers to pay the service charge.

In all of these cases, it is a difficult balancing act between championing your client's interests and the other Principles - ultimately the decision will be an ethical one. The ethical solicitor will always act in a completely transparent way to ensure that all mistakes and misunderstandings are cleared up before an agreement is entered into.

Regulatory Principles clash

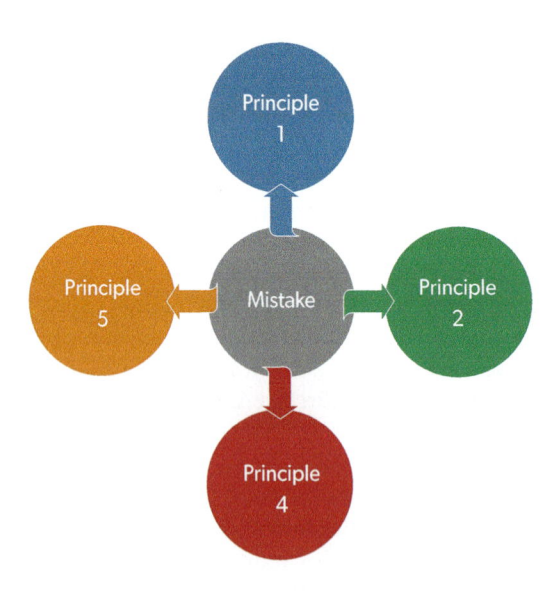

Fig 25: When regulatory Principles clash

5.8 Mistakes where the other side is a litigant in person

The Principles and the Codes of Conduct are not explicit in this area - it is difficult for solicitors to proceed on the basis of a mistake, particularly where the other side is not represented (Code of Conduct for Solicitors and Code of Conduct for Firms Paragraph 1.2). The Law Society have a practice note on dealing with Litigants in Person (LiPs) which should be consulted as it provides excellent practical guidance.

When is a LiP a LiP?

It is, however, sometimes difficult to ascertain if LiPs are actually unrepresented as LiPs can be:

- completely without legal advice because they can't afford it;
- completely without legal advice because they don't want it;
- advised by a legal adviser who isn't on the record as acting;
- advised at court but not in the conduct of litigation generally.

Ask yourself these questions:

(1) What category does the other side fall into?

(2) How does that impact on your ethical responsibility to deal with mistakes?

(3) What are your regulatory and ethical considerations?

There are shades of grey in the above categories and your ethical compass will need to be fully engaged in these situations.

Scenario: Litigant in Person

Facts

The LiP husband is represented in Family Court proceedings by a direct access barrister. There are no solicitors on record for the LiP.

The barrister makes a mistake when drafting an order which means that his client (the applicant) will be responsible for the payment of costs of implementation of certain parts of the order. [We do not propose to consider the barrister's regulatory, conduct and ethical issues within the confines of this book.]

Rules

Principles: **1, 2, 4** and **5** as above.

Ethical considerations

You are a solicitor acting for the respondent and you decide not to say anything to highlight the barrister's mistake, which comes from the barrister's lack of knowledge rather than an administrative error. You take the view that you aren't taking advantage of a third party as the barrister is a professional who is responsible for their own work. They don't bring up the issue of costs and you therefore choose to remain silent. The default position will leave his client bearing the administrative costs of implementation.

When dealing with the implementation of the order you are once again dealing with the LiP who doesn't engage the services of a solicitor when out of court. You ask him for the costs of the implementation of the order (£1,000 plus VAT) so that the order can be implemented in your client's favour. The LiP won't pay as he says that he didn't know anything about the costs. You make him aware that he may have a claim against his barrister but that the deal is done and he needs to pay up.

Outcome

This isn't necessarily a fantastic result for the public perception of the law and solicitors in general. You may have done the best thing for your client in the short term, saving them fees of £1,000.

Have you taken "unfair" advantage of the barrister who should have known about the charge? Although the barrister is qualified it is possible (in the view of the SRA and new Codes) for a solicitor to take advantage of a barrister. It isn't wholly transparent (or honest?) that you didn't raise the issue of the costs at the hearing. The other side's redress may be against the barrister rather than you as the solicitor. The regulatory position is slightly murky on this point.

The question is whether the actions of the solicitor are **ethical** or not. In the long term your client may not prosper as this is likely to cause the need for the matter to return to court for enforcement proceedings if the applicant refuses to pay the costs. Implementation of the order will be delayed as the costs aren't paid. Keeping quiet to secure an advantage isn't transparent and so might not be viewed as entirely ethical.

Arguably, Principles 2 and 7 have not been met; there will be a further delay to the conclusion of matters for your client. The LiP will certainly feel let down by the legal system but whether this is rectified by pursuing the barrister or not is outside the scope of this book.

Solicitors are dealing with increasing numbers of LiPs in practice and you need to be aware of the duty owed to them from a regulatory standpoint. Ethically, it is obvious that the need to be fully open and transparent with the LiP is absolute as in the following example[2].

Scenario: Abuse of process

Facts

In 2015 a father (H) made an application to the High Court seeking to put his ex-partner's solicitor in prison for the way that she acted during Children Act proceedings. He also made applications against other professionals who were joined to the action.

The defendants made an application to strike out the committal application as an abuse of process.

Father alleged that the solicitor deceived him and the lay justices about the state of the law when they were at a final hearing. He alleged that as the solicitor is a specialist in international law, "her deception and contempt" was not an accidental matter.

He also complained that the matter should have been dealt with at a higher judicial level and that the solicitor should have brought this to the attention of the law justices.

In support of his application, he produced a number of audio tapes of illicit recordings he had taken at the court.

Regulations (2011 Code of Conduct)

As above - *Principles 1, 2, 4*, and *6* and *Outcome (11.7)*

---

[2] *H v Dent & Ors [2015] EWHC 2090 (Fam).*

Outcome

The court stated that the complaints against the solicitor "completely ignores the fact that her professional duties lay with her own client".

The judge in that matter went on to say: "She had no contractual relationship with H and at no time was her professional relationship with him impressed with any fiduciary or legal obligations".

The court acknowledged that the solicitor had a duty not to mislead the court and that there was no evidence that she had done so. There was no evidence that he didn't give his true consent to the terms of the order at the final hearing.

H's applications for committal were struck out as there were no disclosable grounds for bringing the application and it was an abuse of process to do so. The applicant had failed to observe procedural matters and the judge would not allow him to rectify those matters.

Ethical matters

If the father in this case made a complaint to the SRA it may be that the result would be the same. After all, the criminal standard of proof must be met in both cases (the SDT has now adopted the civil standard of proof as the standard to apply from 25 November 2019). However, it may be that the information the solicitor gave the father fell short of the transparent ethical manner in which she should have dealt with a LiP (although there is nothing to suggest in reading this judgment that this was the case).

The point is that the public at large feel that solicitors owe them a "duty of care" even if they aren't paying for their services. They feel that they should be able to trust the information (falling short of advice) given to them by a solicitor.

The new Codes clarify matters at the Code of Conduct for Solicitors at Paragraph 2.7 and the Code of Conduct for Firms at Paragraph 7.1(a) that: "You draw the court's attention to relevant cases and statutory provisions, or procedural irregularities of which you are aware, and which are likely to have a material effect on the outcome of proceedings." This is a positive obligation to do much more than act in your client's best interests whilst at court. All relevant cases and irregularities should be made known to the court and not just the ones favourable to your client's case.

Paragraph 2.4 of the Code of Conduct for Solicitors is also new and has serious implications to those who conduct litigation: "You only make assertions or put forward statements, representations or submissions to the court or others which are properly arguable". Weak cases that are brought to attempt to secure negotiations which aren't properly arguable should not be brought, even if those are your client's instructions. This will be considered further in Chapter 8.

5.9 The proper administration of oaths, affirmations or declarations

In the administration of oaths, affirmations and declarations, the solicitor owes a duty to more people and organisations than just their own client.

Although the regulations don't specify the rules about making changes to other documents, it is largely accepted that documents shouldn't be changed after signature.

Scenario: Forging signatures

Facts

A solicitor's clerk was accused of forging various solicitors' signatures on a number of documents - one was a certified copy of a document, and another was a statutory declaration.

Although in this case there was found to be no case to answer due to the quality of the evidence, it highlights that a solicitor's signature on a document is an important matter.

Rules (2011 Code of Conduct)

The SRA wished to prove that the fee earner was guilty of breaches of Principles 1, 2 and 6. Although his guilt wasn't established, it is important to note that the issues were treated on a par despite the fact that the regulations specifically mention the administration of oaths and not signing other documents.

Outcomes

The matter was dismissed against the clerk, albeit he had initially accepted his wrongdoing in respect of one matter during an internal disciplinary meeting.

Ethical considerations

Solicitors should know that altering a document after signature without consent of the client is not ethical behaviour.

5.10 Fees paid by third parties

Litigation solicitors will know that often their client's fees can now be paid for by third parties. It is quite common for groups with stakes in the outcome of a case to provide funds, where the litigant themselves may have difficulty doing so. Insurance companies, trade unions, charities and various pressure groups may pay the litigation fees for particular cases as they have an interest in the outcome.

Scenario: Third party funding

Facts

In a recent family litigation case, the fees of the wife were paid for by investors for the first time. After the case was disposed of by the High Court, with an award of £20 million to the wife, the investors are allegedly about to sue her for breach for contract. The investors allege that the wife used some of the money they gave her for purposes other than to fund her legal fees. She denies the allegations.

In these situations, it is important that the solicitor remembers that the duty is to the client, not to the party who is actually paying the fees. As the matter progresses the interests of the litigant and the third party may diverge, as can be seen in the example above.

Third party litigation funding is more common in commercial cases and research indicates that its use has shot up over the last six years. The Justice NOT Profit campaign says that the industry has outgrown self-regulation.

In 2009, Lord Justice Jackson said that if the use of this type of funding increased to a point of significance then the full statutory regulation would be required. Falling short of that, ethical considerations become ever more important. 63% of those polled said they were either quite or very concerned about the increase in for-profit third party funding.

Fees paid by third parties give rise to many compliance and ethical issues:

- Confidentiality (Code of Conduct for Solicitors Paragraph 6.3);

- Acting in the best interests of each client (Principle 7);

- Behaving in a way that upholds public trust and confidence in the solicitors' profession and in legal services provided by authorised persons (Principle 2).

The ethical issues arise when there is likely to be a conflict between what is in the best interests of the client and what is best for the entity funding the case.

It is advisable for the solicitor in this situation to be clear with the client and third party how the solicitor will deal with the case. This is likely to come in the form of agreements drawn up by the funder as to how the litigation should be conducted. After all, a "for-profit" funder will want to ensure that there will be success at the end of the day otherwise there will be no profit to share. At the start of the case the interests of the client and the funder are aligned; both want to achieve financial redress at the end of the case. There are a few issues that the solicitor will need to think about at that stage .

However, as the matter moves forward, the way in which the litigation progresses may illicit different responses from the funder and the client. The client may have emotional reasons for wanting to proceed to a trial and cross-examination. The client may have unrealistic ideas of success and may not recognise a good offer of settlement when they see one. On the other hand, a professional third party litigation funder will have very fixed ideas about the progress of litigation and settlement options. There will be no emotion attached to the decision; the decisions will centre on profit for the funder. This is where the solicitor may feel a conflict between the two parties.

From a regulatory perspective, it is important to record the boundaries that exist between the client and the funder. More often than not, the funder will have strict terms under which it is willing to proceed. These duties will be documented, and the solicitor must ensure that the client is aware of them and that they are willing and able to fulfil those obligations.

It can be difficult to tread the ethical line between the client and the funder regarding the case, its merits and the evidence. Solicitors can very easily find themselves in a difficult position where their obligations to the funder and the client conflict.

5.11 Contacting the opposing party or their McKenzie Friend

Whereas there were rules under the 2011 regulations about contacting a party directly those rules are no longer in the new STaRs. As a rule a solicitor should not contact the other party directly if they have legal representation. The 2011 Code of Conduct was quite explicit about this as it states:

> *"You do not communicate with another party when you are aware that the other party has retained a lawyer in a matter, except:*
>
> *(a) to request the name and address of the other party's lawyer; or*
>
> *(b) the other party's lawyer consents to you communicating with the client; or*
>
> *(c) where there are exceptional circumstances."*

The Law Society practice note on dealing with Litigants in Person[3] is very helpful in circumstances where contact with the other side is unavoidable and where the new Codes do not have any particular rules to follow. A solicitor can be accused of (Code of Conduct for Solicitors and Firms at Paragraph 1.2) taking unfair advantage of an opposing party's lack of legal knowledge where they have not instructed a lawyer. This is discussed above and needs to be borne in mind. It is also possible that the LiP isn't clear about the role of the solicitor in proceedings and can view them with hostility, making it very difficult for the client to observe his or her regulatory functions.

In the case where the opposing party has engaged the services of an unqualified person, then ethical issues arise alongside regulatory concerns. In the current legal market place, there are unregulated paralegal firms and McKenzie Friend services who compete against solicitors for work. Where this is the case, the qualified solicitor needs to tread carefully in his or her

---

[3] *Produced by The Law Society in conjunction with CILEx and the Bar Council. Available on The Law Society website, June 2015.*

You v The Rest Of The World

communication with unqualified and unregulated entities.

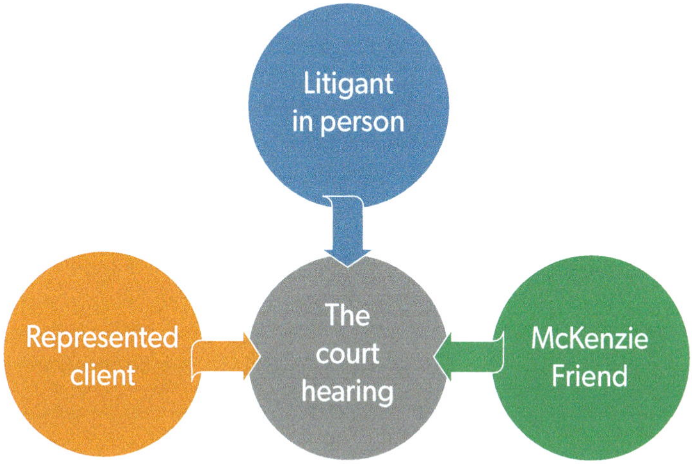

Fig 26: Parties attending a court hearing

All parties are permitted to attend hearings (McKenzie Friends only with permission); however the court should not accept any communication with the McKenzie Friend that would be covered under the banner "reserved legal activities". Unless the McKenzie Friend is given permission by the court they are not permitted to provide advocacy services or conduct litigation. If they do this they will commit a criminal offence. This extends to paralegal firms as they are not authorised entities.

This means that the solicitor should not entertain correspondence with the unregulated firm as this could be a breach of duty to their own client. Bear in mind that the unregulated entity may have no data protection in place; they have no regulated Code of Conduct and may even distribute your client's information deliberately if instructed to do so by their client. Often these firms are not only unregulated but also uninsured. Whilst their "client" will want you to communicate with them, your duty is to your client in this situation and not the third party.

Any dealings with an unqualified person fall under Code of Conduct for Solicitors and Code of Conduct for Firms Paragraph 1.2: "You do not abuse your position by taking unfair advantage of clients or others". Any communications you have with an unregulated third party should be civil.

It some circumstances it might be helpful to be able to communicate with the McKenzie Friend who might be able to bring about a settlement or narrow issues. However, only the LiP has the right to conduct the litigation and no other person. They're not in a position to authorise another person in their place, even by way of a power of attorney. The problem then can be the fact that the best thing for your client will be to communicate with the third party but by doing so you would be encouraging them to break the law by conducting litigation. If you find that you are in this position, the court has the power to authorise the McKenzie Friend to conduct litigation. This is much rarer than a McKenzie Friend being permitted to advocate on behalf of a client in court. The Law Society practice note indicates that:

> *"You should not communicate directly with an MF, but address all communications to the LiP. If a LiP uses an MF, the MF cannot appear in court unless the LiP is also present."*

5.12 Stealing clients

Is it ethical for a solicitor to take another solicitor's client?

This is an ethical conundrum that comes up in all practice areas, some more so than others. To put the issue in sharper focus we will use the example below.

Scenario: Stealing clients

Facts

Solicitor A takes on a client to do some work which isn't in his specialist area. He is hoping to expand his work base and as he is a sole practitioner it would suit him (and his profit margins) to develop a new work stream. The client has received his client care letter and his terms and conditions of business. She has agreed an hourly rate that is more than the published solicitor's guidance hourly rates for a solicitor of his experience.

As part of his job to find suitable funding for the client to pursue her case, she needs to get some advice about the funding agreement from an independent solicitor so she makes an appointment to see Solicitor B. Solicitor B is a specialist in this field of work with more than 12 years' experience.

Both Solicitor A and B are sole practitioners; Solicitor A undertakes a variety of work and Solicitor B only takes on work in his specialist field.

Solicitor A receives an email from Solicitor B asking for the file of papers to be transferred to him as the client has decided to move firms. He attaches an authority from the client requesting the transfer.

The client suffers from depression and is seeing a counsellor. The client refuses to communicate with Solicitor A following the appointment with Solicitor B.

Regulations

Principles

You act:

Principle 2: in a way that upholds public trust and confidence in the solicitors' profession and in legal services provided by authorised persons.

Principle 3: with honesty.

Principle 4: with integrity.

Principle 7: in the best interests of your client.

Code of Conduct for Solicitors

Paragraph 1.2: You do not abuse your position by taking unfair advantage of clients or others.

Paragraph 3.2: You ensure that the service you provide to clients is competent and delivered in a timely manner.

Paragraph 3.3: You maintain your competence to carry out your role and keep your professional knowledge and skills up to date.

Paragraph 7.11: You are honest and open with clients if things go wrong, and if a client suffers loss or harm as a result you put matters right (if possible) and explain fully and promptly what has happened and the likely impact. If requested to do so by the SRA you investigate whether anyone may have a claim against you, provide the SRA with a report on the outcome of your investigation, and notify relevant persons that they may have such a claim, accordingly.

Potential ethical/regulatory breaches

Solicitor A

He has taken on work in a field that he is not an expert in. However, he does meet the required standard of competence as set out by the SRA for a day 1 qualified solicitor in the new area of work. He has undertaken a number of courses in the new field and he isn't holding himself out as a specialist. He should therefore meet the competence requirements in the Code of Conduct for Solicitors. It is not unusual for solicitors to practise in more than one area of law and to adapt their practice over time.

He has not done anything that would result in a claim being made against him.

He might be billing the client more than an experienced solicitor would but the client has had all the billing information that the solicitor is required to send.

There are no apparent regulatory breaches by Solicitor A.

Are there any ethical breaches as Solicitor A isn't a specialist in the field and is charging more than the guideline rates for his year of qualification and location? This isn't a regulatory breach but when taking on board a new area of work should the solicitor be charging lower fees while he finds his feet so that the client doesn't suffer from his lack of experience? Would the public believe that his actions are not trustworthy for a solicitor?

Solicitor B

Solicitor B was engaged to give advice about a funding arrangement and not the case as a whole. It is not known what Solicitor B said to the client to persuade her to change solicitors. It would however appear that he overstepped the boundaries of his retainer - this is not in itself a regulatory breach.

Taking into account the fact that the client is vulnerable, did Solicitor B take these steps to protect the client or has Solicitor B taken advantage of her vulnerable position? At the time that Solicitor B spoke to the client, he owed her a duty as she was his client as well as Solicitor A's client. He was under an obligation to treat her fairly and not to take unfair advantage of her (Code of Conduct for Solicitors Paragraph 1.2). Solicitor B may have believed that his own experience as a specialist solicitor was greater than that being offered by Solicitor A and that the client should be made aware of that matter.

He also owed Solicitor A a duty to ensure that he treated him professionally and he was under an obligation not to take unfair advantage of him as a third party (Code of Conduct for Solicitors Paragraph 1.2). It is not known if Solicitor B used his greater experience to persuade the client to change firms.

Neither is it known if Solicitor B was acting with honesty and integrity in his communications with the client about Solicitor A. It is questionable whether this type of client poaching is considered acceptable by the public or if this would be considered to be a breach of trust issue.

It would appear from the facts of the case that there is no regulatory issue in taking a client from another firm in the way that Solicitor B has done. Depending on the specific circumstances of the case and what was said to the client by Solicitor B, he may have believed that he was acting in the client's best interests if Solicitor A was charging over the guideline hourly rates.

Solicitor B's charging rates were slightly higher than Solicitor A's but also in excess of the hourly rates guidelines. Could the higher charging rate easily be justified as he had many years of specialist experience? Is it ever ethically acceptable to charge more than the guideline rates and should both solicitors have informed the client that they are charging more than recommended?

Suggested reaction

Both solicitors should revisit their hourly charging rate to see if they are happy charging more than the guideline hourly rates. If they decide to charge these rates going forward should they highlight to prospective clients why they believe they should charge more?

Solicitor A should not send his clients to firms that he doesn't have a business relationship with. He should ensure in future that the firms he refers these clients to are not going to take his clients. Whilst the behaviour isn't likely to be a breach of regulations, it may be viewed in many sectors as unethical behaviour.

In a more commercial setting this issue is unlikely to cause much consternation as commercial clients are savvy enough to make sensible buying decisions about legal services. They are aware of their choices, buying power, experience of solicitors and guideline hourly rates.

In a more personal legal situation the client might not be a sophisticated purchaser of legal services or they may be vulnerable and an approach to change solicitor must be viewed in the proper context.

Solicitor B should be careful about populating his clients from other firms as this may damage his reputation and that of his firm in the future. It is likely that once reputational damage is done to the firm that other solicitors will not refer clients to the firm if it is believed that the solicitor has acted unethically.

Code of Conduct for Solicitors Paragraph 2.4

You only make assertions or put forward statements, representations or submissions to the court or others which are properly arguable.

This new provision in the STaRs is one that requires thought and balance; the solicitor can't mislead the court or waste the court's time by making assertions that are wrong or misleading.

Scenario: Recoverable costs

Facts

A solicitor acting for a judgment creditor writes to the judgment debtor setting out the case. If the debt isn't paid with interest within 7 days then enforcement proceedings will be sought and a costs order will be pursued. The debt isn't paid and the solicitor writes once more stating that an application has been sent for a charging order and that the judgment creditor will seek a costs order, the costs incurred so far being £1,000 plus VAT and court fees.

Regulations

The issue with the above scenario is the fact that the only costs that can be recovered in this type of action are fixed costs. The fact that the costs are £1,000 plus VAT will have no bearing on that fact that the costs are fixed at £110 plus reasonable disbursements. Is the solicitor doing the best for the client? Or is the solicitor taking advantage of an unrepresented third party and in breach of Code of Conduct for Solicitors Paragraph 1.2?

Ethical considerations

Is it ethical to lead a third party to believe that they could be liable for costs of £1,000 plus VAT or should the solicitor be explicit that the costs will be capped at £110? The letter itself doesn't say that the costs order will be made in the sum of £1,000 plus VAT. It doesn't even say that the costs order requested will be for the sum of £1,000 plus VAT but it certainly gives the impression that the costs that could be ordered will be £1,000 plus VAT.

Is it ethical to allow a LiP believe something that isn't be true?

It would most certainly be a breach of the Code of Conduct for Solicitors Paragraph 1.2 to do so.

5.13 An abuse of your position in personal circumstances

The Code of Conduct for Solicitors Paragraph 1.2 isn't limited to abuse of your position in a work based situation but could apply personally too. Have you ever sent a personal letter or email and added "solicitor" or "LLB

Hons" at the foot of your signature to make an impression? Were you hoping that your letter of complaint to John Lewis would be taken more seriously if they see your qualifications and worry about the next steps you will take?

If so you may have behaved in a way that the SRA would see as being in breach. You intended to use your position of professional influence to work in your favour against a third party. This would include any comments along the line of "I'm a solicitor, I know the law" when returning (faulty) goods and hoping for a refund rather than store credit.

This should give all solicitors pause for thought.

5.14 Conclusion

Although solicitors would like to ensure that his or her client has the best possible opportunity of securing the best result, this must be done within regulatory and ethical guidelines.

It can be seen from the example above that a solicitor suggesting a proposed course of settlement of a case can be easily misconstrued by a LiP as securing an unfair advantage. There is a fine line to be walked and solicitors must be careful to ensure that they are mindful of zealously representing their own client's interests and infringing those of third parties.

The ethical solicitor should therefore have in the front of his or her mind the fact that being a professional brings with it serious obligations to the world at large. The ethical solicitor will always err on the side of caution in his or her dealings with third parties, especially where those parties are LiPs. The SRA has also indicated that it is possible for a solicitor to take unfair advantage of counsel as a third party and this is an additional burden to bear. One can't assume equality of arms against another legal professional if they are younger, less experienced or just not very good at their job - it is possible that the SRA will see this as a solicitor's breach.

The ethically minimalist solicitor will often make decisions which are not the same as their more ethical peers. They will not err on the side of caution. Instead, they hope that they stay on the right side of regulations and compliance without really assessing whether this will be the case.

The way you choose to practise will change and develop over time but the way the world sees you is just as important as the way your client sees you. The only difference is that your client is probably the one paying your bill.

Chapter 6: Complaints and negligence

6.1 Complaints

Solicitors may be the recipient of complaints, especially in those areas of law that are quite emotional or stressful for clients. For example the Legal Ombudsman's statistics show that family law, residential conveyancing and wills and probate are areas that receive the highest number of complaints. These are all areas of law where the consumer is seeking advice about a personal matter. At the other end of the spectrum commercial conveyancing receives very few complaints. This is the wrong forum to discuss the mechanics of the complaints process; suffice to say it is important for solicitors to treat their clients fairly where complaints arise as the first stage of the complaint process is dealt with by the firm. Indeed, the Code of Conduct for Solicitors (which applies identically to firms) states at Paragraph 8.13 that complaints should be dealt with "promptly, fairly, and free of charge". There is a heightened need for ethical thinking when dealing with situations where something might have gone wrong. The fact that the new Code states that complaints must be dealt with "free of charge" suggests that previously some firms were charging to deal with complaints! The new Codes have become more specific about how individuals and firms should deal with complaints, which is unusual given the streamlining process that has taken place.

6.2 What is a complaint?

The SRA defines a complaint as:

> *"An oral or written expression of dissatisfaction which alleges that the complainant has suffered (or may suffer) financial loss, distress, inconvenience or other detriment".*

LeO adopts this definition as well, given that they are the body that deals with client complaints.

The first dilemma is when to differentiate between a complaint and a 'grumble'. This is a judgement call by the person who hears the complaint; in the first instance this might not be a fee earner but someone in a supporting role, who should be trained to pass on all expressions of dissatisfaction to the fee earner or COLP. The quicker a 'grumble' is passed on and dealt with, the less likely it will be that the grumble turns into a more serious complaint.

Some expressions of dissatisfaction may be easy to resolve in the moment - for example, if a client complains about their telephone call not being returned then an apology and explanation may suffice. Not every expression of dissatisfaction requires a full investigation; if the matter can be resolved to the client's satisfaction the complaint can be closed (Code of Conduct for Solicitors Paragraph 8.7).

A person who hears an expression of dissatisfaction can respond in a number of ways depending on their role within the firm, their training and of course their personal viewpoint. For example, a receptionist at a busy firm may hear several clients per day complaining that they haven't had their calls returned. The receptionist may be untrained in referring complaints to the relevant person and they may also take the view the matter has nothing to do with them. Their approach could be described as disinterested as they have no view on the complaints that are made and might not recognise that they have a role to play in overall client satisfaction.

That same receptionist may say that all clients complain because they are expecting a *"Rolls Royce service for the price of a Lada!"*. This is a phrase that is often heard - there is sometimes a belief that clients shouldn't expect a platinum plated service if they are paying low prices. Of course, this is not reflected in the Codes of Conduct which do not differentiate between the price being paid for a service and the level of service delivered.

A similar receptionist with a highly developed client experience will report every complaint to the relevant person so that the complaints process can be invoked. There are ethical judgements to be made every day by people who are not qualified solicitors but should be trained to recognise and refer issues onward. The person receiving the complaint will have the hard work of deciding how to approach the complainant and the solicitor to resolve the complaint quickly and to the satisfaction of the client. It can't be overlooked that the solicitor complained of will also need to feel that their voice is heard in the client's complaint so whoever is looking into the matter will need to balance those competing interests.

6.3 The framework for dealing with complaints

The main SRA Principles that will be invoked when dealing with complaints are:

- Principle 2: You act in a way that upholds public trust and confidence in the solicitors' profession and in legal services provided by authorised persons.

- The client will need to feel that the decision made is the right one and the decision would uphold the public's trust.

- Principle 4: You act with honesty.

  - The person investigating the complaint needs to deal with the client with honesty, making admissions where there has been a mistake and offering appropriate compensation.

- Principle 5: You act with integrity.

  - The solicitor acting and the person investigating the complaint must both act with integrity. There can be no suggestion of a cover up to protect the solicitor from the complaint. The client's complaint must be fairly considered.

- Principle 6: You act in a way that encourages equality, diversity and inclusion.

  - There can be no difference in the way the client's complaint is looked into due to any protected characteristic they have.

- Principle 7: You act in the best interests of each client.

  - It is important for the person investigating the complaint to understand that the client's best interests need to be held above the interests of the solicitor against whom the complaint is levied. If the complaint is against the firm as an entity, the client's best interests are held above those of the firm. This is likely to be a difficult balancing act.

Client care and complaints is one of the more prescriptive and onerous areas of the SRA Standards and Regulations. Paragraphs 8.2 to 8.6 set out what information the solicitor or firm should give a client about their right to make a complaint. There should be an appropriate complaints handling process for the type of work offered. This will be different depending on whether the solicitor is operating as a freelancer, in-house solicitor or working for a firm. If a complaint is made, the solicitor or firm has eight weeks to resolve the complaint to the satisfaction of the client. If this isn't achieved, the client should be informed of their right to complain to the legal ombudsman (the solicitor or firm should also inform the client how to contact the legal ombudsman).

Paragraph 8.4 specifies that if a complaint can't be resolved by the solicitor or firm within the eight weeks time period then they must provide the details of an Alternative Dispute Resolution approved body that would be competent to resolve the complaint. This information must be given to the client in writing and the solicitor or firm must state whether or not they are willing to use the ADR service. This in itself is an ethical decision - more on the matter of ADR is dealt with in Chapter 8.

A knock-on effect of having a more refined rules-based approach now is that it is more compliance orientated. It can be suggested that this is necessary to protect the client and ensure there is a proper focus on consumer protection. One of the major reasons for this area being more prescriptive is that it is an area where the client's interests and the solicitor's interests can diverge.

It is easy to imagine how difficult it could be for a solicitor or firm to accept that they haven't dealt with matters in the best way possible for the client. Acting with honesty and integrity in respect of client complaints is likely to test any solicitor's ethical compass. It is not unknown for solicitors to respond poorly to complaints. It is not unheard of for firms to respond by asking the client to collect their file of papers, waive their fees and ask the client to never to darken their doors again. No apology offered, no investigation of the complaint. Solicitors can often assume a complaint is simply being made in order to avoid payment of fees, without considering any genuine service complaints made by the client. Firms can often have no intention of addressing complaints, instead responding in the most efficient way to "get rid" of a complaining client.

The Legal Ombudsman's website publishes decisions about complaints upheld; one example shows a complaint made for failure to give costs information, and failure to investigate the complaint internally. A finding of poor service is made against the firm and the firm was made to pay compensation for emotional impact and/or disruption caused and to refund fees already paid. The remedy amount is described to be between £10,000 and £14,999. This is quite a considerable sum to pay for what most solicitors would deem to be straightforward failures.

6.4 Main areas for client complaints

Client complaints usually arise from a breakdown in communication between the solicitor and the client. The onus is on the solicitor to manage the relationship to ensure that an open communication channel always exists between themselves and their client and the client has a good understanding of the matter and its consequences.

During the progress of a matter, client complaints come from three main areas:

- Service standards;
- Costs information;
- The client's ability to make an informed decision based on the information provided by their solicitor.

6.5 Client service

The main issues for client service are clarity and managing client expectations. Solicitors should present a client with terms of business before they proceed to engage in any work and manage client expectations.

In these terms of business and accompanying letters the firm needs to set out the scope of the matter they will deal with, define what is in and out of scope and discuss the foreseeable outcomes and knock-on effects. Paragraph 8.6 of the Code of Conduct for Solicitors sets out that clients should receive information in a way that they understand. This is very important and cautions the solicitor to check not only that certain information is sent to a client, but also that it is understood.

Paragraph 8.7 of the Code of Conduct for Solicitors states that the client *"receives the best possible information about how their matter will be priced and, both at the time of engagement and when appropriate as their matter progresses, about the likely overall cost of the matter and any costs incurred"*. This paragraph is intended to ensure that possible complaints about costs are averted as the solicitor is required to keep this information updated through matters. Where solicitors act in a fixed fee capacity this is not likely to be a problem unless they have to undertake work which is outside the fixed fee retainer. If that happens, the solicitor will need to carefully explain what the additional work is and how it will be priced. This can often be a source of dissatisfaction with a client as they might not be ready to incur additional expenses.

There is some necessary prescriptive information which is generally pre-designed within firms so that this isn't forgotten. The problem areas can be when the service standards expected are not met by the firm.

Many complaints upheld by the Legal Ombudsman are that the solicitor

How To Be An Ethical Solicitor

has failed to reply or that they have failed to follow instructions. It is difficult to understand why the solicitor would do this without any detailed information about the complaint. These actions will, if found to be true, result in compensatory awards being levied against the firm. The failure to follow instructions is not a level of service that any firm or individual solicitor aspires to.

Scenario: Lying to cover oversight

Facts

A client gives his solicitor instructions to issue an application in a dispute between two neighbours. The solicitor delays in making the application and does not issue proceedings, despite specific instructions to do so. When the client chases the solicitor, the solicitor says that he is waiting for the court to issue the application. The solicitor doesn't tell the client that the application has not been sent to the court as a result of his oversight, even though this is the truth. The client telephones the court and discovers that the application has not been received by the court and raises the matter as a complaint with the firm.

Rules

Principle 2: Act in a way that upholds public trust and confidence in the solicitors' profession and in legal services provided by authorised persons.

Principle 4: Act with honesty.

Principle 5: Act with integrity.

Principle 7: Act in the best interests of each client.

Potential ethical issues/professional breaches

Lying to a client to cover up wrongdoing is both ethically wrong and a regulatory breach. It is not acting in the best interests of the client to mislead them about their case, particularly as this is an example of failure to provide a good level of service which is a regulatory breach (Code of Conduct for Solicitors Paragraph 3.2). When faced with the ethical decision to tell the client a difficult truth or telling a lie, it should go without saying that the truth should always be the choice made.

A solicitor could be accused of failing to act with both honesty and possibly integrity and if it was proven they had lied, the SDT could strike that solicitor off. Once again, any attempt to cover up the poor service issue is ethically worse than the poor service issue it- self. The regulatory penalty is much higher for the latter behaviour. The reason to tell the truth isn't to avoid sanction - it is to ensure compliance with the Principles set out above. Self-preservation for the solicitor should have no part in the decision-making process. The right decision should be made for the right reason.

Possible approaches

It is much more honest for the solicitor to admit that the client's instructions haven't been followed and offer immediate correction, apology and even compensation. This would also comply with Principles 2 and 5.

If the firm attempts to restrict the right of the client to go to LeO to seek redress, or fails to inform the client about that right (Code of Conduct for Solicitors Paragraph 8.2), the solicitor or firm could find itself involved in a bigger regulatory mess. The SRA would view this action as an attempt to take advantage of a third party and would impose penalties for failing to notify the client of their rights to complain.

Suggested reaction/steps to avoid

Don't mislead the client (Code of Conduct for Solicitors Paragraph 1.4) about steps that have/have not been taken in accordance with their instructions.

Always avoid the cover up!

Attempt to resolve the complaint yourself first and if this can't be achieved ensure that the client receives the relevant complaints information set out in Code of Conduct for Solicitors Paragraphs 8.3 to 8.13.

The best way to ensure that the client doesn't go to LeO after a complaint is received is to offer restitution that the client is satisfied with. If this is done, then the client will not feel the need to approach LeO about this issue.

After receiving a complaint, it is important that the solicitor/firm reflects on the reasons why the complaint was made. In doing so the firm can try to ensure that this doesn't happen again.

6.6 Pricing information

Alongside scoping out the nature of the work to be undertaken the solicitor must give an outline of what the matter is expected to cost (Code of Conduct for Solicitors/Code of Conduct for Firms Paragraph 8.7). The client must also be made aware of the potential financial liabilities they may incur if the matter goes against them.

There are a number of ways in which costs information may be deficient or the cause of a complaint:

(1) No pricing information is given to the client at all. This is not compliant with the rules and certainly doesn't hold the profession in a good light.

(2) Broad pricing information is given, which is linked to an hourly rate but this isn't updated as the case progresses and by the end of the case this is wrong. This is not compliant with the rules and doesn't hold the profession in a good light. A complaint about deficient information will result in compensation being paid if LeO is involved.

(3) A quote is given for a fixed fee but the firm seeks to depart from this agreement during the retainer due to unforeseen circumstances. The firm should have been clear about the scope of the fixed fee from the outset. It would be wrong to renege on a fixed fee quote and would amount to a substantiated complaint of poor service.

(4) A quote is given for a fixed fee which has no bearing on the complexity of the case or the hours that would be spent on the case; for example, if the work was straightforward form filling and the client is charged on a fixed fee ten times what the hourly rate would be. There are many ethical issues in this particular context - how should fixed fees be designed and should the client be told what the hourly rate equivalent would be?

Scenario: Inadequate pricing information

Facts

The client complains about the fact that the solicitor has given inadequate pricing information and the matter is investigated by the nominated complaints person (not the fee earner). The solicitor who reviews the file likes the fee earner and has always held them in high regard. However, the file is not in great order and shows that costs information has been scant and not properly updated throughout the matter.

Rules

Principles

You act:

Principle 2: in a way that upholds public trust and confidence in the solicitors' profession and in legal services provided by authorised persons.

Code of Conduct for Solicitors

Paragraph 3.2: You ensure that the service you provide to clients is competent and delivered in a timely manner.

Paragraph 8.7: You ensure that clients receive the best possible information about how their matter will be priced and, both at the time of engagement and when appropriate as their matter progresses, about the likely overall cost of the matter and any costs incurred.

Potential ethical issues/professional breaches

Not only is there a regulatory requirement to keep the client in- formed about their costs, it is ethically right to do so. Clients should know what they are being charged and who will be doing the work on their matters, so they can make an informed decision as to whether to use your firm's services or not (Paragraph 8.6 of the Code of Conduct for Solicitors). Without good information at the outset, the client's decision-making is hindered and this does not produce an ethical result as the client is lacking information. For example, estate agents often quote high selling prices for houses in order to secure a contract and defend their own high rates. It is not ethical for them to do this knowing that the information is false or the price is unachievable. The same principles apply in the legal environment and is subject to regulatory sanction (unlike the position estate agents find themselves in).

Possible approaches

The supervising solicitor could find that the complaint has no validity on the basis that the solicitor is usually good at giving this information and this is just a simple oversight. This is not in the best interests of this particular client who hasn't received the prescriptive costs information. That decision might not be in keeping with the Principals of honesty and integrity either; either the solicitor has or hasn't given the costs information. The fact that the solicitor has failed to comply in this case is all that is relevant.

If the wrong decision is made about the complaint, the client could take matters further and go to the Ombudsman. Therefore nothing is gained by the short-sighted decision to sweep the complaint under the carpet. Further, that decision might give the solicitor the impression that their approach to costs/pricing information has been sanctioned by the firm and may continue in the same vein in the future. This may then encourage poor practice within the firm - a bad apple is turning the barrel bad.

A client who is not satisfied with the proposed resolution may approach LeO, the firm will pay the flat fee of £400 and may face a compensatory payment to the client. The loss of money and fee earning time in dealing with the complaint with LeO will be considerable.

Suggested reaction/steps to avoid

A better approach, which is more reflective of the Principles and the Codes of Conduct, would be to review the file, note what information the client was given and whether it was accurate. If not, the firm should recognise the error and offer the client an appropriate reduction in their bill and perhaps even refund money that has already been paid. Apologising to the client may also be warranted in the circumstances.

The solicitor should be given further training on the issue of costs information and the need to provide it accurately. This approach would address both short and long term issues. If the client was still unhappy with the level of redress and escalated their complaint to LeO, the complaint would be investigated but if they considered the resolution offered was satisfactory, the flat fee of £400 may well be waived.

6.7 Making an informed decision

Ultimately it is down to the ability of the client, based on the information provided, to make an informed decision about the matter in hand, how it will be dealt with and by whom, and the scope of the options available to them in how to proceed as to whether they will complain or not. Clients will always be disappointed if a matter does not end favourably for them but the solicitor can take much preventative action so that the client does not blame them no matter what the outcome. If the solicitor is careful in advising the client to enable them to make choices during the proceedings, it is more difficult for the client to blame the solicitor for the outcome.

6.8 Complaints handling

Dealing with the complaint internally

Paragraph 8.2 of the Code of Conduct for Solicitors outlines that every firm and solicitor not practising within a firm structure should have a complaints procedure which relates to the services provided.

Paragraph 8.3 of the Code of Conduct for Solicitors states that the client should be informed in writing at the time of engagement about their right to complain about services and charges, how to complain and who to address the complaint to, and that they have the right to complain to the legal ombudsman. The client should be given details of when such a complaint could be made to the ombudsman.

It is important that someone independent investigates the complaint and that they have sufficient power to come to an independent conclusion. There should be a transparent methodology for documenting the complaint, gathering the evidence and documenting the logic used to make the final decision. This would support the principle of integrity; it would not look good if the person who is the subject of the complaint is actually the person investigating the complaint.

If the firm appoints the person who had primary control of the file to investigate the complaint, it might not be considered to be a fair investigation by the client. This is an ethical consideration for the firm to take into account - many people would not believe that the fee earner could have sufficient objectivity to investigate a complaint against them.

If the complaint is then raised with the Legal Ombudsman, the firm or solicitor should co-operate fully and transparently in an effort to get the complaint satisfactorily resolved in the swiftest manner possible. Paragraphs 7.3/3.2 of the Code of Conduct for Solicitors/Code of Conduct for Firms require that the individual solicitor/firm cooperates with the SRA and other regulators specifically naming the ombudsman.

Solicitors and firms should behave in a professional manner throughout the period of the complaint.

Scenario: Backdated attendance note

Facts

The client complains that the solicitor hasn't given advice on a particular issue and they raise the matter as a complaint. The solicitor needs to identify the issue as a complaint and activate the complaints process. The solicitor knows that if the client goes to LeO then they will ask to see evidence of the advice given to the client which will be in the form of written advice or a note of oral advice given to the client. The solicitor is sure that they gave advice to the client orally about the matter but there is no evidence on the file to support that. The solicitor is certain that the client has been properly advised but the file lacks evidence to support that.

The solicitor decides to backdate an attendance note to support the advice that they believe they have given, believing that they could not get caught doing this. Although the attendance note might be backdated, the advice was given.

Rules

Principles

You act:

Principle 2: in a way that upholds public trust and confidence in the solicitors' profession and in legal services provided by authorised persons.

Principle 4: with honesty.

Principle 5: with integrity.

Principle 7: in the best interests of each client.

Potential ethical issues/professional breaches

Even if the solicitor did give the relevant advice to the client, back-dating evidence of this is professional misconduct. It is not in keeping with Principles 4 or 5, which require the solicitor to act with honesty and integrity. Fabricating evidence to support the solicitor's recall of advice given isn't in keeping with these principles and neither is it acting in the client's best interests.

The solicitor cannot rely on their memory of advice that was given orally - only an attendance note made contemporaneously would be good evidence of what advice was given at the time. It is better if the solicitor follows up oral advice with written confirmation to the client, for the avoidance of doubt. Although this isn't a requirement of the new Codes it is good practice. Ethically, it lacks integrity to manufacture a document to prevent a complaint being made. It is a short term fix as the act of creating the document is a more serious breach than the issue of poor service.

Possible approaches

The solicitor should admit the oversight and make amends to the client. If no detriment has been caused by the failure to advise then a compensatory offer should be made to the client to reflect the poor service element. The firm will save time and costs of a LeO investigation by reaching an agreement with the client. LeO charges firms £400 for every complaint it investigates and this is borne in mind when an offer of settlement is made.

Suggested reaction/steps to avoid

It is not advisable to fabricate attendance notes, emails or letters to circumvent a complaint from a client. Not only are there serious regulatory concerns, it is unethical to do so. Taking this route could lead to a solicitor being struck off for committing a dishonesty offence. The act of covering up poor service is a worse regulatory breach than the poor service element.

6.9 Negligence

The circumstances that give rise to a complaint of poor service and a claim in negligence can often be the same set of circumstances. It may be that the client feels the level of compensation they are looking for will not be provided by LeO and they therefore may decide it is appropriate to bring a claim in negligence. LeO will not look at a complaint where a negligence claim has been initiated. However, they can look at the complaint first and as long as the client does not accept their resolution, the client can still raise a claim in negligence.

The governing Principle in this area is Principle 7: You act in the best interests of each client.

Paragraph 3.2 of the Code of Conduct for Solicitors and Paragraph 4.2 of the Code of Conduct for Firms state that the service you (the solicitor or the firm) provide client is competent, delivered in a timely manner and takes into account your client's needs and circumstances. This means that each client will need something different from their solicitor. The transaction or case might be straightforward, but the client might need more advice or a different level of service from the solicitor or firm.

Occasionally, reporting a solicitor to the professional body may not provide sufficient monetary or disciplinary remedy for the client's circumstances so they may have to resort to bringing the solicitor to court for negligence or breach of contract. Whilst this might address the monetary complaint, disciplinary sanctions are imposed by professional bodies and not the court. Sometimes, a client can feel that the sanctions imposed by the professional bodies to do not remedy the wrong that they have suffered and then they take the matter further.

Normally it is quite easy to establish whether a contract is in place as the solicitor would have supplied the client with terms and conditions before starting the matter. Sometimes there can be ambiguous scenarios, such as third parties relying on a solicitor's advice, where you need to establish whether a contract is in place or not. If there is no contract in place between the solicitor and the "client" then no court proceedings for negligence can take place.

6.10 What are the principles of negligence?

In order for a client to show that a solicitor was negligent there must be three elements present:

(1) The solicitor owed a duty of care;

(2) The solicitor breached that duty of care; and

(3) The client suffered a loss as a result of a breach of that duty.

Proving negligence is usually a rules-based approach, with a few ethical issues that arise.

6.11 Does the solicitor owe a duty of care?

There are three factors that need to be assessed when considering whether a duty of care is owed which are foreseeability, proximity and justice and reasonableness.

(1) The foreseeability test is whether it was foreseeable that the solicitor might harm their client by their actions;

(2) The proximity test measures whether the two parties were close, either physically or in a relationship;

(3) The justice and reasonableness test is whether is it just and reasonable to impose a duty of care.

If it can be shown that a client relationship exists then it is easy to prove a duty of care. It is more difficult where this relationship is in doubt or does not exist.

6.12 Duty of care to third parties

Normally a solicitor gives advice to a client in the knowledge that the advice is only for them and not to be relied upon by third parties. There are some situations where third parties do place reliance on advice given to another party such as the beneficiaries of a will. In these scenarios the solicitor must be able to reasonably deduce that the advice will be relied upon by specific third parties. A client telling a separate third party about advice given by a solicitor, where the solicitor has no knowledge of that third party, will not establish a duty of care.

6.13 Breach of duty of due care and skill

To show that a solicitor has breached their duty of due care and skill the solicitor has to be shown to have exercised a lower level of due care and skill than that of a reasonable solicitor in that situation. It is also vital to show that the solicitor showed a lack of due care and skill in relation to the scope of their retainer. The retainer should have been set out before or at the point the solicitor accepted instructions to act.

How To Be An Ethical Solicitor

It is also important to note that a solicitor cannot be found negligent for merely losing a case. However, in matters where there is a definitive objective which is within the means of a reasonably competent solicitor, and where it is reasonable to assume that the solicitor has control of the outcome, such as the drafting of a will, non-production or defective production of the final outcome can lead to a claim of negligence.

6.14 Is a solicitor culpable for lack of knowledge of the law?

Due to the depth, breadth and complexity of the law and its ever evolving nature there is no way that solicitors would be expected to have an in depth knowledge of all of it. However, if they do not have a sufficient level of knowledge in that area to provide their client with a sufficient level of due care and skill then they need to research those areas or defer to another legal expert in the particular field in question. We have explored the solicitor's obligation to maintain their competence to practise in the context of the new Competence Statement in Chapter 2: Rules-based ethics and regulation.

Lack of knowledge of the law is looked upon dimly by the courts. However, the advice given by a solicitor has to be judged upon its reasonableness at the time. If a solicitor acts or gives advice in what is seen to be standard at the time then they will be deemed not to be negligent. However, this standard has to be free of foreseeable and/or avoidable risk.

If a solicitor can show that they reasonably followed the SRA Codes of Conduct and good practice as it relates to those Codes, it would be highly unlikely that a court would find a solicitor to be negligent.

6.15 Complex cases and specialist lawyers

If a solicitor gets involved in a matter and then discovers that more specialist legal knowledge than they can provide is required, should the solicitor declare this to the client and excuse themselves? Ethically, it is the right thing to do to admit that one's knowledge is insufficient and refer the matter onwards or acquire the knowledge required in order to complete the matter.

In matters where the legal points are complex and the solicitor does not hold themselves out to be an expert in these points they would need to show they sought a Counsel's or expert's advice or both. Not to do so would open themselves up to accusations of negligence were the matter not to proceed favourably for their client. Ethical decision-making that goes wrong could end up with an action for negligence.

Another related point would be that work needs to be allocated to a person of suitable standing and expertise to complete the work to the professional standard the matter deserves. If overly complex work is given to a trainee or junior member of staff without adequate supervision or support the firm could open themselves up to a negligence claim.

6.16 Can a lawyer be found negligent for not following the instructions of a client?

This very much depends on the circumstances of the matter. If the client gave a reasonable legal instruction that was within the capabilities of the solicitor then, nine times out of ten, if the solicitor did not carry out that instruction they would be negligent. However, clients don't always give reasonable, actionable, legal or ethical instructions.

Scenario: Deceiving clients

Facts

The client instructed the solicitor to proceed with litigation in circumstances where the solicitor did not think the client would win. The client did not agree to proceed with ADR processes despite good advice to do so. The solicitor deceived the client into believing that proceedings had been issued when they had not. The solicitor had hoped that the client would negotiate a settlement rather than issue proceedings. The client discovered the deception and complained.

The firm apologised and offered remedies which were accepted by the client and no negligence action was taken.

The solicitor agreed that he should have been more firm with the client about issuing the proceedings against his advice, rather than lie to the client in the hope that he would negotiate a settlement.

What the solicitor needs to do is to inform and advise the client of the possible courses of action and the reasonable expectable consequences of action or inaction. Once the solicitor is satisfied that their advice has been understood by the client it is the client's decision as to the course of action to take. The solicitor has to then make the ethical decision whether they can carry out the client's instructions or refuse to act. If the solicitor refuses to act then they need to document the exact circumstances and reasoning they undertook when they decided not to act.

6.17 Can a solicitor be found negligent for advice given in relation to settlements?

A solicitor can only give reasonable advice based on the circumstances of the case and making a professional judgement on what spectrum of results the client should expect. Therefore if a solicitor can show that they exercised reasonable due care and skill when giving the advice on the amount a client should settle for, for example, a client cannot say they were negligent if the final settlement is lower. Ethically, the solicitor needs to ensure that the reason that they are encouraging a settlement is in the best interests of the client. If there are overwhelming personal reasons that the solicitor is encouraging settlement then this would be ethically wrong.

Scenario: Encouraging settlement

Facts

The settlement figure to the client is £100,000 with costs to the firm of £25,000. The solicitor knows that the costs figure is probably higher than they would get outside the terms of the offer but that the settlement figure for the client should possibly be £125,000. The solicitor should not encourage settlement just to get the higher fees that are on offer.

6.18 Following the advice of a barrister

If a solicitor is following the advice of a barrister are they absolved of any claims of negligence? Again, it largely revolves around the circumstances of the case and the balance of knowledge between the two individuals. If it is a complex case in a specialist area of law and the barrister is such a specialist, then it would be reasonable that any claims of negligence should fall solely on the barrister. But in no circumstances does the solicitor get off scot-free. The solicitor must always apply reasonable care and judgement to any advice they may receive from a barrister to ensure that it is fair and relevant to their client and subsequently the best course of action to follow.

6.19 Wasted costs orders

Is it ethical for a solicitor to pursue an action that they know is doomed to failure or is an action that will only incur costs for the other side? These types of action can be known as:

(a) nuisance claims; or

(b) speculative claims; or

(c) vexatious claims.

Sometimes the claims are made with the intent of securing a settlement rather than the paying party incurring disproportionate legal costs. There are two instances where this would occur.

(1) Where the client instructs the solicitor to pursue the order (in spite of advice to the contrary);

(2) Where the solicitor advises the client to pursue the order (costs proportionality would need to be taken into account).

Some solicitors might take the view that it is his or her job to outline options to the client. Ultimately, the decision of how to proceed is for the client and not the solicitor. In this scenario, the law recognises that the solicitor has a duty to third parties.

According to Section 51(7) of the Senior Courts Act 1981:

""wasted costs" means any costs incurred by a party:

(a) as a result of any improper, unreasonable or negligent act or omission on the part of any legal or other representative or any employee of such a representative; or

(b) which, in the light of any such act or omission occurring after they were incurred, the court considers it is unreasonable to expect that party to pay".

Therefore, if the court deems the application improper, unreasonable or negligent then the court may hold that the solicitor who brought the case is liable for all or part of the incurred costs.

At this point the interests of the solicitor and their client would diverge as the section is meant to act as a deterrent to prevent unnecessary applications. A solicitor should therefore make an ethical decision regarding an application before the risk of a wasted cost order arises, and advise their client accordingly.

6.20 Summary

It is inevitable that a client may reach the end of proceedings and feel that their experience has not been as expected. Professionals should be subjected to an external and objective complaints procedure and even negligence claims for the work they do. If we were told that we could never complain about the service of a medical professional we would feel very vulnerable.

There are ethical dimensions to complaints or negligence actions and solicitors should try to be objective when dealing with them. They should do their best to rectify any areas where it is agreed that service has not been as expected. Clearly, covering up a complaint, failing to deal with it or dealing with it rudely does the reputation of the firm and the profession no good.

Chapter 7: Ethics and social media

7.1 Introduction

It is very difficult to associate the idea of sites such as Facebook and Twitter as having any relevance to legal regulation and professional ethics. However, the technological developments in electronic communication dragged the legal profession kicking and screaming into the 21st century.

The Law Society defines social media as:

> *"websites and applications that enable users to create and share content or to participate in social networking.* **Social media are web-based and mobile technologies that turn communication into active dialogue**. *Some channels may be more appropriate for a practice's or individual's business needs than others, particularly in relation to social networking"*[1].

Essentially social media is any form of online application that allows its users to (publicly or otherwise) share information amongst networks they are connected to, or even to the public in general. Social media sites can often be accessed in a variety of ways, be it by way of an internet browser or through an application on a tablet or mobile device.

Some practitioners less familiar with the concept of social media may raise an eyebrow about the relevance of a chapter regarding social media in a handbook about the professional ethics of solicitors in practice. Consider, however, that from a marketing perspective social media is an increasingly popular and effective way of expanding a firm's advertising and networking circles in order to communicate the firm's ethos to a wide range of individuals. This is leading firms and solicitors to use

> Readers who have a firm understanding of social media may want to skip to section 7.6 which discusses the ethics of utilising social media

social media more and more. As a result of this increased use in social media, solicitors are quickly becoming acutely aware (and some learning the hard way) that their online interactions are subject to the regulatory and ethical principles of the profession in equal measures to their offline interactions. Two years on from the first edition of this book, recent decisions from the Solicitor's Disciplinary Tribunal indicate social media is still very

---

[1] *https://www.lawsociety.org.uk/support-services/advice/practice-notes/social-media/.*

How To Be An Ethical Solicitor

much a danger zone for solicitors, and one in which the SRA are taking a particular interest.

The majority of firms now accept that social media has evolved beyond a tool purely utilised for networking personally to become powerful marketing devices for both firms themselves and also the individual solicitors within those firms. It is now considered commonplace for law firms to have their own Twitter and Facebook pages; consumers can often associate the lack of an online presence as somewhat of a warning sign.

Social media exploded into the legal profession around 2011, but it is only recently that most firms have embraced the potential rewards it offers. Equally, individual solicitors have understood that social media offers an easy way for them to develop their own separate online identity, independent from that of their firm. Compared to other industries, the application of social media by the legal profession is relatively in its infancy. As a result of this relative infancy, lawyers have been extremely reticent to fully appreciate the application of professional ethical issues to their interactions online, and in particular, through social media. The key issue for solicitors who use social media regularly is that the Standards and Regulations will apply to their actions, regardless of whether they are at work or "off the clock" in their own personal time. The last thing on most solicitor's minds after a few drinks on a Saturday night is the SRA's Standards and Regulations!

This chapter will seek to discuss the ethical and regulatory issues which apply to the online interactions of solicitors both in a professional and personal capacity, and discuss actions which can be taken to ensure that this exposure is limited.

7.2 The rise of social media and online interactions

The rapid expansion of the legal profession's use of social media and electronic communication should not come as a surprise. The benefits of electronic communication are well known and we do not propose to have great levels of discussion regarding this; very few practitioners will now solely send correspondence by way of letter as a result of the widespread use of email. Social media operates on the same wavelength and offers many professional and personal benefits to both a firm and individual solicitors in that firm.

7.3 Social media in the legal profession

It is important to remember that in its infancy, social media was used primarily for online interactions between individuals, purely for the purpose of socialisation; it was not until social media sites began to possess serious traction and data on its users that could be sold that social media was properly utilised for business purposes. It was even later that the legal profession began to understand its significant benefits.

Social media is typically used by solicitors in two ways:

(1) **A marketing tool for the firm**. A nominated individual, or the firm's marketing department, may use social media sites as a way of promoting the firm to the general public. This is done in a variety of ways, for example:

- Posting about the firm's objectives;

- Providing an insight into the firm's ethos and practice style;

- Offering comments on the changing legal landscape;

- Posting photographs of their employees engaging with the local community (such as charity events hosted by the firm);

- Posting "offers", such as particular fixed fee packages for example;

- Posting links to the firm's "blog" for potential clients to consider.

(2) **A marketing tool for the individual solicitor**. An individual solicitor may use social media as a way of establishing and promoting their own services, or for their own private reasons unrelated to professional promotion. Whilst an individual solicitor may utilise their social media accounts to promote the services of the firm they are currently employed by, they will also be promoting their identity and offerings independently of the firm by using social media. In a similar way to how a firm might operate a social media account, individual solicitors will often promote themselves and their firms in the following ways:

- Publishing comments and blogs on developments in their individual practice areas;

- Posting photographs of their "extra-curricular" activities;

- Engaging with other firms and practitioners;
- Interacting with clients (albeit less common).

Individual solicitors may not consciously promote either themselves or their firms through social media. Many simply comment on areas of law through these platforms out of curiosity without self-promotion in mind. Additionally, many individual solicitors will use social media for purely personal reasons and interactions, with absolutely no professional intentions in mind. It is therefore necessary to differentiate between different accounts for individual solicitors:

- **Professional accounts**: these will be accounts where solicitors use social media for the purpose of promoting their services or the services of a firm. These accounts will tend to post content publicly and will contain mostly professional posts regarding their own practice areas or content which promotes their or their firm's personal ethos and practice style.

- **Personal accounts**: personal accounts conversely will be accounts which solicitors use for non-professional purposes, such as corresponding with friends and family and keeping their networks updated on more personal updates like holidays and relationships. These accounts tend to be private and viewable only by those people the solicitor has authorised to view their private network (e.g. their friends).

We will see that certain platforms of social media will lend themselves more towards personal accounts and others will lend themselves more towards professional matters.

To complicate matters even further, some solicitors will not appreciate that there is a distinction to be had between these two forms of use and will often use one for both professional and personal accounts which can lead to complications.

7.4 The benefits of social media

We will briefly consider the potential benefits that social media offers to firms and individual solicitors, although you may be aware of many of these.

- Social media raises the profile of the firm and individuals for little or no cost regardless of the size of the firm in question. Even the smallest of firms will be able to appoint an individual (albeit under supervision) to promote the firm by way of social media. Unlike traditional advertising the basic functions of most social media sites are free and therefore, other than any business overheads, the cost of social media compared to more traditional methods is refreshingly cost effective. In any event, even where firms subscribe to paid advertisements on social media, the costs of social media campaigns compared to traditional print campaigns are inherently minimal and are much more likely to reach a wider and targeted audience.

- Social media provides an opportunity for a firm to determine what information is available online about both itself and other solicitors, rather than relying on the word of mouth of third parties. For example, legal recruiters now have the benefit of LinkedIn to search for profiles of solicitors, allowing them to trawl through various solicitor profiles and match potential suitors to their client's needs. Equally, firms can do this where they require a particular solicitor for a role, allowing them to head-hunt candidates effectively.

- Most social media sites allow posts to be directed to individual people or target audiences, provided that particular market possesses an online presence. This allows the ethos and sales pitches of the firm that are communicated by way of social media to be specifically directed at the desired market of the firm, ensuring marketing campaigns reach their intended audiences. This is a significant improvement over the more "scatter-gun" approach of traditional marketing.

- In a world dominated by the use of the internet, many clients will expect firms to possess an online presence and to interact by way of electronic communication. In the same way as you may express some concern over an opponent firm which possesses no website, many clients will consider a lack of online and social media presence as somewhat of a red flag. An online presence and ability to market the firm effectively by social media suggests that the firm possesses a very forward-thinking attitude and is able to adapt to evolution and change.

- Social media removes the geographical barriers that more traditional marketing simply cannot achieve. Online posts and marketing can be targeted towards markets that the firm previously could not reach. This is particularly useful for firms with specialisms in niche practice areas as they are able to specifically communicate and advertise their services nationally, attracting clients who may never have been aware of the firm in the absence of social media.

7.5 The risks of social media

Whilst the benefits of social media are many, the ability to quickly communicate content to a wide public audience does of course carry with it a large amount of risk, particularly from the perspective of professional regulation.

- Solicitors are by their very nature very vocal about areas of law they are passionate about; it is a requirement of the job! When combined with the instantaneous nature of social media, any rash comments, particularly where untruthful, could lead to liability for both the firm and the individual solicitor in tort for some form of defamation. Equally, boisterous or unsubstantiated claims made on social media have the potential to mislead the public, a breach of Paragraph 1.4 of the Code of Conduct for Solicitors.

- More seriously, any posts which could be considered to breach the Principles, such as the duty to act with integrity, could easily attract the disciplinary attention of the SRA. If anything, social media is more likely to attract the attention of the SRA given that posts are publicly made available and permanent, meaning even where a person regrets a post and deletes it is not always the case that the message has not already been seen by others or recorded in some way.

- It is all too easy to indirectly and inadvertently make the private affairs of a client (over which solicitors of course owe a duty of confidentiality) public by way of social media. As we will see this can easily occur through inferences drawn from social media posts, even where the solicitor does not intend it to occur.

- The risks of social media apply not only to you, but also your clients. Your client's social media posts can be produced as evidence in litigation. It would, for example, be difficult for you to maintain a personal injury claim for reduced mobility if your opponents are able to adduce photographic evidence of your client's recent skiing holiday from their Facebook page.

- The removal of geographical barriers also carries with it some element of risk. Of course it carries the firm to markets it hasn't previously had access to; however this also presents an element of danger where the firm does not understand the market it is entering into. Particularly where these new markets are international, the risk of misunderstanding market elements through social media posts could cause offence, and may raise certain diversity issues.

- Whilst firms can place controls on their employees' social media usage regarding what they can and cannot utilise social media accounts for whilst under the firm's employment, ultimately if an employee does post something irresponsible, unprofessional or unethical, it can undermine the firm's image and expose a risk to its integrity. Whilst the firm can take disciplinary proceedings against their employee for this, the damage done to the firm may well already have been spread potentially globally and even if the employee deletes the post, it may well already have been permanently captured or commented upon by a third party.

7.6 The ethics of social media

The interactions of solicitors on social media, both during office hours and outside them, presents multiple ethical dilemmas for solicitors. It is often difficult for solicitors to appreciate this because social media is fairly new to the legal profession, and therefore many solicitors struggle to take it seriously when contemplating breaches of the Standards and Regulations. As a result of this solicitors rarely contemplate ethics and regulatory conduct when utilising social media; most solicitors think of serious ethical issues as including only accounts breaches or serious criminal actions.

After all, how on earth could putting something on Facebook result in a striking off?

7.7 Why do ethics apply to social media?

The risks of social media can be contextualised by comparing the issues to that of the interaction between lawyers and the "traditional" media, which has long sat uneasily alongside the profession.

Lord Woolfe has previously suggested that parties to litigation and their respective solicitors should not make comments to the media in reference to ongoing litigation without the express leave of the court. His reasoning behind this was that he argued that the parties were entitled to have their issues determined before the court without "improper interference with the course of justice"[2]. We should assume that the same dicta applies equally to statements that have been issued by solicitors through social media.

---

[2] *Hodgson v Imperial Tobacco Limited [1998] EWCA Civ 224.*

Statements made online by solicitors have the capacity to be perceived by the public and the media to carry authority even where the content of that statement is completely inaccurate. As Lord Woolfe stated:

> *"The professionalism and sense of duty to legal advisers who conduct litigation of this nature should mean that the courts are able to rely on the legal advisers to exercise great self-restraint when making comment [to the media]…"*

In considering this statement it is easy to see how the risk of communication between solicitors and the wider public on an instantaneous platform could result in ethical and regulatory breaches. Simply put, social media makes it a lot easier for inappropriate or accidental comments made by solicitors to be communicated on a mass basis. If, for example, a solicitor makes an inappropriate comment on their social media account regarding ongoing proceedings then there is a real risk that they will prejudice current or anticipated proceedings, undermining the authority of the court and the trust in the profession.

Of course, the risk of professional breaches in the context of social media is not restricted to matters involving ongoing litigation; in theory any of the Principles can be breached, often unwittingly, by a solicitor utilising social media. As we have previously seen, this is also complicated by the fact that many solicitors will combine their professional and private social media accounts, blurring the boundaries between what is a personal interaction on social media and what is a professional one. Solicitors may be surprised to learn that unethical posts on their private social media accounts made outside of work hours can still be considered regulatory breaches by the SRA.

The Principles that are the most likely to be tested when an individual is engaged in social media activity are:

You act:

(1) **Principle 2**: in a way that upholds public trust and confidence in the solicitors' profession and in legal services provided by authorised persons;

(2) **Principle 4**: with honesty;

(3) **Principle 5**: with integrity;

(4) **Principle 6**: in a way that encourages equality, diversity and inclusion.

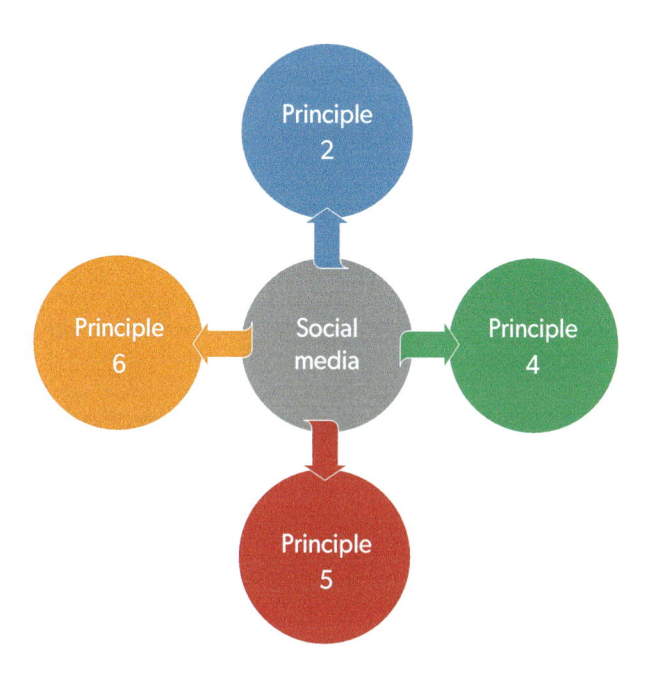

Fig 27: Social media and the Principles

Of these Principles it is Principles 2 and 5 which are most easily breached by solicitors through social media.

It is also extremely important that ethics are applied to social media due to the speed at which content can not only be posted, but also shared. Controversial posts have known to become "viral" (that is they are shared between multiple networks extremely quickly, and ultimately to thousands of site users) within hours of the post being made. Social media is therefore particularly dangerous to an individual solicitor, a firm and the profession as a whole because it is a public forum where anything can become accessible to thousands of people extremely quickly, and the record will be permanent.

It can often seem somewhat bizarre to suggest, but in the most serious of breaches of the Code of Conduct, a solicitor could face being struck off the roll as a result of their actions. Being struck off the roll for an absent minded post on a social media site may seem ludicrous, but where the post is a serious breach of professional conduct this may well be the appropriate sanction. By way of comparison consider that whilst most people may not believe not paying for a train ticket to be anything serious, because of the dishonesty status of this offence, solicitors have been struck off for this in the past.

Above all, social media remains such a significant risk for solicitors purely because its novelty means that it appears to be innocuous. However, remember at all times that social media is a public forum, and where comments are made in that forum they can be communicated to other networks with frightening speed.

7.8 The importance of social media in the legal profession

Despite this and given the benefits of social media it is not surprising that the legal profession has been quick to monetise upon the benefits it offers. But why is social media so important to the legal profession, and why should we even consider ethical principles when utilising it?

The main reason behind the importance of social media is that it allows solicitors to engage with their colleagues, other solicitors and even the judiciary, allowing instantaneous mass debate on topics such as law reforms or changes to court services. This collaboration between various legal professionals, particularly those who practice in areas affected by reforms, is an excellent way for the profession to collaborate with one another. For example, forums on LinkedIn allow users to discuss and comment upon developments in their practice areas. Before the advent of social media, outside of large scale meetings of practitioners, this was not possible with such ease and transparency.

It may seem extreme, but the widespread use of social media by the legal profession is now helping to shape how the rule of law evolves; as social media is an instantaneous platform for commentary and debate on the changing legal environment it can be suggested that it acts like a pulse for how the profession perceive certain legal issues.

7.9 Understanding different social media platforms

One key thing to understand about social media is that there are various social media sites available for practitioners to promote their businesses, and that all of these sites employ various different functions and privacy settings.

There are many types of social networks with which solicitors may engage during their careers; in a response to an SRA consultation one firm responded that it utilised as many as 16! Fortunately, most firms are unlikely to use anywhere near that number and are more likely to simply use sites such as LinkedIn or Twitter. However, the social media sites which potentially could be of use in a law firm in order of relevance are:

- The firm's website
- LinkedIn
- Twitter
- YouTube
- Forums of legal debate
- YouTube
- Facebook

How To Be An Ethical Solicitor

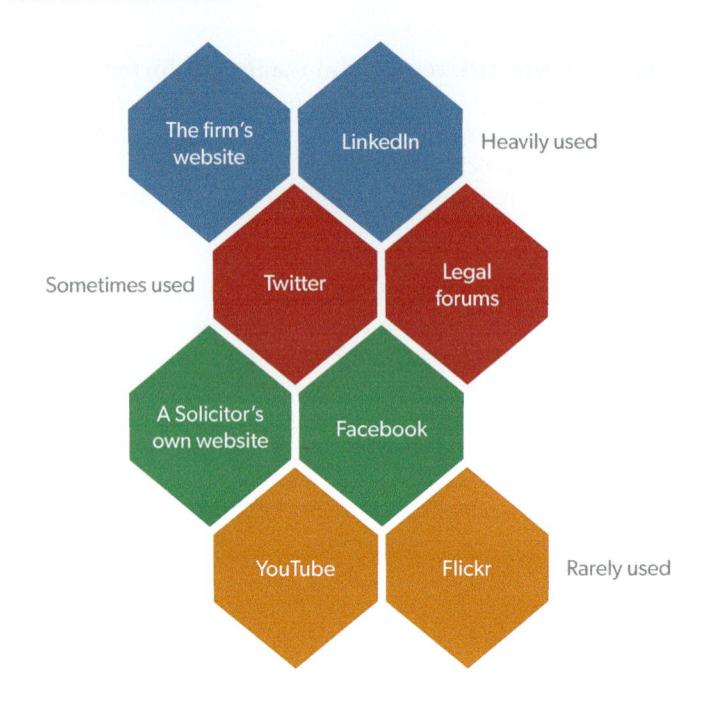

Fig 28: Types of social networks used by law firms

A crucial element of remaining ethically vigilant on social media is understanding that different social media sites employ different privacy options. You should also remember that just because a post is not made publicly available on one social media site does not mean that it is not publicly available on another! Equally, one site may well change their privacy settings, making private posts public, or vice versa. The terms and conditions of certain sites may have unintended consequences, such as the relinquishing of your rights to content that you post on these sites or providing licenses to the social media site and other users to use your content.

This chapter focuses on the most common social media applications utilised by the legal profession; however, when utilising social media or any other form of online interaction, you should have the SRA Standards and Regulations at the forefront of your mind.

7.10 Facebook

Most practitioners will be familiar with the social media site Facebook due to the fact it is one of the oldest and largest social media platforms available,

Ethics And Social Media

with an almost universal recognition amongst the general public. Facebook has become so inoculated within the majority of the public's daily lives that phrases such as "send me a message" have been replaced with "Facebook me".

The popularity of Facebook means that law firms are likely to want to capitalise upon its large user network, and indeed Facebook certainly offers the possibility to do this. Businesses can set up their own "pages" (which are much like individual user profiles) that users of Facebook can follow (known as "liking a page") and receive posts from that page. It is now extremely common for law firms to have their own Facebook pages, which are used to post updates about the firm and its services.

The main issue with Facebook within the legal profession is that it bases its roots so firmly within private social interactions between individuals, and thus possesses a more relaxed environment which is considered detached from the world of professional regulation. After all, Facebook began its days as a site for Harvard University students to share updates on their lives between the Harvard networks. With this foundation in mind it is very difficult to see how Facebook has progressed to a marketing tool for solicitors.

Facebook is also increasingly dangerous because individuals automatically assume that the content they post on their Facebook account can only be viewed by their friends (i.e. other users who have been authorised to view content). This is an incorrect assumption; the default settings of Facebook are indeed such that only friends can see posts, but individuals who misunderstand the privacy settings can easily change settings, making posts they assume are private, public. Additionally, some parts of a user's profile will be viewable publicly by default, such as the profile picture selected by the user. It is important to recall that not only inappropriate words can cause issues on Facebook, but also photos.

The personal basis of Facebook is such that the network channels have evolved primarily for personal use, and as such their audiences are typically more responsive towards content that their friends have shared on their networks, rather than the business minded posts of law firms. This has the result that an individual posting photos of their recent holiday is likely to attract far more than a post by a solicitor's firm about the reforms of a particular legal sector.

Because of this firms tend to approach Facebook with caution. However, arguably the main concern with Facebook is its use by individual solicitors. Most solicitors will possess their own Facebook account, and utilise it purely for their personal interactions outside of work. The issue with this is that a solicitor using Facebook outside of the office may, by virtue of the private and relaxed nature of the site, completely forget that their professional obligations apply to this online environment, even if their posts are restricted to their "friends". Consider this example:

Scenario: Facebook post

Facts

You are a solicitor in a small High Street firm. You have just arrived home after a week-long trial for a particularly vulnerable client. Unfortunately, the trial was not successful and judgment was made against your client, and the costs order is such that your client is likely to lose their home to pay for the costs. You feel that part of the reason you lost is because your opponent and their solicitors adduced key evidence extremely late and were very bullish regarding the application to admit this at the trial out of time. After one too many glasses of wine you log into your Facebook account and post:

> "Terrible time at the Royal Courts of Justice this week. Just goes to show that 99% of solicitors are corrupt and will do anything to win!"

Whilst your profile settings are such that only your friends will see this post, what issues are there regarding this post?

Rules

Principles

You act:

Principle 2: in a way that upholds public trust and confidence in the solicitors' profession and in legal services provided by authorised persons.

Principle 5: with integrity.

Code of Conduct for Solicitors

Paragraph 6.3: You keep the affairs of current and former clients confidential unless disclosure is required or permitted by law or the client consents.

Potential ethical issues/professional breaches

The mistake in this scenario is to assume that purely because Facebook is a private social media site, and the solicitor is not at work, means that there are no regulatory breaches. This is not true. This post, when viewed by the friends of the solicitor, is extremely likely to damage the trust the public places in the provision of legal services.

Equally, consider that even though the message is private now, any member of the solicitor's network could copy the message and display it on a more public forum. On a side note, consider that mentioning that the case is at the RCJ could draw an inference to who you act for. If this post became public and the other firm were identified, you could potentially face proceedings for defamation.

Possible approaches

Delete the post and inform your compliance officer (even though you are not at work).

Maintain a policy of not posting negative comments about your job on your Facebook page.

Suggested reaction/steps to avoid

This is a scenario where the best advice is simply to maintain a policy against sharing content of this nature on your private Facebook account.

It is extremely common for solicitors to utilise Facebook purely for personal reasons and use it to share photographs of holidays and accounts of their day to day activities. It is key to understand that anything placed on Facebook, whilst it may appear private within its relaxed environment, is still subject to the SRA Standards and Regulations.

7.11 Twitter

Twitter is generally considered to be the main competitor of Facebook and most practitioners will be familiar with the site and the concept of "tweeting", purely because Twitter is more commonly employed by the legal profession than Facebook. Twitter is a social media site where users can post text based content up to a maximum of 280 characters.

Similarly to Facebook, Twitter possesses a massive network of users which law firms are equally keen to impress their services upon. Firms can set up their own Twitter accounts which can then be followed by users on Twitter in order to receive updates from the firm's page.

Generally speaking it is more common for a firm to use a Twitter account than a Facebook account, and the reasoning behind this is fairly obvious when the nature of Twitter is properly understood. By default, posts on Twitter are made public, and the public can view the profile of any individual account. This is the default setting on all Twitter accounts and will apply unless the user deactivates it by making their account "private", having a similar effect to a Facebook account in that a user's content will only be viewable to those members of the network who are authorised by that user.

Additionally, the 280 character restriction imposed by Twitter (which was previously 140) raises certain issues that solicitors will need to be aware of. Unlike other social media sites messages will have to be tailored to fit into the restricted allowance. Many users of Twitter do this simply by deleting or abbreviating words in their overall message; however as solicitors will know, altering words and phrases can alter the entire meaning of the overall sentence! This is coupled with the fact that solicitors tend to prefer long explanations of legal concept, and it is often extremely difficult to make a sophisticated legal opinion within 280 characters. To visualise this, consider shortening the last judgment you read into 280 characters.

A unique feature of Twitter (which is creeping into other social media sites) is the use of the hashtag ("#"). Users are able to tag a specific word within their short posts by putting a hashtag immediately before it (for example a post about legal aid cuts may utilise the hashtag #LegalAid). Other users of Twitter will be able to search through all of the posts made to Twitter by searching hashtags, and if the same hashtag is used by a significant number of users in a short period of time then Twitter will notify other users that this specific hashtag is "trending", i.e. that a large body of Twitter users are posting about the same subject. To continue the legal aid example, during the amendments to criminal legal aid in 2012, posts primarily by the legal profession started the trend of the hashtag #SaveUKJustice.

The risks associated with a message (whether negatively or positively) "going viral" are also extrapolated with Twitter due to the fact that any message you make can be instantly posted to their own profile, known as "re-tweeting". The result of this is that any re-tweeted message is quickly seen by multiple networks outside the original poster's intended audience.

This should not put you off Twitter so long as you give thought to your ethical obligations. An unethical post can of course be disastrous when a damaging post is made on Twitter, but extremely beneficial if it is a positive and engaging sales message about the firm, hence its appeal to firms and individual solicitors!

7.12 LinkedIn

LinkedIn is a social media site that is more nuanced than Facebook, and is pitched as a bespoke social network for professionals, encouraging various professional networks to engage with one another for the purposes of doing business, offering employment and commenting upon one another's services. In the legal profession a great deal of LinkedIn is utilised for discussing legal matters and the publishing of blogs.

LinkedIn offers a similar network to Facebook in that it allows users to create a profile and post updates from that profile, with the difference being that a LinkedIn profile reads somewhat like a CV, with the user detailing their current job position and any other ongoing projects, along with their employment history, references and their skills. Other users are able to write recommendations for users on LinkedIn, and these will appear on that person's profile.

Unlike Facebook however, the entirety of a user's LinkedIn profile is viewable by any other member of LinkedIn, regardless of whether the two users are connected with one another or not. Users are also notified when a certain person views their profile, and will be given the name and job title of that person. It is, however, possible to anonymise yourself on LinkedIn, the downside of this being that you will not be notified of the people who view your profile.

LinkedIn operates a similar concept to Facebook's "friends" feature, meaning that users of LinkedIn can request to connect with other profiles on LinkedIn and become connections. Once two profiles have connected with each other they will be able to see one another's interactions on LinkedIn. For example, if one of the parties then opts to connect with another user then their connections will be notified of this. Equally, if you were to comment on a post on LinkedIn your connections would be able to see not only that you have commented on another user's post, but also view that comment.

LinkedIn is similar to Twitter in its public nature, to the extent that all posts and profiles are by default viewable by the public and any user of LinkedIn.

You should be aware that this is slightly more nuanced on LinkedIn than Twitter. For example if you were to comment on a colleague's post, others who you have connected to on LinkedIn may also get a notification that you have made a comment on that person's post, even if they are not connected with the person whose post you commented on.

Because LinkedIn is both a public facing and specific professional networking site, even connecting with a client may breach your confidentiality requirements as it may suggest to your network that you act for your client! Linkedin also allows you to include examples of your past work on your profile. If you include projects and client names on this then there is a risk that you could be in breach of your confidentiality obligations by publicly disclosing this information.

7.13 YouTube

YouTube is a commonly known social media platform that focuses explicitly on the creation and sharing of video content. Users create video content, typically below 10 minutes in length, and then upload it to YouTube where other users of the site are able to not only view it but also comment upon it in a public forum. YouTube is another site where the default privacy settings are such that any user of the site, regardless of whether they are a connection of the user or a member of the public, will be able to view the content uploaded. You are able to share videos on YouTube privately, but this somewhat defeats the point of the network.

YouTube is becoming slightly more relevant to the legal profession, although is still less utilised than the other social media networks referred to in this chapter. This is largely for the same reason as Facebook, in that the network is more focused towards social interaction on a personal level; popular videos on YouTube tend to include music videos, reviews of video games and films and independent film makers making a name for themselves. Whilst for this reason it is less geared towards the legal profession, there is a weighty amount of legal content on YouTube, and some firms have been keen to capitalise on the large network of potential clients. YouTube is also used by some firms as a convenient way of sharing and displaying any webinars they may have produced, since YouTube is both free and a public forum. Some solicitors are now exploring YouTube as a platform, and we are now seeing YouTube channels springing up that provide pro-bono advice, help junior solicitors navigate the difficulties of entering the profession and even the critiques of the accuracy of popular legal films.

7.14 WhatsApp

WhatsApp is a popular instant messaging service (owned by Facebook) that allows two or more people to communicate with one another and share photographs.

Like Facebook, WhatsApp (and any other instant messaging service) is often overlooked as not falling under the remit of professional conduct because it involves private conversations between two or more of its users. However, the same guidance to other social media apply equally to WhatsApp messages. WhatsApp messages are frequently perceived to be private but can easily become public through screenshots by any user involved in the chat. Whilst WhatsApp now allows users to delete messages previously sent, this does not provide anonymity.

7.15 Online forums and social media sites which encourage discussion

We have seen that one of the key benefits of social media in the legal profession is that it affords solicitors the ability to share their experiences, whether negative or positive, in their practice areas as well as allowing them to provide their opinions on new or reformed areas of law with one another. Professional sites such as LinkedIn certainly offer a platform to do this; however there is a multitude of online forums specifically devoted and tailored to these forms of discussion.

We mentioned earlier that these online discussions can act as the "pulse of the profession", but when discussing previous experiences or offering comments on areas of reform there is a substantial risk that professional and ethical obligations could be breached as a result of these comments. Sharing your experiences and opinions invariably means drawing upon your previous experiences, and ultimately confidential information about your previous and current clients. This has the potential, albeit sometimes unintentionally, to breach client confidentiality if a post is not structured in such a way as to protect your client's confidential information. Consider the following:

Scenario: LinkedIn post

Facts

You are a family solicitor in a High Street firm. A dispute resolution solicitor who is a connection of yours on LinkedIn posts a question seeking advice on their client's prospects of an application in the family courts. You reply to the comment as the facts seem similar to a previous matter you acted on some years ago:

> *"I acted for a client with similar circumstances a few years ago. In my experience the courts are quite amenable to granting these sorts of applications in circumstances such as this. I would imagine you will be successful."*

Are there any potential issues that might arise from your comment?

Rules

Principles

You act:

Principle 2: in a way that upholds public trust and confidence in the solicitors' profession and in legal services provided by authorised persons.

Principle 5: with integrity.

Principle 7: in the best interests of each client.

Code of Conduct for Solicitors

Paragraph 4.1: You keep the affairs of current and former clients confidential unless disclosure is required or permitted by law or the client consents.

Potential ethical issues/professional breaches

You should consider that the above comment may breach the duty of confidentiality you owe to your previous client. This is because someone who knows your previous client's circumstances could identify them from your comment that you "acted for a client with similar circumstances a few years ago". This is particularly relevant on LinkedIn where your professional circles frequently mix, and there is the possibility that a connection might know your client.

Possible approaches

There are several ways to approach this situation:

- Amend your comment, removing your reference to your previous client, i.e. "In my experience the courts are quite amenable to granting these sorts of applications in circumstances such as this, so I would imagine you will be successful." This reduces the risks of another connection associating the facts with your client because it removes the association of your experience with that particular set of circumstances.

- Seek your previous client's permission to discuss the matter with the solicitor on LinkedIn, making reference to the fact you wish to expressly say you have an experience in similar circumstances.

- Privately message the solicitor with your comment rather than comment on the public post.

- Don't comment.

Suggested reaction/steps to avoid

In this instance it is probably best to amend the comment and remove the reference to you having dealt with a similar matter. This reduces the risk that someone will associate the facts with your client. You should, however, appreciate that any reference to your previous experiences may draw inferences to previous clients of yours.

The potential risk does not stop at breaching client confidentiality. A solicitor could inadvertently make a negative or offensive comment about the actions of another solicitor, and even where true, posts of this nature could quite easily breach the obligation to act with integrity or decrease the public's perception of the profession. In commenting upon these discussions a solicitor will need to consider how their and their firm's professional image might be affected by any comments made. For example, the forum and news website, www.RollOnFriday.co.uk frequently discusses the more risky "gossip" of the firms of the legal profession, but even an anonymous comment made about fellow members of the profession on sites such as these could be picked up by the media, linked back to the solicitor, and be considered as an action which brings the profession into disrepute. Whilst anonymity on online sites encourages more risky comments, it is crucial to remember that purely because a site states you are posting anonymously this is not an excuse to act unethically, or assume that your actions cannot be traced back to you.

7.16 Blogs

Blogs are (typically) short online articles written by individual solicitors which are then posted on their own websites, social media platforms or on the firm's website. Blogs can in general be about anything related to the legal profession, from commenting upon areas of law requiring reform or change in government policies, all the way to blogs listing the top ten most attractive barristers in London.

Blogs pose ethical risks in a number of ways, primarily as they will usually be more lengthy in nature than short social media posts. This is somewhat of a double-edged sword; whilst a greater length will often mean that a solicitor will consider more thoroughly the content of the work (unlike a post on social media which can be done instantaneously), the chance that some part of the content will be unethical rises exponentially.

Consider also that an individual solicitor's opinion of a certain matter might differ from their firm's; a solicitor's blog may suggest to the wider public that this is the opinion of the firm, or even the profession itself.

Blogs will be either incorporated in the firm's or solicitor's website, published on LinkedIn or hosted on an individual social media site which is dedicated to the publication of blogs.

7.17 Websites

One commonly overlooked social network (albeit somewhat of a hybrid) is of course the firm's website. A firm's website is not a social network in the traditional sense; however on most websites visitors (i.e. prospective clients) will be able to interact with the firm by reading and commenting upon the content of that site. A firm's website will usually be the first port of call for potential clients when considering which firm to instruct. Equally, when a firm is heavily featured in the media, interested parties (opponents/potential employees) will usually consider the firm's website in order to uncover further information regarding the firm. Incorrect information on a firm's website will potentially attract breaches of Paragraph 1.4 of the Code of Conduct for Firms , that you do not mislead your clients or others.

7.18 Other social media platforms

This book has considered only the social media platforms which are most likely to be relevant to the legal profession; however remember that a wide variant of social media exists which utilises different mediums of networking. At the time of writing there are some 211 major social media sites worldwide! We will briefly discuss some of more frequently used social media accounts in the event that you come across them when engaging through social media;

- **Flickr**; a social network site where photographers share the works that they have produced. The default privacy setting of Flickr is that all posts are shared publicly.

- **Instagram**; social networking site where the users share personal photographs of their day to day activities. Some businesses utilise this social networking as a slightly alternative way of updating their customer base as to their day to day work or product development. The default privacy setting is that all posts on Instagram are shared publicly.

- **WordPress**; a social network dedicated to the publishing of blogs. Users are able to create a mini-website for themselves which focuses upon articles posted by that user. It tends to be more widely used by undergraduate students who are required to host their own blog sites as they do not have access to a firm's website or another posting forum.

- **Snapchat**; Snapchat is a photo sharing form of social media where the majority of photos sent between users disappear after being viewed. Whilst many brands use Snapchat as a way of communicating branded content to Snapchat users, in the legal profession you are much more likely to find Snapchat used by individuals, rather than law firms.

How To Be An Ethical Solicitor

It is important that you understand broadly the privacy settings of these social media sites if you come across them, and appreciate that the niche opportunity to market presented by these networks may encourage your firm to utilise them.

It is also worth bearing in mind that social media is an evolving market, and therefore there will no doubt be new emerging social media concepts which post-date this book, and may well be interacted through mediums that are entirely unappreciated today.

7.19 Engaging with social media ethically

It is hopefully quite clear from above that whilst social media is considered to attract ethical considerations, it carries with it a considerable amount of risk from a compliance perspective. As a result of this, engaging with social media should always be approached with certain ethical safeguards in mind.

Two Accounts: One Private and One Personal

We have seen that social media bases its foundations on interactions on a more personal level, and that the use of social media for business promotion is not the primary purpose of social media. Solicitors will manage their social media accounts in the following ways:

- An account that they utilise for personal social interactions with a network comprised of their friends and family. The privacy settings of these accounts tend to be private.

- An account that they utilise for professional interactions with a network comprised of their business contacts. The privacy settings of these accounts tend to be public.

- An account that they utilise for personal and professional interactions with a network comprised of their friends, family and business contacts. The privacy settings of these accounts are more likely to be a combination of public and private.

You will no doubt not be surprised to learn that it is the third use of social media that exposes a solicitor and their firm to the highest amount of risk. This is because it can often be difficult to appreciate where the line between personal and professional behaviour lies and where your professional obligations start and end. It can also be increasingly difficult to distinguish between casual interactions with clients and more formal communications. Many people will share photographs of their stories and experiences on their personal social media accounts, and it is probably true that every member of the profession who utilises social media for personal reasons has a post or photograph they would rather their clients did not see! In deciding whether it is appropriate to combine your private and professional accounts you should consider primarily whether this act is likely to breach your obligation under Principle 5 (to act with integrity), or Principle 2 (to maintain the trust the public places in the legal profession).

From a purely professional point of view your clients will probably consider personal updates about their solicitor's personal lives to be inappropriate; most clients will not care for updates about their solicitor's significant other, or photographs of their cat. On a more extreme note, however, images from a drunken weekend of a solicitor acting unethically, if serious enough and viewed by clients, could attract the attention of the SRA.

Of course, even when utilising a personal account with private settings you should consider that this content may either not be private (due to a settings misunderstanding) or later become public. When considering whether the content you post on your private account is appropriate it is worth asking yourself the question posed in Chapter 1:

Would you be happy for the following people to view the post you have placed on your private social media account?

- An unknown person on public transport;
- A colleague;
- A friend;
- Your supervisor;
- A journalist;
- Your partner;
- Your parents;
- A judge;
- The Solicitor's Disciplinary Tribunal.

It is therefore typically good practice for a solicitor to maintain two separate accounts:

(1) An account that they utilise for personal social interactions with a network comprised of their friends and family. The privacy settings of these accounts tend to be private.

(2) An account that they utilise for professional interactions with a network comprised of their business contacts. The privacy settings of these accounts tend to be public.

Having two accounts is effective because it allows you to consider the content you are posting and then post that to the account you consider it appropriate for, be it your professional or private account.

7.20 Understanding privacy settings

It cannot be stressed enough that **all information you share on social media may well be accessible to a much wider audience than you initially intended**, and it is therefore crucial that when you engage in any form of online interaction you fully appreciate and understand the privacy settings of the particular site you are using.

The issue of a potentially unexpected audience is amplified by the fact that social media sites rarely delete historical content you may have posted; posts you may have made to the site years ago (perhaps even before you qualified) could still be viewable to a wider audience than you intended initially! Newly qualified solicitors in particular are encouraged to review their historical posts to ensure that their accounts comply with their newly acquired ethical obligations and ensure that there is no content within it which:

- reflects badly on your own image as a solicitor;

- reflects badly on the profession itself.

It is strongly recommended that any posts that do not comply with either of the above ethical obligations are made "private", or preferably, deleted altogether.

You will have noted from the breakdowns of all the differing social media platforms that a great deal of exposure comes from not understanding the nature of social media. It is therefore vital that a firm and its individual solicitors understand and appreciate the privacy settings of each particular social media site they utilise. As we have seen this is not necessarily a straightforward lesson to learn; different sites employ different types of privacy settings, be it public posts or posts restricted to certain groups or individuals, and these settings are subject to revision and change by the site owners themselves.

In practice a firm will usually take charge of ensuring that its solicitors understand the social media sites they are using in order to promote the firm, but mitigate against any potential breaches. This means a firm will need to do two things:

(1) Understand the privacy settings of each site; and

(2) Ensure that all members of staff understand the privacy settings of each individual site they are using.

It is sensible for whoever is heading the social media management at a firm to fully familiarise themselves with the privacy settings of all social media sites typically employed by solicitors. However, even where the firm has considered and adopted the strongest privacy settings this does not necessarily mean that the information posted to the social media sites is protected. Some sites may default to public settings and even sites with the most stringent privacy settings are vulnerable to attacks by cyber criminals.

7.21 Being your client's friend

A "friend request" from a client is both a personal and professional conundrum. If you do choose to connect with a client on a social media site then you will need to evaluate whether this will affect any of your professional ethical obligations. It may well not be immediately obvious how interacting with a client on a social media site may impact upon your professional obligations. However consider the following scenario:

Scenario: LinkedIn request from a client

Facts

You have recently conducted an interview with a high value and well known individual in connection with his divorce from his wife. At the interview you agreed to act for the client and he signed the necessary client care paperwork. Upon returning home from the office that evening you notice that you have a connection request from the client on LinkedIn. On your LinkedIn profile it states that you are a solicitor specialising in divorce and financial remedy.

Should you accept your client's connection request?

Rules

Principles

You act:

Principle 5: in the best interests of each client.

Principle 7: with integrity.

Code of Conduct for Solicitors

Paragraph 6.3: You keep the affairs of current and former clients confidential unless disclosure is required or permitted by law or the client consents.

Potential ethical issues/professional breaches

In this scenario you should consider the nature of the client in question before deciding whether or not to accept their request. If you accept the request both you and your client's connections will be able to see that you have connected, and they will be able to view your profile and your job title. Viewers, including the media, may be able to infer from this that your client are seeking advice about a divorce, which may not be public knowledge. You may well breach Paragraph 6.3 of the Code of Conduct for Solicitors in accepting the connection request.

Ethics And Social Media

Possible approaches

You could reject your client's connection request, and this would not notify you or your client's connections that you are interacting in some way. Alternatively, you could make contact with your client before accepting or rejecting it, notifying them that you have an obligation to keep his affairs confidential, and warning him that it might be best to avoid connecting at this point in time to avoid any discovery. Your client may advise you that he does not mind this, and give his consent for the connection to go ahead, mindful of the potential issues.

Suggested reaction/steps to avoid

In this scenario it is probably preferable not to connect with the client, as you may breach Principle 7 or Paragraph 6.3 of the Code of Conduct for Solicitors by acknowledging that you have a connection with that person.

Would it make a difference if...?

Your client was to "follow you" on your professional Twitter account?

This scenario is a good example of how an ethical breach can easily occur through social media without the individual consciously intending it. The solicitor in question may not appreciate, for example, that fellow connections may be able to see their new connection, or may not appreciate that an inference could be drawn from the connection and the job title on their LinkedIn account.

But what if you were already connected with your client before they became a client? This could occur where a personal friend instructs you or your firm to act for them, or where a professional contact you have afforded a great deal of networking to finally decides to offer you the work you have been pitching for.

The situation is somewhat difficult if you have already established an online relationship with someone who later becomes a client. In these circumstances it is more acceptable to maintain that personal relationship; however you should at all times consider that the relationship you have with that person must now operate with even more awareness against the backdrop of your professional obligations.

7.22 Social media policies

Avoiding breaches of the Code of Conduct for Solicitors that could occur through social media can be a logistical nightmare for a firm because social media usage by employees is extremely difficult to control, particularly because social media is very commonly used by employees in non-core hours for their own personal purposes. Breaches can be committed by any employee of the firm, from a legal secretary, to paralegals, to partners.

The Law Society has suggested that safely and ethically establishing a social media presence requires a great deal of planning and preparation through the use of policies governing the firm's parameters for social media use and the permitted engagements between employees and their professional contacts.

Robust and regularly updated policies are generally considered to be very good ways of ensuring, or demonstrating that a firm has at least attempted to ensure, that social media mistakes do not become full blown regulatory breaches. A firm should ensure that it not only has a social media policy but that it also takes active steps to review and update it on a regular basis, particularly as we now know that social media is a fluid forum and is constantly evolving. Any policy should therefore take account of the possibilities that privacy settings may change or that a completely new social media platform may enter the market. Of course, what this policy looks like in reality will depend on the size of the particular firm. A smaller firm may have a more concise, more relaxed and broader policy, whilst a larger one may have a much more detailed and targeted set of policies that apply across various jurisdictions.

As a guide, social media policies should address the firm's purpose of utilising social media, make staff and management aware of their ethical and regulatory obligations when using it and ultimately protect the firm from inappropriate use of social media. We would suggest that the following points be considered when preparing such a policy:

(1) Provide clear guidelines as to how staff and management should communicate with the general public through social media (this should be a primary consideration);

(2) Inform everyone as to which individuals in the firm will be overseeing day to day management of social media accounts, and which member of management will oversee the firm's social media accounts and the content being posted by staff on those channels;

(3) Details as to who will oversee (and how) ensuring that the firm's use of social media is compliant with the SRA Standards and Regulations.

(4) The steps to be taken to ensure confidentiality is maintained when using the firm's social media and by individual fee earners;

(5) Decision on whether the firm requires employees to utilise disclaimers on their own personal social media accounts.

For their own sake and the firm's, employees should also read, understand and adhere to these policies in order to ensure that they are acting within the parameters of their obligations not only to their employers, but also their professional and ethical responsibilities.

The existence of a social media policy is good practice because it not only mitigates risk, but it also provides employers with a more solid ground to take action against employees who frequently flaunt policies, and who potentially put the firm at risk through negligent and unprofessional conduct on social media. This also demonstrates to the SRA that the firm in no way endorses any unethical behaviour on social media, and has taken active steps to prevent breaches of this nature.

A firm's social media policy will not always cover purely social media and may instead expand to all "electronic communications". Consider how a social media policy may assist in the below scenario:

Scenario: Derisory emails about client

Facts

You are a solicitor in a large city firm. You are working in a team of three solicitors on a divorce for a client who you perceive to be making unreasonable demands of their ex-partner, and is generally quite short and rude to all three of you.

The two solicitors who you are working with on the case have been sending derisory emails about the client to each other, copying you in.

How should you react to this situation? Would you reply?

Rules

Principles

You act:

Principle 2: in a way that upholds public trust and confidence in the solicitors' profession and in legal services provided by authorised persons.

Principle 5: with integrity.

Potential ethical issues/professional breaches

Offensive emails about both clients and other members of the profession can attract, and have attracted, the attention of the SDT. Offensive comments in general can attract regulatory sanctions. However, due to the easily shared nature of electronic communication, they tend to attract more issues. A few negative comments among colleagues about a client in the kitchen may never come to light, but it is easy for an email to be sent to the wrong person, shared to every firm email address or even picked up by managers during a review of staff email correspondence.

Derisory comments about your client can breach both Principle 5 (the obligation to act with integrity), but also Principle 2 (to uphold public trust in the profession) because if a client (or the wider public) discovers that they are being discussed disrespectfully as a result of their giving of instructions, then this will undoubtedly reduce their trust in the provision of legal services.

You should also consider that, even if the client does not have sight of these emails, merely writing or sending them technically constitutes a breach of the Code of Conduct for Solicitors or the Principles. In any event many would consider the negative discussion of a person in a difficult situation who is also paying for your services to be unethical. Derogatory comments towards clients over colleagues are likely to breach Principle 6 (to promote equality, diversity and inclusion) with greater severity and thus will attract a greater magnitude of potential sanctions.

Ethics And Social Media

Possible approaches

- Respond to your colleagues that you do not agree with their comments, and report the solicitors to your firm's compliance officer.

- Reply to your colleagues indicating that you do not wish to get involved in discussing the client in such a way and do not agree with it. You could add that they also should not respond.

Suggested reaction/steps to avoid

Ideally you should report your colleague's behaviour to your firm's nominated compliance officer, indicating that you do not agree with the behaviour and are uneasy about being copied into the conversation. Certain solicitors, particularly junior ones, may be less willing to refer their colleagues and friends to the compliance officer for a multitude of reasons.

7.23 Dealing with social media backlash

It is very easy for users of social media to come under fire (whether rightly or wrongly) from other users of social media in response to controversial, posts, events or reputations.

(1) Agree a strategy for responding to comments, which may well be simply to ignore the comments;

(2) At all times consider your ethical and regulatory obligations when responding to such comments;

(3) Consider posting one clear message on social media rather than responding to individuals who may use your response to add fuel to the fire.

Sometimes users may face a backlash for no reason at all. Where a toxic individual is using social media (that is, a user who simply wishes to cause upset and capitalise upon the anonymity of the platform), this causes both distress to the firm's employees and can damage its reputation. Often the best approach is to follow the first rule of the internet which is: '*don't feed the trolls*'. This essentially means not responding to the user (or blocking them from contacting you altogether).

7.24 Recent developments and the future

The BSB and SRA have published guidelines on their website for barristers and solicitors who use social media. Neither are extensive documents (nor are they intended to be), but they come as a result of a number of "slip ups" on social media by barristers and solicitors, including one QC whose website included a testimony that *"he could get Stevie Wonder a driver's licence"*. Whilst perhaps not quite to that extent, it is not unheard of for solicitors to exaggerate their abilities online; referring to themselves as "experts" or "the leading firm" in certain practice areas, often without any formal accreditation of this fact, and unaware that this could potentially be a misleading advertisement which would breach Paragraph 1.4 of the Code of Conduct for Solicitors.

The BSB's guidelines highlight certain maxims that solicitors will see reflected in their own Code, such as the duty not to act in a way which is likely to diminish the trust and confidence which the public places in you or the profession. The BSB guidelines helpfully remind us that comments which are constructed to be offensive or demean a person are likely to diminish this trust. Indeed, the BSB recently disbarred a barrister for insinuating through Twitter that Michael Gove was *"pro-Zionist"* and *"pro-Jew"*, amongst other anti-Semitic posts. The barrister in this instance attempted to rely on the fact that he had not directly attacked anyone by addressing them on Twitter. However, this was rejected by the BSB, who focused upon the fact that the tweets, which were in the public domain, would diminish the trust and confidence the public placed in the profession. The SDT took a similar view on this in response to a solicitor who had been receiving anti-Semitic abuse from other users on a number of popular social media site. In response to one public message in particular that wished death upon the solicitor, the solicitor replied that they 'wished death' upon that user as well. A complaint was made regarding this to the SRA who referred the matter to the SDT, who ultimately fined the solicitor £2,500 and made a costs order against them of £10,000, notwithstanding the horrendous comments made against the solicitor initially. The SRA stated that: *"We prosecute solicitors and their firms where we believe they have breached our standards. We believed that was the case here and the tribunal agreed with us."*

Interestingly, both guidelines also suggest that heated arguments and online debates are inadvisable on the basis it may contradict Principles 2 and 5 of the Code of Conduct for Solicitors respectively. Certainly, on LinkedIn there can often be heated debates between solicitors regarding areas of law and if you do enter debates of this nature on social media you should consider if any of the comments you make could fall foul of Principles 5 or 2.

Ethics And Social Media

The BSB guidelines also repeat our warnings that even unqualified members of the profession should consider the guidelines on the pretext that they are members of the profession and expected to adhere to the same standards as qualified members.

It is hoped that as social media becomes commonplace within the legal profession (indeed perhaps it already is) the risks associated with it will also be more easily identified by solicitors. The first edition of this book suggested that the profession would be aided by the publication of a formal set of guidelines by the SRA, which have of course now been published. These guidelines demonstrate that the SRA is likely to focus on the following areas of the Standards and Regulations:

Principles:

(1) **Principle 2**: That comments and posts made by solicitors do not diminish the trust the public places in them. Attention would likely be focused towards thinking through each online interaction made by a solicitor at the time of publishing and reviewing historic posts.

(2) **Principle 5:** That comments and posts made by solicitors do not compromise their integrity.

(3) **Principle 6:** That online interactions encourage equality, diversity and inclusion.

Code of Conduct for Solicitors:

(4) **Paragraph 6.3**: That you do not inadvertently breach the duty of confidentiality a solicitor owes to their clients through social media posts.

(5) **Paragraph 1.4**: That solicitors ensure the fast-paced nature of social media does not mean that any marketing advanced through social media about themselves or their firm is misleading.

(6) **Paragraph 3.2**: Due to the complexity of social media and its various privacy settings any firm utilising social media should, in theory, have controls and systems in place to ensure compliance with the Code. Equally, any guidance is likely to suggest that firms provide social media training to their employees together with appropriate social media policies.

7.25 Conclusion

It is hoped that after reading this chapter you will appreciate that there is a great deal of ethical consideration to be afforded to social media, despite the fact that usually sites like Facebook and Twitter usually do not concern themselves with ethical considerations.

The ethical solicitor in utilising social media ethically will consider the following:

(1) They consider their ethical and regulatory obligations during **every** post they make, regardless of whether that post is made on a private or personal social media network;

(2) They understand and appreciate the particular privacy settings of each and every social media network they utilise, and keep abreast of changes in site privacy settings;

(3) Appreciate that ethical and regulatory breaches can occur in subtle and completely unintended ways, and apply caution to all online interactions;

(4) Maintain separate social media networks for personal and professional interactions on social media;

(5) Appreciate and adhere to any social media policies established by their firm.

Ethics And Social Media

Social network	Regularly used by the legal profession?	Default privacy setting	Specific risks
Facebook	Yes	**Private** - only connections can see posts and user profiles.	Tends to suggest a more relaxed and personal environment due to the private nature of this social network.
Twitter	Yes	**Public** - any user can see posts and user profiles.	It can be difficult to shorten complex legal points to 140 characters. Messages can go "viral" within an extremely short space of time
LinkedIn	Yes	**Public** - any user can see posts and user profiles.	Profile is public and can be viewed by anybody accessing the site.
YouTube	No	**Public** - any user can see posts and user profiles.	Rarely utilised by solicitors, and therefore the privacy settings are under-appreciated.
Blogs	Yes	Will differ from site to site, but **usually public** - any user can access the post.	In drawing on previous matters to populate blogs client confidentiality can be easily breached.
Websites	Yes	**Usually public** - it would be unusual for a firm or individual to have a private website.	Incorrect information can constitute a regulatory breach due to the fact the website is always public facing.

197

Social network	Regularly used by the legal profession?	Default privacy setting	Specific risks
Online forums	Yes	Will differ from site to site.	Easy to breach client confidentiality by drawing on previous experiences. Anonymity on online forums encourages more risky comments.

Chapter 8: Litigation v ADR

8.1 Is litigation ethical?

In 2015, Mr Justice Turner, dismissing a first stage application for wasted costs, bluntly summarised the unforgiving environment of litigation:

> *"A cigarette packet carries the warning that smoking can kill you. Solicitors' standard terms of business should carry a warning that litigation can cost you. For litigation is an inherently risky business: there are no certain winners; and very often even the fruits of success are never recovered…*
>
> *…**The moral is caveat litigator**.*"[1]

It is commonly accepted amongst litigious solicitors that clients who expose themselves to the contentious environment of litigation seldom have cause to thank their lawyers at the conclusion of the process. In fact, many litigation solicitors consider it a fair result if both parties are unhappy with the end result. Whilst conveyancers will ultimately provide their clients with a new home, and commercial solicitors with a profitable business asset, the litigation process is adversarial and seldom offers anything but stress, financial pressure and a result that is often short of the desired resolution. The unpredictability of litigation, coupled with the unbending confines of the cost rules of the Civil Procedure Rules ("CPR"), often force a solicitor to consider difficult ethical issues when advising their client.

Indeed, in undertaking to enter the arena of litigation a client will often agree (perhaps unknowingly) to suspend normal life until the conclusion of their case. Even where the client is successful, they may not necessarily receive their desired outcome or remedy, and if they do, it often comes at a high cost. As a result of Lord Justice Jackson's review of the cost rules in 2013 it is now commonplace for litigators to advise their clients that litigation is an unpleasant cocktail of cost, delays, risk and stress. The act of conducting (or even threatening) litigation can sour even the healthiest of relationships; age old business and familial relationships alike have been irreparably shattered by litigation.

Litigation is not only expensive for individuals, but also for the courts and the public purse. As a result of this the government and the courts place heavy encouragement upon the parties utilising alternative dispute resolu-

---

[1] *Kagalovsky & Anor v Balmore Invest Ltd & Ors [2015] EWHC 1337 (QB).*

tion ("ADR") methods to resolve disputes rather than referring their matters to the courts and tribunals. ADR is considered by many practitioners to be a less stressful and more informal medium of resolving a dispute. This is particularly advocated in the arena of family law, where there is a heavy emphasis towards mediation with a view to minimising the acrimony between parties. For this reason ADR is often (but not always) a more cost effective way of settling a dispute without irreparably damaging the relationship between the parties.

For solicitors, there are strong incentives to persuade parties involved in litigation to at least consider some form of ADR, either prior to the commencement of formal litigation or during it. The courts actively encourage parties to settle their disputes without its involvement where possible. The CPR attaches a great deal of weight to ADR, encompassed largely by the overriding objective at Part 1.1, *"to deal with cases justly and at a proportionate cost"*. Going further than the overriding objective, CPR 1.4(2)(e) states that the court's duty to provide active case management under CPR 1.4 includes:

> *"...encouraging the parties to use an alternative dispute resolution procedure if the court considers that appropriate and facilitating the use of such procedure..."*

It is arguably because of this that the commonly adopted position by solicitors regarding ADR and litigation is that litigation is bad and therefore unethical and to be discouraged. The natural extension of this is that ADR is good and ethical and should be facilitated and encouraged by solicitors where possible. However, as is always the way with ethics, it is not quite as simple as this!

This chapter will consider:

(1) The purpose of litigation and ADR from an ethical standpoint;

(2) Whether you are ethically obliged to consider and encourage the use of ADR;

(3) If litigation is unethical.

8.2 The purpose of litigation

To determine if litigation is indeed unethical we need to consider its purpose. At its simplest, litigation offers a remedy and solution to bad behaviour in society. Criminal litigation addresses criminal behaviour on behalf of the crown and civil litigation addresses civil breaches of the law. For the most part, litigation takes place between citizens who are trying to protect or establish their rights. If the law has no enforcement mechanism, then it and the rule of law ceases to have any purpose. Litigation is therefore force behind the law and possesses great weight. To put this in a more poetic context:

> *"Litigation is about making order out of chaos"*[2]

Consider what would happen if remedies for civil breaches (such as breach of contract) did not exist. If individuals were free to commit a breach of contract without consequence, then this would have disastrous penalties for society. If there is no sanction to face for refusing to comply with a contractual obligation, then why should anyone bother to comply at all? Our common law system also demands litigation in order to determine and analyse the law and provide rigidity in its application from case to case. Without litigation, deciphering the law would be guesswork at best. Litigious practitioners will therefore be happy to note that for these reasons alone we cannot simply conclude that litigation is unethical.

That being said, whilst there is a need for a system of litigation, it has been argued that the current adversarial system for civil and family litigation might not be best suited for fostering an ethical society.

8.3 The adversarial system

You will be aware that the litigation system of England and Wales is an adversarial one; each party will independently submit the best evidence available to it to support its case, then the court will weigh up the quality of this evidence and make a judgment accordingly.

Some solicitors do not agree with our adversarial system approach because it can sometimes lead to injustice on the basis that the financially stronger party is in a better position to obtain legal advice and present their case. Consider where one party is able to submit its best case due to deep pockets for funding solicitors and a barrister (or two if you have particularly deep pockets) and the other party has limited means and submits a weak case; it could follow that justice has not been necessarily served if judgment goes against the weaker party. In such circumstances it is difficult to argue that

---

[2] *Fundamental Principles of Civil Procedure: Order out of Chaos in Civil Litigation in a Globalising World (Neil Andrews, Springer, 2012).*

justice has been properly and ethically delivered.

These arguments sit uneasily with an individual's freedom of autonomy in litigation; that is to say that each party has the freedom to choose how to present their case, and what defence they wish to advance[3]. Some practitioners are unsettled by civil jurisdictions in which evidence is collected and adjudicated by the presiding judge because it removes the autonomy of the parties' when deciding how best to plead their case.

It is important to consider these underlying issues when considering your ethical obligations to your clients as, under the adversarial system, success very much turns on the performance on the day. Systems which reject the adversarial system can be said to have the advantage that the scales of justice are not merely tipped in the favour of the party who best pleads their case. In our system, the ability to best plead a case is often incumbent upon an individual's ability to obtain legal assistance and have that assistance prepare their case. Arguably, where access to legal advice due to financial constraints is suppressed, an adversarial system does not always offer the best ethical or justice focused outcomes. This is more dangerous than ever given the current state of legal aid and the severe underfunding of the court system.

8.4 The ethics of the cost rules of the CPR

Litigation is dominated by the harsh cost rules of the CPR. With or without the involvement of solicitors, litigation is inherently expensive. As a result of this a solicitor's initial advice to a client may often be to accept a lower sum to avoid the headache of litigation, or simply abandon the claim entirely. Many solicitors accept the fact that due to the recoverability of legal costs being set at between 60% and 75% it is often simply uneconomical to issue proceedings for any amount below £20,000. This is before one assumes that the other party will be in a position to pay any amount that is ordered. Once again, the system places difficult ethical burdens on the solicitor.

As we suggested above, the progression of a litigious matter to trial is considered by most to be a failure in most cases, except those optimistic clients who simply want *"their day in court"*. The primary reason (outside of the small claims track) is because of the financial cost involved with doing so. The default costs rule means that the losing party at trial will be ordered to pay the successful party's costs. The cost for the state in court and judicial time is also particularly substantial. It is therefore not surprising that on

---

[3] *The Downside of Procedural Reform (D Barnhizer, Solicitor's Journal, 29 March 2002, 1142).*

average around 60% to 80% of all issued proceedings are likely to settle before reaching trial.

The ethical dilemmas contained within the CPR mostly concern whether the fear of costs consequences, and the incentives to deter the use of the courts, should ever pressure a person with a valid claim into settling for less than they are entitled to, or even to abandon their claim altogether. Do you have an obligation to advise your client solely on the commercial reality of bringing their claim, or should the principles of justice prevail?

That is not to say any solicitor has a great amount of choice in this respect. Solicitors have little choice but to comply with the CPR and the ethical issues that arise from these rules.

8.5 Ethical considerations of the CPR[4]

Consider the following ethical observations of the CPR:

(1) The CPR demand cooperation between the parties engaged in the dispute. This in itself is contrary to the adversarial approach of our litigious system;

(2) The CPR dictate that the judge actively takes part in ensuring compliance with court timetables and the setting down of directions, which conflicts with an individual's right of autonomy;

(3) The CPR actively encourage settlement in a rigid way such that it can be said that they restrict access to justice and a court hearing[5];

(4) Is it ethical to limit access to justice based on a party's financial strength?

Against these points, consider the following scenario:

---

[4] *The Downside of Procedural Reform (T Aldridge, Solicitors Journal, 29 March 2002, 1142).*

[5] *Group Litigation, Class Actions and Collective Redress: An Anniversary Reappraisal of Lord Woolf's Three Objectives, (S McGibbons) in Civil Procedure, Ten Years On (D Dwyer, Oxford University Press, 2009).*

Scenario: Part 36 offer

Facts

You act for a medium sized company, ABC Limited, who are seeking damages for breach of contract from XYZ Limited for £17,500. The claim has been issued and both parties have filed their statements of case but the court has not yet listed the matter for a Case Management Conference. Having sought counsel's advice both you and the client are aware that the prospects of success in this matter are above 75% and your client is very likely to succeed at trial.

XYZ's solicitors send you a Part 36 offer to settle for £10,000, alleging that the offer is advanced purely for commercial reasons and claim that they believe (contrary to your advice) that their client has a strong defence to your client's claim. Your costs estimate to your client is that costs to trial are likely to be £48,000. On the basis that your client wins at trial and recovers 90% of its costs, you have estimated that your client's best position (winning at trial and recovering 90% of its costs) is that its net position will be that it loses £4,800, recovering the £17,500.

From a commercial perspective, would you advise your client to accept XYZ's Part 36 offer?

From an ethical perspective, would you advise your client to accept XYZ's Part 36 offer?

Rules

The SRA principles likely to apply to this situation are that you act:

Principle 1: in a way that upholds the constitutional principle of the rule of law, and the proper administration of justice.

Principle 2: in a way that upholds public trust and confidence in the solicitors' profession and in legal services provided by authorised persons.

Principle 7: in the best interests of each client.

Potential ethical issues/professional breaches

This is a common conflict between the commercial reality of a matter and an ethical approach. In this scenario the client is likely to win at trial but stands to lose money in exercising their legal rights. There is a conflict between acting in the best interests of the client (securing the best monetary outcome) and upholding the rule of law (demonstrating that the breach by the other party can be remedied fully). On one hand it appears that the client has an ethical right to pursue and obtain a judgment in their favour and the recovery of the full amount owed to them (Principle 1). They stand to lose money pursuing this, and therefore it may not be in the client's best interests (Principle 7).

Possible approaches

- Advise the client that in the circumstances it may be best to accept the Part 36 offer on the basis that the legal costs may soon outweigh the amounts being pursued. Additionally, advise the client that if the defendant is unable to pay the amount owed plus costs at trial they stand to lose the entirety of their fees.

- Advise the client that they have a good claim and should push to recover the full amount, with £10,000 being far below the amount they are fully entitled to.

- Consider offering a counter offer in the knowledge that your opponent will likely have made similar calculations as to your client's costs position.

Suggested reaction/steps to avoid

In this situation you best serve your client by providing them with all of the information to allow them to make an informed decision on the matter. Stressing that your client should accept the £10,000 offer purely because of costs implications might not be ethical or acting in their best interests.

Additionally, you should consider whether your client wishes to have the matter subjected to judicial scrutiny, and that upon obtaining judgment they could have other avenues of remedy available to them, such as the ability to wind up the defendant company, which may well be a desirable outcome for your client.

Without wanting to render this chapter pointless, there is ultimately little an individual solicitor can do regarding the ethical status of the CPR, and in particular the implications of the costs rules. Solicitors simply have an obligation under those rules to advise their clients regarding ADR. However, it is important that you recognise that there is an underlying concern about the ethical standard of the costs rules because of the pressure they put on parties to settle their disputes without judicial intervention. Arguably a less favourable settlement achieved purely as a result of the fear of costs sanctions is not justice being performed.

The ethics of the CPR's costs rules is particularly relevant when we consider the point raised above that, however undesirable, the individual wealth of a claimant or defendant plays a large part in their prospects of success. Wealth allows individuals to present their cases on a stronger footing and provides access to tactical offers being made. Wealthy litigants can drag cases out, employ multiple experts in their field to offer their opinion or simply bury opponents under reams of legal paperwork. Particularly where there is no court timetable in place the ADR process is open to abuse; this is done with a view to the wealthy litigant placing pressure upon the less affluent opponent.

8.6   The ethics of ADR?

With litigation having been viewed under the ethical microscope it is only fair that we now analyse whether ADR is in fact the good and ethical poster child it is commonly promoted to be. ADR is an inescapable variable in modern day litigation but is (in theory at least) an optional process. Every solicitor who acts in a litigious capacity will have to advise their client of the requirement to consider ADR as an alternative to traditional litigation. It is, however, worth considering that ADR is still, relatively speaking, in its infancy in this jurisdiction.

In some circumstances the court can award costs against a party who unreasonably refuses to consider ADR. The full reality of this is realised when you consider that this penalty can be ordered even where the party has been successful at trial[6]. We have also seen that the court has a duty under CPR 1.4(2)(e) to encourage the use of ADR, and in general solicitors are urged to do the same. This is not necessarily a negative concept; solicitors will of course be aware of the numerous advantages that certain types of ADR offer over the courts. When ADR is utilised correctly it can provide a cheaper and more expedited conclusion to litigious matters, and can usually achieve

---

[6]   *Dunnett v Railtrack [2002] EWCA Civ 302.*

these in a private environment away from the publicity of the courts.

In family litigation, the attendance of the applicant at a Mediation Information & Assessment Meeting (MIAM) has been compulsory since 2013, when issuing certain types of application. However, it is not unknown for solicitors who do not wish to lose their clients to the ADR processes to simply not mention the possibility that there is an alternative to court. This is dubious unethical behaviour which does nothing to help the client or the public perception of the profession. The rules are clear that there can be costs consequences if a party fails to attend the initial mediation appointment without a valid exception being claimed. It is worth adding that the family courts have separate cost rules under the Family Procedure Rules, which are quite different than those in civil litigation. The family courts rarely make an order that one party pays another's costs where both litigants have acted reasonably. Even when a party has acted "unreasonably", it is still rare for a cost order to be made. This means that the pressure to seriously consider ADR is almost non-existent.

Staying with the family courts briefly, statistics released from the Ministry of Justice show that the number of MIAMs fell by 16% in 2015 compared to 2014. In fact, after the introduction of the mandatory requirement for the applicant to attend that meeting, there was a sharp drop in these meetings taking place. Despite the introduction of legislation requiring an applicant to attend a MIAM, the numbers of applicants attending is lower than it was in 2013 when legal aid was withdrawn for most family work. If there is little access to justice, then parties are not aware of the existence of ADR options and proceed straight to court. The system for parties to attend a MIAM is poorly structured and results in fewer than 10% of all issued private law children applications being preceded by attendance at the meeting. Without the threat of consequences those with and without solicitors can simply do as they please. The ethical issue for family solicitors who never bring this to the attention of the client is very clear; it is difficult to suggest you are acting in the best interests of your client if you deny them the right to choose a non-court route to resolve their issues.

There are rather complex ethical considerations that must be afforded to ADR options before deciding whether it is indeed suitable for your client's case. Because the litigation environment promotes ADR in such a positive light and provides costs sanctions, the ethical considerations can be overlooked by solicitors. There has been a reported case dealt with by the SDT where the solicitor was so sure that a matter would settle that the solicitor did not issue proceedings despite instructions to do so. In that case, the solicitor was so convinced that the client would not benefit from litigating the case that they did not tell the client that he would not or did not issue proceedings.

The matters that the solicitor should bear in mind from an ethical standpoint include:

(1) Is there a genuine commitment from the parties and the solicitors to use ADR?

(2) Is the referral to ADR an attempt to delay proceedings to enable a party to hide evidence, assets or create delay?

(3) Is the client capable of negotiating a good settlement at mediation without legal representation on the day?

(4) What type of ADR is the best for this client and this dispute?

Scenario: Lying to your client

Facts

You are a newly qualified solicitor employed in the dispute resolution department of a medium sized regional firm. You are acting for a client whose managing director is notoriously quick to litigate and he has instructed you to write a letter before action to the potential defendant on a fairly straightforward debt matter for £123,000. When you receive the reply to your letter before action by email it appears that the defendant's purported defence is extremely weak.

The potential defendant's solicitor calls you shortly after sending an email on a without prejudice basis to explain that their client is in the process of advancing what you consider to be a very sensible offer. When you explain this to your client you are instructed to ignore the prospect of settlement and issue proceedings immediately.

You have always placed great importance on settling cases where possible, always stating that the cost of litigation is rarely worth it. You also think the case will settle shortly and don't want the client to have to incur unnecessary court and solicitor's fees. You tell the client that you have issued proceedings, knowing you will receive an offer your client will accept shortly.

What ethical issues, if any, arise in this situation? What should you do in this situation?

Rules

The SRA principles likely to apply to this situation are that you act:

Principle 1: in a way that upholds the constitutional principle of the rule of law, and the proper administration of justice.

Principle 2: in a way that upholds public trust and confidence in the solicitors' profession and in legal services provided by authorised persons.

Principle 5: with integrity.

Principle 7: in the best interests of each client.

Potential ethical issues/professional breaches

The issues within this scenario are immediately obvious. The junior solicitor has lied to the client, albeit with the intention of acting in the client's best interests (in that they believe the case will settle shortly). This is both unethical and a regulatory breach as it involves lying to the client and deceiving them as to the actual state of litigation. The fact that it is purported to be in the client's and the court's best interests is essentially irrelevant in this scenario.

Possible approaches

Realistically there is only one option in this matter. The solicitor should not have misled their client and must self-report to the firm's compliance officer. Ultimately the firm should advise the client of the situation.

Suggested reaction/steps to avoid

Whilst this scenario may seem extreme there are cases where experienced solicitors have been struck off for doing exactly this. To avoid this situation arising the fee earner should not submit to the pressures of ADR and costs, fully explaining to the client the need to consider ADR and never to deceive the client as to the status of a matter.

How To Be An Ethical Solicitor

The ethics of this selection process are often overlooked by many solicitors who are quick to advise their clients simply to adopt their *"go to"* choice of ADR. For example, some lawyers favour mediation and negotiation because it generally incorporates a great deal of solicitor time which captures more work for them and therefore more fees. Other solicitors are more comfortable utilising tried and tested ADR processes rather than engaging with more novel ones. A solicitor is unlikely to suggest an ADR process that they are trained to engage in as this would lose them a client - is this ethical?

In selecting the correct and ethical route of ADR for your client you will need to have recourse to:

(1) Whether a third party is required to resolve the dispute, and if necessary:

    (a) what the role of that third party will be; and

    (b) whether the effect of the third party's decision will be binding or non-binding.

(2) The role of the solicitors during the ADR process; and

(3) The role of the law.

Fig 29: Considerations for selecting the appropriate method of ADR for your client

It is crucial that an ethical solicitor selecting the right form of ADR considers all three of these variables as the interaction between them will differ substantially depending upon the ADR mechanism in question. We will briefly consider the various forms of ADR which are used in England and Wales, and discuss the potential ethical issues associated with them, focusing in more detail upon the ethical considerations of negotiation, arbitration and mediation.

The primary ethical obligation to arise in the use of ADR is simply that the legal system exists for a reason. We saw in Chapter 1 that the enforcement mechanisms of the justice system operate to ensure that where people have their rights breached they are able to utilise enforcement mechanisms. It is therefore odd that the rise of ADR operates to restrict an individual's autonomy to utilise this system without being penalised financially. Equally, it seems contrary to our adversarial system that a person is essentially forced by the costs rules to sit down and negotiate with a party they believe has wronged them. It is even more ethically reprehensible to suggest that the wronged individual has a duty to consider accepting less than they are actually entitled to, and deny them their day in court. This ultimately means that there is a risk that the severe pressure for parties to consider and utilise ADR is in part unethical because it undermines the importance of the legal system, and a person's individual right to apply to the court for remedy where they have been wronged.

There is also an issue with the ADR mechanisms globally lacking regulation. The majority of individuals who are involved in facilitating agreements between disputing parties are unregulated, and with the exception of arbitration, ADR mechanisms generally have no regulatory framework for its users to fall back upon if their facilitators act unethically or negligently. Unethical settlements may be achieved purely because the third parties fail to understand the underlying legal issues, or are focused on achieving settlement at any cost, regardless of the legal position of the parties. In these circumstances, third parties could facilitate settlements that might work in theory for the parties, but do not actually work practically or legally. Additionally, the settlement might not take account of third parties in the same way in which a court might; for example, any children the parties may have between them or other debtors of one party.

Consider also that ADR is a private resolution process, hidden from public and judicial scrutiny. Some may think that as a result ADR has fewer ethical guidelines, and as such fewer incentives for parties to behave in an ethical way. You should be aware that, whilst an unattractive thought, there will be some solicitors who seek to utilise this hidden variable of mediation

How To Be An Ethical Solicitor

deliberately in order to obtain settlements that are more beneficial for their clients, or to avoid the scrutiny of less ethical tactics in open court. In the alternative, others may believe that because ADR is cost efficient and a low impact alternative to court, it is actually a more ethical methodology. The lack of regulation may be seen to be an adherence to a higher ethical code and this may be attractive to parties and solicitors alike.

To decide whether your ADR is suitable for your client you will need to consider all variables mentioned in this chapter, as well as whether your client has a suitable character to engage in the ADR process you are suggesting.

8.7   ADR processes with no third party

The most basic forms of ADR are those where no third party is involved other than the parties (and often, their lawyers). These processes will usually involve the parties discussing potential avenues of settlement with one another directly, with or without the assistance of solicitors. Because they do not involve the expense of third parties or the hiring of venues to conduct the ADR process, they tend to be significantly cheaper than their facilitative ADR counterparts.

It is extremely tempting to assume that simply because the parties are engaging directly with one another you have no ethical considerations to make; however as we will see, this is far from the truth and can in certain circumstances be heightened purely because of the lack of a regulatory framework.

Ethical considerations

Is any potential delay to allow these negotiations going to jeopardise the preservation of evidence, assets or litigation advantage?

Is this process going to assist the parties to reach a settlement?

The solicitor should not be putting their fee target over and above the client's best interests in reaching a fair settlement early on.

8.8   Negotiation

Negotiation is arguably the most flexible and informal mechanism of ADR, depending on its approach. Many solicitors are comfortable with this type of ADR process; written and oral negotiations are fairly typical processes which can necessitate a lot of fee earner time.

Negotiation of course does not necessarily need the involvement of solicitors. Parties involved in negotiation essentially attempt to reach an agreement between themselves. If solicitors are not instructed, then notwithstanding the personal overheads of the parties, the costs are virtually non-existent. Negotiation is normally conducted on a without prejudice basis in private, ensuring that the parties' positions are protected in the event that the discussions do not result in an agreed settlement.

Negotiation requires the consent of both parties to the dispute. It is actively encouraged by the courts and demanded in certain pre-action protocols (for example, Part 9 of the Pre-action Protocol for Construction and Engineering Disputes requires the parties to conduct a round table meeting for the purpose of narrowing the position).

The fact that negotiation offers such flexibility and a lack of official rules does of course require solicitors to be aware of certain ethical situations.

Ethical considerations

The primary purpose of a negotiation is finding your opponent's minimum position, i.e. the lowest amount that they are prepared to accept in order to bring the matter to a conclusion. This must be combined with concealing the weaknesses in your client's case. It has been suggested therefore that the test of whether a solicitor is a good negotiator is gauged on their ability to lie!

Whilst white lies permeate the daily interactions in society[7] many solicitors are uncomfortable with the idea that a willingness to lie is central to effective negotiation[8]. The accepted ethical workaround for this is to distinguish between two different types of lies in negotiation;

- **Bad lies**. Making a statement to an opponent about evidence that you know to be untrue is clearly unethical. This will attract the attention of the SRA and if found out a solicitor will be struck off for dishonesty offences.

- **White lies**. Stating that your client is *"unwilling to settle for less than*

---

[7] *Doing The Right Thing: An Empirical Study of Attorney Negotiation Ethics* (A Hinshaw & J Alberts (2011) 16 Harvard Negotiation Law Review 95).

[8] G. Wetlaufer -'The ethics of lying in negotiation' (1990) 76 Iowa Law Review 1219, 1221.

£14,000" when they perhaps may be willing to settle for £13,000 is more likely to be considered tactical whilst technically still a lie.

Many solicitors will negotiate on the basis that *"my client has instructed me to offer £14,000"*; this makes no comment about the willingness of the client to offer more or the merits of the case. A solicitor who puts forward this offer has done nothing wrong on the fact of the facts. The solicitor may however be acting in an amoral position; being ethically neutral is in itself an ethical choice.

Some solicitors form the view that white lies are harmless in negotiation and serve to oil the gears, saving court time and reducing the costs of litigation in the process.

A common ethical consideration in negotiation is whether or not to remain silent on an issue, for example, actively choosing to not bring an omission by your opponent to their attention. Is this ethically neutral? Generally speaking you do not owe your opponent any obligation; litigation is not a form of sport and litigators are not required to be friendly to one another.

Consider the following two mantras when considering the ethical considerations of remaining silent:

- You are under no general obligation to be open with an opposing solicitor[9].

- Silence does not constitute lying[10].

Paragraph 1.2 of the Code of Conduct for Solicitors states that you should not take unfair advantage of your opponent. You will of course have to consider this against your obligation not to place yourself in contempt of court, and you must comply with court orders which place obligations on you (Paragraph 2.5).

Finally, practitioners should beware of the "shadow of the law" that their involvement casts upon a negotiation. Generally speaking, two parties who are negotiating directly are completely at liberty to abandon those negotiations when they please, and typically conduct their negotiation purely on what they think is fair as opposed to any underlying legal reasoning.

---

[9] *Thompson v Arnold [2007] EWHC 1875 (QB).*
[10] *Thames Trains v Adams [2006] EWHC 3291.*

When solicitors become engaged in the process, however, negotiation will of course be conducted upon the basis of legal principles as opposed to the parties just agreeing "*what they think is fair*". Solicitors therefore drastically alter the atmosphere of the negotiation, producing a potentially different outcome. It may therefore be ethical and appropriate for you to suggest that your client negotiates without your formal assistance in the early stages of a dispute, particularly where their claim is more grounded in the fairness of the situation rather than being legally sound.

Scenario: Omission on consent order

Facts

You are a solicitor employed in the dispute resolution department of a medium sized regional firm.

You are in court for the trial of a long-standing matter and are negotiating the dispute with the solicitor acting on behalf of the defendant before going into court.

After much negotiation your clients have reached a compromise and your opponent begins to draw up the consent order for the court. When your opponent hands you the consent order to approve you notice that a key definition of one of the consent order provisions has been omitted, which would make it very difficult for your client's opponent to enforce the terms of the order if your client was to default on the agreement.

Do you point out your opponent's omission, or stay silent?

Rules

The SRA principles likely to apply to this situation are that you act:

Principle 1: in a way that upholds the constitutional principle of the rule of law, and the proper administration of justice.

Principle 2: in a way that upholds public trust and confidence in the solicitors' profession and in legal services provided by authorised persons.

Principle 5: with integrity.

Principle 7: in the best interests of each client.

Code of Conduct for Solicitors

Paragraph 1.2: You do not abuse your position by taking unfair advantage of clients or others.

Paragraph 1.4: You do not mislead or attempt to mislead your clients, the court or others, either by your own acts or omissions or allowing or being complicit in the acts or omissions of others (including your client).

Paragraph 2.6: You do not waste the court's time.

Paragraph 2.7: You draw the court's attention to relevant cases and statutory provisions, or procedural irregularities of which you are aware, and which are likely to have a material effect on the outcome of the proceedings.

Paragraph 3.2: You ensure that the service you provide to clients is competent and delivered in a timely manner.

Potential ethical/regulatory breaches

The issue in this scenario is whether it is incumbent upon you to point out errors by an opposing solicitor to the detriment of your client. You will need to balance your obligation to act in your client's best interests and provide a proper service against not taking unfair advantage of a third party. Additionally, you will need to consider that this silence could be considered a controversial tactic.

Possible approaches

- Point out your opponent's error, with the reasoning being that being faced with a further complex litigation is not in the best interests of your client.

- Remain silent as you have no obligation to disclose this to your opponent and it benefits your client.

Suggested reaction/steps to avoid

This is a good example of litigious tactics that may be regulatory compliant (silence is not lying and you have no obligation to your opponent) but are ethically controversial. The reaction therefore will depend on the solicitor, and client, in question.

Would it make a difference if?

You had made the omission on the consent order to the detriment of your opponent?

8.9 Mediation

Mediation is a popular mechanism of ADR endorsed by both solicitors and the courts. In a mediation process the parties meet, with the assistance of a third party (*"the mediator(s)"*) who will identify and narrow the issues between the parties with a view to achieving settlement.

Mediation is conducted on a without prejudice basis and in private. Any settlements that take place within mediation are not binding upon the parties until the parties sign a settlement agreement or file the appropriate consent order with the court (if the parties are in court proceedings).

There are many different types of mediation used in England and Wales. The family mediation model is very different to that of the commercial mediation. Thus the role of the mediator is tailored to suit the dispute in question. The most common form of mediation in England and Wales is facilitative mediation where the mediator will actively play a role in attempting to encourage settlement between the parties by narrowing their positions. The mediator can only identify and suggest points of compromise between the parties and has no power to comment upon the merits of either party's case or make a binding agreement upon their dispute.

Ethical considerations

Mediation's popularity has risen so drastically that it has been suggested that the natural format of concluding litigation will be a hybrid between litigation and mediation, known as "liti-mediation". The parties begin their dispute with traditional litigation, but ultimately settle the matter by way of a mediation conducted after proceedings are issued[11].

Despite this widespread popularity and support, the vastly diverse body of mediators who conduct this form of ADR remains largely unregulated. Many mediators are not required to even submit to some form of accreditation although this is starting to change. As regulation and ethics are so

---

[11] J Lande - 'How will lawyering and mediation practices transform each other?' (1997) 24 Florida Law Review 839.

closely linked, it is worth noting this issue.

In theory anybody can hold themselves out to be a mediator regardless of their legal knowledge; this is regarded by some to be a benefit as the settlement of a dispute at mediation is not solely dependent on legal determination. As a result of this there is a great deal of debate amongst practitioners about whether all mediators have the requisite legal knowledge to consider more complex areas of law, and therefore consider all the potential ramifications of any settlement they are attempting to facilitate.

Ethically, mediation also falls foul of the same issues that have been made against our litigation system. A party who is unable to plead a strong case against a party who pleads a strong one may be overwhelmed with the pressure to settle. This would easily be addressed by the mediator when assessing the parties' suitability to attend mediation at the outset. In many forms of commercial mediation the parties are assisted by the lawyers throughout and any power imbalances are redressed that way.

Scenario: Terms of a consent order

Facts

You are a family solicitor employed in a small high street firm. You act for the petitioning wife in the divorce from her husband. The parties have two young children and the husband is acting in person.

The marriage ended mutually and the couple have parted on fairly good terms, disagreeing only on a few points, in particular about the division of pension funds. You select a mediator who you know is very good at settling matters and has a very good understanding of pension assets. However, that mediator has very little understanding of children law which you know due to your past dealings with them.

You suggest that your client and her estranged husband attend a mediation with this mediator as you fully expect that they will reach settlement shortly and see no reason why they should engage with the court process. As expected the parties reach settlement after only one session of mediation and your client asks you to draft the consent order for submission to the court. Whilst drafting the consent order it occurs to you that your client may not be paying enough child maintenance to her husband; the parties have agreed that he will have primary residence of the children. As they have already settled on this matter you merely draft the consent order as instructed and submit it to the court.

Have you acted ethically in this situation?

Rules

The SRA principles likely to apply to this situation are that you act:

Principle 1: in a way that upholds the constitutional principle of the rule of law, and the proper administration of justice.

Principle 2: in a way that upholds public trust and confidence in the solicitors' profession and in legal services provided by authorised persons.

Principle 5: with integrity.

Principle 7: in the best interests of each client.

Code of Conduct for Solicitors

Paragraph 1.2: You do not abuse your position by taking unfair advantage of clients or others.

Paragraph 1.4: You do not mislead or attempt to mislead your clients, the court or others, either by your own acts or omissions or allowing or being complicit in the acts or omissions of others (including your client).

Paragraph 3.4: You consider and take account of your client's attributes, needs and circumstances.

Potential ethical/regulatory breaches

The issue in this scenario is twofold; whether the solicitor has acted in the client's best interests by not selecting a mediator that gives proper consideration to their client's children, and whether they have taken advantage of the unrepresented party by submitting the consent order fully aware that the opponent may be entitled to more. This is unlikely to mirror the position had the matter proceeded to trial in the courts.

Also, the solicitor has to act with integrity and by being seen to act with integrity fulfils their obligation under Principle 5. Whilst mediation may take place in private, by acting with integrity the solicitor promotes the service of mediation by showing it can be used to resolve potentially difficult issues for the mutual benefit of all parties.

Possible approaches

- Inform your client of your assessment of child maintenance, identifying that you believe she should be making higher payments.
- Inform the court of your actions and ask it to make directions accordingly.
- Take the view that as the court must sanction the consent order, it is for the presiding judge to make a decision on this point.

Suggested reaction/steps to avoid

Avoiding situations like this in mediation matters largely involve considering the nature of the parties and the preferred mediator. The solicitor in this matter has potentially put excessive focus on settlement and one particular part of the dispute in selecting a mediator, without reference to a mediator who would consider the needs of the children in greater detail.

A more common issue in family mediation is the solicitor selecting the mediator on the basis that they will not be able to help the parties reach a settlement, thereby protecting the client who will be forced to litigate.

Ultimately the main reason clients may wish to avoid mediation is simply because they may arrive at a settlement which is less than they are entitled to in court. There is evidence that suggests claimants receive less compensation through mediation when compared to litigation[12].

8.10 Arbitration

Arbitration is a relatively new method of ADR regulated by the Arbitration Act 1996 and it shares many similarities with the formal court-based litigation process. Arbitration has a semblance to formal litigation and it is particularly popular with commercial litigators who have been using this route for many years. It is gaining a significant amount of traction in family law as a method of resolving financial disputes on divorce and relationship breakdown. However, it is a *"novel"* approach in the family law arena and solicitors are hesitant to use an ADR method that they know little about. This impacts on the client's choice as the solicitor may not be wholly forthright about the availability of the process to the client.

In a similar form to mediation the process is extremely flexible, with the parties being able to conduct the hearings over Skype or by way of telephone conference, outside of core hours. If the parties agree they can both submit written submissions only and have the matter decided without the need for a hearing at all. Not only is this method more convenient but it is also normally completely private as the parties do not need to attend a public hearing centre to resolve their dispute and can attend their solicitor's office to conduct the hearings if necessary. For this reason arbitration has found much attraction between notorious members of society who would rather keep their legal disputes out of the public eye!

Arbitration is a voluntary process, but is unique in that parties can be forced to engage in the process where a clause in a contract dictates that the parties must resolve any disputes that arise under the contract by way of arbitration.

The key regulatory difference to other forms of ADR is that arbitration is regulated by the Chartered Institute of Arbitrators (CIArb).

Ethical considerations

Arbitration shares many of its core ethical dilemmas with litigation, which is unsurprising given that there are so many similarities. The major ethical concern for solicitors at the outset of an arbitration should be selecting an appropriate third party to conduct the arbitration.

---

[12] *Central London County Court Mediation Scheme (H Genn, Department for Constitutional Affairs, 1998).*

This is particularly so considering that the role of the arbitrator will be tantamount to that of a judicial position; that position should be protected and an objective arbitrator should be sought. In commercial disputes this isn't such an issue as there will usually be a panel of three arbitrators, thus any bias in appointing one will be balanced out by the other two. However, in family arbitration, there is only one arbitrator and bias can exist in the appointment process.

Scenario: Arbitration

Facts

You are a family solicitor in a medium sized practice acting for the applicant husband in a divorce. Both parties are successful business owners and both want to have the matter dealt with as quickly and privately as possible. However, there are points they disagree upon such as the complex division of the business assets.

Your opponent is a family law arbitrator and has suggested that your clients engage in arbitration to settle the matter. You have no in-depth knowledge of arbitration in a family law context and understand that it is relatively novel and untested. Your client asks you for advice on this proposal. You are hesitant to suggest arbitration due to your unfamiliarity and its general novelty.

How should you advise your client?

Rules

The SRA principles likely to apply to this situation are that you act:

Principle 2: in a way that upholds public trust and confidence in the solicitors' profession and in legal services provided by authorised persons.

Principle 7: in the best interests of each client.

Code of Conduct for Solicitors

Paragraph 3.2: You ensure that the service you provide to clients is competent and delivered in a timely manner.

You consider and take account of your client's attributes, needs and circumstances.

Potential ethical issues/professional breaches

You should be cautious about rejecting *any* method of ADR simply on the basis that you do not fully understand it, or that it is a novel concept. If you fail to sufficiently consider all of your client's needs in selecting an appropriate medium of ADR then it is difficult to suggest that you are acting in the client's best interests. Equally if you do not fully understand new and evolving methods of ADR and how to apply them to your client's situation then you are unlikely to be providing a proper standard of service to your client.

Possible approaches

- Explain to your client that arbitration is a new method of ADR in family law proceedings, and as a result you are unable to recommend it to him without carrying out further research or training into arbitration.

- Advise your client that arbitration is new, and if he was to select it you may need to pass the client to someone more experienced in the practice.

Suggested reaction/steps to avoid

Where you are unable to determine the suitability of an ADR process due to your inexperience, it is crucial that you do not dismiss a method of ADR purely for this reason. The most appropriate response is to research further into arbitration to determine fully whether it is an appropriate ADR mechanism for your client. To avoid coming across this issue, if ADR is something you encounter regularly in your professional obligation, then consider ensuring that you look at all areas of ADR when undergoing your annual professional development.

Arguably, a family solicitor who knows nothing about family arbitration could not declare ongoing competency in the area of family law.

8.11 Collaborative law

Collaborative law is another type of ADR typically found within family law disputes. Each party will instruct a trained collaborative solicitor who agrees to commit their efforts to facilitating an agreement between the parties using the collaborative process. Collaborative law works through a series of without prejudice meetings held between the parties and their solicitors. At the start of the process the parties and their solicitors sign an agreement that says if the solicitors are unable to facilitate a settlement then they must cease acting for their clients. The collaborative solicitors are not permitted to litigate for clients who were committed to the collaborative process. The thought behind this is that the solicitors will focus all their efforts on settlement, rather than half-heartedly approaching it in the hope that a lucrative piece of litigation will arise instead.

The parties organise meetings and negotiate. They are able to take legal advice during the negotiations. The main benefit of collaborative law as a means of ADR is that it aims to preserve the relationship between the parties in a way which traditional litigation cannot due to its adversarial nature. This is of particular importance in family law matters where the parties may be required to maintain contact after settlement, for example if they have children together.

Ethical considerations

Collaborative law is a mechanism which attracts particular ethical consideration from a solicitor as it is suitable in only certain situations. Consider whether it would be inappropriate to look at collaborative law between parties who have been involved in domestic violence, where one party has not accepted that their relationship is over and therefore will find it difficult to independently focus upon settlement or there is distrust in the situation. Collaborative law, perhaps more than any other element of ADR, requires an in-depth understanding of the interaction between your client and their partner; if there is an imbalance of power between the parties there is a risk your client may well be overpowered by them. Generally, collaborative law is suited towards parties with lower levels of conflict who can focus on the best outcome for the family unit objectively with a view to obtaining a solution as opposed to a rights-based approach.

Although collaborative law was introduced as an ADR process more than a decade ago, it has not enjoyed widespread uptake by clients. Many family solicitors trained in the process but found that clients were not using it. In order to meet the perceived issues for clients, some practitioners developed a "Collaborative Lite" process. In this process the parties use the collaborative model to attempt to resolve the dispute but they don't sign the agreement at the outset. This means that if the process breaks down the parties can use the same solicitors to litigate the matter. This is deemed by purist practitioners to be unethical. The central agreement between the solicitors to the clients is that they won't litigate if the process breaks down. Those practitioners who use the process argue that they are meeting a demand and others feel that this is breaching the core tenet of the process. How can the clients trust that the solicitors are committed to a negotiated outcome if they won't sign the paperwork?

8.12 Executive tribunal

An executive tribunal is an ADR processes more commonly employed to informally resolve a dispute between two commercial bodies. A representative of each party, or their solicitor, will make representations regarding the party's case or defence to a panel comprised of the senior executives of the disputing parties. The panel will be chaired by an independent chairperson appointed by the parties, who assumes the role of the mediator. You should therefore consider the ethical considerations raised in this chapter regarding mediation in the selection of this chairperson.

After hearing the representations from the parties the panel of executives will retire to discuss the representations, with the independent chairperson exercising their role as a mediator in order to facilitate settlement between the parties. Again, here the role of the mediator is typically purely facilitative; however, again, the independent chairperson can also evaluate each party's case. In an executive tribunal the role of the mediator can sometimes go further, with the parties agreeing to the mediator becoming an arbitrator and making a binding agreement between the parties if they are unable to reach an agreement.

8.13 Conciliation

Conciliation is a variation of mediation in which a third party attempts to facilitate an agreement between the parties, with the difference being that the third party will actively pursue and encourage the parties to reach a settlement.

This is a commonly used (and mandatory) ADR process in employment disputes. You may be familiar with the conciliation process offered by ACAS in which parties must initially refer their matters to ACAS prior to issuing proceedings in the Employment Tribunal. Whilst ACAS conciliation is mandatory, in a similar way to the ethical position of the Civil Procedure Rules, you should consider whether it is appropriate for wronged employees to be forced to attempt to compromise with employers who may have caused them immense emotional pressures (the reverse situation would of course also be a consideration). This is particularly the case where the third party encouraged to promote settlement may not have received any form of regulated training on the area of law they are conciliating upon.

8.14 Early Neutral Evaluation

Early Neutral Evaluation ("ENE") is another variation of mediation in which the selected independent third party would provide the parties with a non-binding opinion on each party's merits after considering each party's evidence and the law in question. The parties can then decide, fully aware of their positions, to either agree to settle on the outcome of the ENE entirely, or use it as a starting point for negotiation.

In the same way as a mediation in which an assessment of each party's claim is made by the mediator, you should ensure that the party providing the ENE is sufficiently qualified to make an accurate assessment of your client's position - if an ENE is faulty and later used as a basis of settling a matter then the settlement reached is likely to be unethical.

8.15 Expert determinations

An expert determination expands upon the concept of an ENE. An expert determination is essentially an ENE provided by an expert in the field that the claim is relevant to, the distinction being that the decision of the expert is binding upon the parties. As a result of this, expert determinations are significantly more common in disputes that turn upon expert evidence to apportion liability. Expert determinations are more commonly found in disputes over contracts that involve projects like construction but can be found in low value consumer disputes such as the sale of faulty goods.

When using this method of ADR you should consider that the determination is not considered to fall within the legal framework of the Arbitration Act 1996. Therefore the only regulation involved is the general regulation imposed on experts by their respective institutes in providing their determinations.

8.16 Adjudication/Dispute Review Board

An adjudication will be used to determine the disputes which arise over the life of certain projects, most notably in larger construction projects. The adjudicator will be instructed to consider disputes as they arise during the project and make a binding decision on those disputes. This ensures that any disputed elements do not significantly jeopardise the timescale of the project.

A dispute review board is essentially a panel of adjudicators who are utilised in very large projects, typically in the construction of large commercial construction projects. The panel of three neutral adjudicators will be selected at the outset of a project and will visit the site regularly over the lifetime of the project, providing interim binding decisions on any disputes that arise during the process.

8.17 Conclusion

It seems obvious to state but the appropriate ADR method will differ from matter to matter. It would not be appropriate to state "*I always consider mediation in all of my cases*" simply to comply with your obligations to the court to consider ADR. The following table may be used as a quick reference guide to decide whether a particular method of ADR is appropriate or not:

ADR process	Third party?	Binding decision?	Ethical considerations
Negotiation	✗	✗	• No positive obligation for your opponent to disclose their case's weakness if not specifically noticed by you; • The atmosphere and result of abandonment will differ depending on whether your client or you conduct the negotiation.
Mediation	✓	✗	• Unregulated sector; • Must ensure chosen mediator has expertise to deal with the matter; • May not adequately deal with the rights of any interested third parties.
Collaborative law	✗	✗	• Ensure that your client is not leading the negotiation in the absence of your advice to obtain their best position; • Ensure there is not an imbalance of negotiating power between the parties; • Ensure there is no reason for the parties not to negotiate, such as domestic violence.
Executive tribunal	✓	✗	• Are the independent experts appointed as the executive tribunal sufficiently experienced in the area of technical expertise required? • Are the independent experts appointed as the executive tribunal compliant with their own regulatory obligations?
Conciliation	✓	✗	• In the case of compulsory conciliation, is it appropriate for the two parties to be actively forced to consider settlement?

ADR process	Third party?	Binding decision?	Ethical considerations
Early Neutral Evaluation	✓	✗	• Is your client's matter suitable for early neutral evaluation, or is the collection of further evidence necessary?
Arbitration	✓	✓	• Have you selected an appropriate arbitrator for your client's dispute? • Do you sufficiently appreciate the arbitration process? • Is there a risk that the matter will need to be enforced or referred to the court?
Adjudication	✓	✓	• Is the selected adjudicator suitable to deal with the dispute in question? • Is the adjudicator subject to any regulatory body?
Expert determination	✓	✓	• Is the expert sufficiently experienced in the area of the dispute to make a binding decision on the parties? • Is the expert regulated in any form?

You will note from this table that a great deal of consideration goes into ensuring that the third party is suitable for the particular case at hand. It is surprisingly common for solicitors to overlook this. When advising the client, is it correct to conclude that ADR is good and to be encouraged, and that litigation is bad and to be discouraged? It is unlikely that this is an ethical approach to take. At all times you should remember that litigation ultimately exists to allow wronged members of society access to an official forum which will address these wrongs if proven, and punish the individuals that have caused loss as a result of their breaches of the law. ADR can of course offer parties a more cost effective and speedier conclusion to disputes, but it is largely unregulated and private, which can be both a pro and a con. Ultimately this chapter gives solicitors an extremely difficult question to answer: how do you behave ethically within a system which can be suggested to be unethical itself?

Chapter 9: Ethics and the rise of lawtech

9.1 Introduction

> *"Because, if you stop to think of it, the three Rules of Robotics are the essential guiding principles of a good many of the world's ethical systems."*
> Issac Asimov, I, Robot

You've probably heard the phrase '*lawtech*' being muttered amongst the legal profession in quiet, suspicious whispers. The cautious approach by solicitors to legal technology is well justified for (if the legal press is to be believed) the age of organic solicitors is nearing its end. We are (apparently) on the verge of an army of artificially intelligent robot lawyers armed with '*the blockchain*' descending upon our practice areas and ousting us from employment. Whilst robots are less argumentative when it comes to salary and fringe benefit expectations, we can assure you that's not quite the case (for now). However, legal technology (or '*lawtech*') is indeed something that is becoming much more prevalent within the legal sector, and for good reason.

In the first edition of this book the lawtech scene was a much more nuanced one; the legal profession was just about getting used to using social media. As a result, this chapter could not be found within its contents page. However, the 2020 version of this book simply could not ignore it. Lawtech is rushing into the legal profession with some aggression; everyone within the profession seems vaguely aware of 'artificial intelligence' and 'blockchain' in some capacity. Firms are beginning to take note of the value lawtech investment can bring to their practices whilst the courts are dubiously attempting to transition to the digital world. Some have fully automated online portals that allow for the electronic filing of most court forms whilst others lash out in a confused rage if you even so much as dare to send a digital duplicate of a physical bundle to them.

Lawtech is exciting. It speeds up administrative processes and it makes your life easier. It's pitched as your unfailing accomplice in legal practice and it's there to give you more time to focus on being a lawyer. In the same way as social media it is therefore surprising to bring ethics into this shiny new world. Unless you're a big science fiction fan, you're probably wondering what on Earth could be unethical about a piece of software?

9.2 Ethics and lawtech

The ethics behind technology could fill the pages of an entire anthology. In the legal world the ethical conundrums of lawtech are founded on the fact that solicitors operating it usually have no idea how the underlying software functions, and how the results provided to them have been calculated and delivered. By this we do not mean not understanding how your case management system works (for example); we mean the actual functions of the software comprising of computer code that users cannot see working in the background. And why should solicitors know this? The role of a solicitor is one that requires the interpretation and analysis of the law, not to consider the intricacies of code behind the software installed within their firms to make their lives easier. Unfortunately, as is often the way in this job, it's not quite as simple as this anymore.

Consider the following nuanced example to explain how exactly lawtech can engage with the ethical thinking process:

Scenario: Disclosing client information online

Facts

Imagine you are a family solicitor at a medium sized firm who has been qualified for four years.

You have been working on a case for a semi-famous client for several years and the final hearing of the matter has finally been listed. You leave the office very late the night before the hearing, having just finished a three-hour call with your very anxious client. Arriving home, you realise that in your haste you forget to take your copy of the hearing bundle and your work laptop.

You can't get back into the office before the hearing starts, but you remember you scanned a copy of the bundle to yourself the day before. You access your emails from your phone and save a copy of the bundle onto your JCloud, a free online storage system your firm takes advantage of. You have never used JCloud before, but you know it allows you to store files which are quite large. You then log into JCloud on your personal laptop and use it to access the bundle.

You take your personal laptop to court and use it during the hearing to view the bundle. The hearing goes very well and results in a very positive decision for your client. After celebrating with your client, you return to the office and carry on with the rest of your work, forgetting entirely that you saved a copy of the bundle to your JCloud.

Sometime later you receive a call from a reporter looking into your client's case, saying that their court bundle is available to view online as they can see it stored in your JCloud. Checking your JCloud you realise, with horror, that you set the access settings to 'public'. As a result, anyone searching your client's name in a search engine would be able to view and download your client's bundle. When you check your JCloud you can see that it has been downloaded 43 times.

What would you do? What regulatory and ethical decisions are there to be made in this scenario?

Rules

Principles

The SRA principles likely to apply to this situation are that you act:

Principle 1: in a way that upholds the constitutional principle of the rule of law, and the proper administration of justice.

Principle 2: in a way that upholds public trust and confidence in the solicitors' profession and in legal services provided by authorised persons.

Principle 7: in the best interests of each client.

Code of Conduct for Solicitors

Paragraph 3.2: You ensure that the service you provide to clients is competent and delivered in a timely manner.

Paragraph 6.3: You keep the affairs of current and former clients confidential unless disclosure is required or permitted by law or the client consents.

Paragraph 7.2: You are able to justify your decisions and actions in order to demonstrate compliance with your obligations under the SRA's regulatory arrangements.

Potential ethical issues/professional breaches

This scenario is a perfect example of how even simple technology can have serious consequences for solicitors simply trying to act in their client's best interests.

Albeit unintentionally, the actions here have published sensitive client information into the public domain which have been accessed by members of the public.

Possible Approaches

Almost certainly there has been a breach of your duty to ensure your client's affairs have been kept confidential and it would be advisable to report this immediately to your COLP and the client.

It is unlikely that anything permitting the disclosure has been provided by the client to sanction the disclosure of the bundle. In any event court rules would likely prohibit the publishing of various documents without the permission of the court.

Matters are likely to be exasperated if the disclosure is not brought to the attention of your firm and your client immediately for, whilst the innocent omission is not likely to be considered dishonest, covering it up almost certainly will be.

Going forwards, it is crucial that whenever a piece of technology is used, you appreciate precisely how it works.

It may be that the firm in this scenario did not provide adequate training to their staff about the risks of storing confidential information outside of firm's computer system in this way, in which case it may be desirable for the firm to provide training in this respect.

9.3   So, what is lawtech?

In the scenario above, it is easy to dismiss the fictional JCloud as something unexciting. It is inevitable that you will have come across lawtech in some shape or form whilst practicing or studying within the legal sector, either at your firm, university or engaging with the (often perilous) technologies of the courts. Providing an exact definition of lawtech is not a simple one, partly because like ethics it means different things to many people. Many leaders in the lawtech industry label it as anything that is cutting edge in its field, using artificial intelligence or machine learning to develop its functions. Some (unhelpfully) make a distinction between '*LawTech*' and '*LegalTech*'. This book takes a much broader (and we would argue, factual) definition:

> ***Lawtech is any kind of technology developed for or used within the legal system with the specific purpose of increasing its efficiency or access to justice.***

This definition captures not only those products built and designed specifically for the legal profession but also those built with the intention of helping any person hoping to engage with the legal systems itself, for example lay people engaging with the courts. In casting the net so widely it is easy to see how lawtech is so fundamental from an ethical standpoint. At the moment you can organise lawtech into the following categories:

(1) **Research enhancement** – allowing lawyers to research legal points more efficiently and store this information in an easily accessible way;

(2) **Precedent artificial intelligence** – allows lawyers to enter details regarding a matter before them and be presented with predictions regarding prospects of success;

(3) **Smart contract drafting** – pieces of software used for drafting legal documents that either pre-insert precedent wording or analyse and suggest amendments automatically;

(4) **Chatbots** – software that emulates simple conversations for new or existing clients;

(5) **DIY Law** – systems which provide lay-persons with auto-generated forms after they answer a series of questions, or another form of resource that enables lay-persons to do legal tasks without a lawyer;

(6) **Legal practice and risk management** – software developed to assist with running a law firm, for example ensuring compliance with the regulatory obligations of a practice or running a practice in an efficient way.

9.4 Blockchain, AI, big data, what?

The legal media loves a buzzword, so to make matters more confusing, lawtech operates under a guise of different personas; artificial intelligence, blockchain and machine learning to name but a few. All of these words describe the different types of technologies that can be used within lawtech.

We will now briefly consider a few buzzwords and technologies used within the profession to describe lawtech, before analysing and applying the ethical conundrums these technologies present. What we would hasten to point out here is that you do not need to understand these technologies to the extent that you could go and create one tomorrow, only that you understand their application such that you know their risks and know how to question their results.

Artificial Intelligence

The pièce de le résistance of the legal media's buzzwords when it comes to lawtech is *'artificial intelligence'*. At its simplest artificial intelligence is an attempt to simulate human intelligence using a computer. In its purest form an artificially intelligent computer would be self-aware, have a consciousness and be able to think for itself without human intervention. Whilst the lawtech community would like you to believe otherwise, if you take one thing away from this chapter, it should be this: *this kind of artificial intelligence does not yet exist and likely won't for a significant period of time.*

When it comes to lawtech most products are simply what can be described as a *'reactive machine with limited memory'*. This means that when making decisions lawtech can recall their previous experiences to analyse and make future decisions. You see this kind of technology within the legal sector mostly in the form of chatbots, that are placed on the firm's website and used to 'speak' with clients who may wish to become clients in the future, taking initial details and forwarding them to the appropriate fee earner to follow up. The chatbot will analyse the question put to it and select the most appropriate answer from a pre-determined set of responses, even if it doesn't quite make sense. The label of *'simulated intelligence'* is likely a more appropriate definition.

Artificial intelligence is a very interesting ethical conundrum itself, for it raises all sorts of queries about whether human intelligence should ever be emulated on a machine, and if a machine does ever achieve that intelligence, should it be afforded the same rights as a human being? Those are however, discussions for a different book entirely. The word of warning with artificial intelligence is this: simply because a piece of lawtech describes itself as artificially intelligent does not mean it is and you should be wary of placing weight on this description.

Case / Practice Management Systems

Case Management Systems ('CMS') and Practice Management Systems are something most (if not all) lawyers are aware of. CMSs are up front in their naming; they exist to manage cases in a simple and easily accessible way by displaying the various documents involved in a transaction. Some go further and regulate an entire firm's practice, providing management with an overview of fee earner KPIs, handling the accounting system and so on.

Your firm's case management system probably doesn't strike you as lawtech, either because it's not that interesting (they are powerful but boring pieces of software) or because lawtech is sometimes billed only as top end life changing pieces of technology. However, as the tasks in which case management systems provide begin to expand beyond simple administrative assistant and more towards legal work such as the generation of documents, it's important that they are included within the lawtech label.

Blockchain

Blockchain is a favourite buzzword associated with lawtech because it is thought to be a very secure way of logging entries within a system that cannot be easily altered after the event, if at all. This is of course very useful in a profession where the sanctity of evidential security is so important, but a cynical view would be that many lawtech providers simply include a blockchain so that they can make use of the *"using blockchain technology"* catch phrase.

A blockchain is kind of like a ledger and is what it says on the tin; it's a chain of blocks. The blocks are chunks of computer data which are all held together in a specific order. Each block of data compromises a new transaction on the ledger. Each block also contains information about the particular transaction together with a unique 'fingerprint' of who created the block and (crucially) information about the previous block's data. Now, if someone later changes the data about a transaction then the next block will show a mismatch on its data, which is why blockchain is considered to be tamper-resistant. What takes this further is that a blockchain usually doesn't reside on one person's computer, but instead on a large network of computers. Every time a new block is added to the network all of the computers check and verify that the transactions are valid. Provided they are, the block

How To Be An Ethical Solicitor

will be added to the chain. If anyone wanted to change the blockchain (like a computer hacker, for example) they would need to attack and alter all of the computers involved in the network, which can sometimes extend to millions of computers.

| Block 23 ID from 22 | Block 24 ID from 23 | Block 25 ID from 24 |

Fig 30: A simplistic example of a blockchain

This is best imagined using a law firm's accounting system. Imagine a solicitor is moving money from client to office using their case management system. The block on the blockchain would record: *"Moved £900 from client to office on Smith"*. This block would then circulate to all of the other blocks on the system including the data from the previous block, meaning everyone's version will show that the solicitor moved £900 from client to office on Smith. If, to later cover up some mistake, the solicitor attempted to edit the entry to show that they only moved £850 from the client account, then this would be easily detectable because the rest of the blocks in the blockchain would not authenticate this.

The problem with blockchain is that it is often described as infallible because it is difficult to amend an entry or change its timestamp. This is a dangerous label to give a piece of technology. The strength of a blockchain will be the extent to which it exists across numerous computers (known as a public blockchain). In the legal profession public blockchains are difficult to impose because of our confidentiality obligations (even where such information is obscured). Where all the versions of the blockchain are on computer systems which are under the control of one person or company (described as a private blockchain) then the transactions can simply be edited across all of the blockchains. In the scenario involving the £900 above, if the blockchain was under the control of a rogue legal accountant who controlled all instances of the blockchain, then they could easily amend blocks and make it look as if the rest of the chain agreed with these edits.

The important point to take away with blockchain is this: putting '*blockchain*' on something does not mean you can treat it as inalterable. The extent to which the information can be verified or relied upon depends on whether the blockchain is public or private, and if it is private, who controls it.

Bitcoin and digital currencies

Digital currencies are the internet's version of money, made famous by Bitcoin. Bitcoin is a digital currency that exists as a public blockchain. Every time someone makes a Bitcoin transaction (for example, buying something online) then the transaction is anonymously logged within a public blockchain. Whilst Bitcoin has been around since 2008, the price of Bitcoin skyrocketed in 2013 which alerted other users to its presence. At the time of writing one Bitcoin is worth £6,431.16, although this value tends to fluctuate massively on a regular basis.

Blockchain arguably gained so much traction within the legal profession because of Bitcoin. The wide reports of the currency sent the profession into a bit of a tailspin, with law firm partners fearing that their clients would be lining up to pay invoices using Bitcoin.

At their core, digital currencies allow one person to send money to another without having to involve a bank or other third party. People purchase and sell Bitcoins by way of online exchange and transactions are recorded on a public blockchain using a personal but anonymous identifier known as a public key. This means it is possible to hold digital currencies such as Bitcoin in a pseudonymous way, without revealing your identity. For these reasons digital currencies have attracted a bad name for themselves, being seen as criminal repositories for money laundering and buying illicit black-market items. Many prefer using this public ledger of a currency's movements.

Your anti-money laundering alarms are probably working overtime at this point. Digital currencies raise several issues for solicitors. Most notably, as it is very difficult to trace the origins of a Bitcoin, how could a solicitor who accepted payment in a digital currency be sure that the money has not been procured from illicit sources?

Machine learning

The difference between you and a computer is that you learn from your past experiences. Computers, however, need detailed human direction in order to perform a specific task which is done in the form of computer code. Machine learning seeks to move away from this division and is essentially a concept of software development that allows a computer to learn from data which documents their past experiences. It does this by asking the computer to look at large databases and look for patterns so that it can make better decisions in the future and learn automatically without human intervention.

A very simple example of this is to imagine you are trying to teach a computer what a tree frog looks like. To do this you would have to manually use code language to tell the computer that a frog is green and has webbed feet. However, if you wanted to the computer to then tell you what a monkey looked like, it would not be able to use its frog knowledge to determine what the monkey was. This is where machine learning comes in. If you used a database containing pictures of lots of animals, the computer would search through this database, analyse the patterns within it, and determine the characteristics of both the frog and the monkey and be able tell between them. It will then use this information going forward, much in the same way as humans learn from their past experiences.

Machine learning is of use to the legal profession because it allows us to drill down into trends within the law and make predictions based on that data quickly. This of course has applications within litigation, where trends in precedents could be used to predict the prospects of a client's case. Lawtech already exists that suggests cases as you draft various litigious documents and identifies strengths and weaknesses in your case. Sounds great right? Absolutely, but there are some pitfalls to be aware of.

The weakness of machine learning rests on the underlying databases being used. How do you know that the information in the database is correct, or large enough to have any use to the computer? For example, imagine you have a database of 200 answers to the question *"what is the animal in this picture?"* together with a picture of a frog. If your database contains 200 answers incorrectly identifying the frog as a monkey, then the computer now thinks that a frog is a monkey. To extrapolate this to a legal scenario, imagine if a computer thinks the outcome of a case means one thing, when it actually means completely the opposite.

In the example above, how can you be sure that the cases being suggested to you do indeed support or contradict your client's case? How do you know the database has enough knowledge of any pending appeals in that respect? It's possible there is a case in existence that dissents from or revokes the decision being proposed by the software. It's unlikely that you'll be able to review the database of such software, but it is important you do not simply take the information at face value without taking separate steps to verify it (for example, by researching and reading the case). This sounds obvious, but when an answer is readily presented to you by a piece of intelligent software it is easy to be complacent.

Big data

Machine learning takes us nicely onto another favourite buzzword, 'big data'. Big data is simply a way of describing (perhaps obviously) a massive volume of data that it just isn't possible to analyse properly without specifically trained software. It comes as a result of our ever-increasing data hungry society.

Big data is used in the legal profession for a number of reasons, most notably advertising. Social media sites collect a huge amount of data from their users, and this data can be used by paying customers (like law firms) to target their advertising towards a particular group or demographic. Ever wondered why if you look at something on the internet you seem to be followed around by adverts relating to that search term? You have big data to thank for that, because a database is predicting that, based on your age, gender and interests, you may want to buy a particular item. Big data databases are also used in machine learning lawtech to predict trends as we have previously discussed.

The same warnings that apply to machine learning apply to big data. If a trend has been identified or the lawtech has used big data to make a legal prediction, are you satisfied that the data pool is wide enough to substantiate the information being provided to you?

9.5   Lawtech in the wild

Here are few examples of emerging lawtech:

(1) **Chatbots** – as we briefly discussed above, chatbots are usually designed to sit on a firm's website and deal with enquiries from prospective clients without the need for a fee earner to spend time speaking with the client to begin with. Chatbots are also used (usually in non-regulated areas) to provide advice or generate documents. For example, a chatbot could be used to generate parking ticket appeal letters. The user logs onto the chatbot, answers a series of questions and is presented with a fully completed appeal letter without the need for a lawyer at all.

(2) **Smart contract drafting** – heralded as the technology that will replace lawyers (but won't), smart contracts are basically self-executing contracts that also regulate themselves. They are designed to digitally verify and enforce the performance of a contract. Most do this using a (unnecessary) blockchain to log when a contract is

How To Be An Ethical Solicitor

signed and when certain milestones within it are completed by the parties. If you had commissioned a mechanic to repair a scratch on your car in return for £200, the mechanic could send a picture of your repaired car to the smart contract and automatically be paid by it.

(3) **Precedent generators** – at their simplest, precedent generators allow lawyers to enter information into a questionnaire based on their client's individual circumstances and receive a tailored precedent document pre-populated with the client's information. A good example of this that most practitioners will be aware of is Thomas Reuters' PLC 'Fastdraft' tool. There are a few public facing precedent generators in circulation which allow lay people simply to input their details and the lawtech generators produce a tailored precedent document. Some provide for lawyers to cast an eye over the document before the client is provided with it (at a premium), whilst others do not.

(4) **Legal trends predictions precedent** – a form of machine learning and big data, this type of lawtech trawls through a databank of case law and predicts trends in cases depending on a particular client's case and provides you with an overview of that client's prospects of success. Some boast the ability to also take into account variables such as a particular judge and even barristers instructed on the case.

(5) **'Smart' case/practice management systems** – these case management systems are usually based in 'the cloud' (i.e. accessible via the internet) and are therefore accessible from any device, be it a PC, Mac or a mobile device. Smart practice management systems usually go beyond the normal realms of case management and include much of the technologies set out above to aid and streamline administrative burdens on the solicitors using the lawtech.

(6) **Dispute resolution platforms** – these online platforms provide mediation and arbitration services, allowing clients to negotiate settlements over the internet using webcams and chat sites. In the future we may see platforms that allow litigants to simply upload a contract and their respective positions, and have a binding settlement issued by a computer that considers the pros and cons of each party's case.

Some lawtech does not take the law too seriously:

Scenario: Lawtech's flippant approach to the law

Facts

You are a partner in a litigation department of a medium-sized firm.

Recently you have been bombarded with lots of new enquiries relating to cases involving very small sums of money. As these cases fall into the small claims tracks, your advice is usually that it is uneconomical to instruct solicitors to resolve these disputes.

One lunchtime you come across the website law-flip-resolution.com, which is a tongue in cheek piece of lawtech that allows litigants to enter a strange form of resolution, where both parties agree to settle their dispute on the flip of a coin. The parties use law-flip-resolution.com to sign a binding agreement, and the website then flips a coin. The winner of the coin toss then has a binding settlement agreement that can (in theory) be converted into a court order.

When you next receive a call from a consumer, it relates to a small claim about a faulty car tyre installed by a garage, with the value of £45.

You simply suggest that the consumer tries this site to resolve their case in a cost-effective way.

Are there any issues ethically with your suggestion of law-flip-resolution.com?

Rules

The SRA principles likely to apply to this situation are that you act:

Principle 1: in a way that upholds the constitutional principle of the rule of law, and the proper administration of justice.

Principle 2: in a way that upholds public trust and confidence in the solicitors' profession and in legal services provided by authorised persons.

Principle 3: with independence.

Principle 4: with honesty.

Principle 7: in the best interests of each client.

Code of Conduct for Solicitors

Paragraph 3.2: You ensure that the service you provide to clients is competent and delivered in a timely manner.

Paragraph 3.4: You consider and take account of your client's attributes, needs and circumstances.

Paragraph 7.2: You are able to justify your decisions and actions in order to demonstrate compliance with your obligations under the SRA's regulatory arrangements.

Potential ethical issues/professional breaches

Whilst it is unlikely that a solicitor would realistically recommend a potential client to settle their case on the flip of a coin, this scenario serves as a good demonstration of where lawtech may be used chaotically.

Particularly against the points discussed in Chapter 8, it would be difficult to suggest that the solicitor has properly considered the client's needs in recommending this form of ADR.

The lawtech in question does not properly consider the legal basis of either party's claim, nor does it properly analyse the factual basis of each party's claim. For all you know, the defective work may lead to more serious issues, which you may have sanctioned being settled on the flip of a coin. On the other hand, your potential client could be an absolute lunatic pursuing a meritless claim, in which case you may have suggested a settlement option that would legitimise a legally flawed position. Neither route supports the rule of law or administration of justice.

Furthermore, how can you be sure that law-flip-resolution.com actually works on the basis of 50/50 odds? Its programming could be flawed, meaning heads comes up more often than tails, or vice versa.

Possible Approaches

In this instance it would likely be best to contact the client and skilfully retract the suggestion, until (at least) you are able to satisfy yourself of the claim's merits, and the client still wishes to use law-flip-resolution.com regardless.

If the would-be client had already committed themselves to law-flip-resolution.com then this would likely be a breach of the rules set out above and the solicitor should self-report themselves.

Would it make a difference if?

law-flip-resolution.com was not a random process, and used "*artificial intelligence*" to analyse the legal and factual position to produce a judgment?

9.6 The benefits of lawtech

Despite all the doom and gloom contained within this chapter lawtech remains a very exciting frontier for the legal profession. Indeed, it is simply necessary for the profession to adapt and survive within the growing digital economy that is rapidly springing up around the world. For the most part lawtech just exists to make lawyer's lives easier. As we have seen from the examples above, it does this by taking over more administrative functions such as the preparation of court bundles or allowing them to research points of law much more quickly. When properly implemented lawtech has the potential to do the following:

(1) **Save time**: lawtech can perform certain tasks at a much faster rate than humans, picking up anything from spelling and punctuation errors to deficiencies in legal arguments. Research tools are a fantastic example of this; the idea of looking through a book to do legal research is simply alien to some lawyers.

(2) **Identify risk more effectively**: regulatory lawtech (sometimes called regtech) enables law firms to identify when a particular matter may be high risk, or if certain money laundering flags exist due to a client's particular circumstances. In theory this allows a fee earner to 'verify' that they have had the results of their risk assessment independently reviewed, and have it automatically referred to a more senior member of the team if there are any irregularities or concerns.

(3) **Increase the service to clients**: in removing more administrative tasks lawtech frees up more time for lawyers to not only focus on legal work, but also engage more with their clients. Some lawtech is also client facing, for example some case management systems have a client portal which allows them to check the status of their

How To Be An Ethical Solicitor

matter. Instead of calling you for an update the client can simply check this themselves.

(4) **Attract more clients**: if clients see you as an innovative lawyer with the potential to approach a situation in a new and innovative way, you are likely to gain a reputation for being creative in the way you solve your client's legal problems.

(5) **Make you a more efficient lawyer**: unlike us human beings properly programmed lawtech has the potential to be error-free. This therefore streamlines the production quality being produced by a firm by enhancing the output of each of its lawyers.

Lawtech is likely to be beneficial for the future junior lawyers of the profession, for it will likely replace various administrative tasks. Whilst this may reduce the need for administrative positions somewhat it will in theory mean junior lawyers are doing more legal work during their training than administrative tasks like building bundles or photocopying. It is therefore envisaged that this will lead to a better quality of training for junior lawyers who will be regularly exposed to 'pure' legal work during their training.

If lawtech is used by lawyers in the right way, then it often leads to the reduction of overheard costs and an increase in efficiency which are becoming ever necessary for smaller and medium sized firms alike. This in theory then provides a better service for clients of that law firm.

9.7 The pitfalls of lawtech

Now back to the doom and gloom. For all its bells, whistles and promises, lawtech should be approached with caution. Make no mistake, in the wrong hands it is simply dangerous.

In considering how regulatory ethics apply to lawtech it may assist you to consider the following sections of the SRA Code of Conduct:

Principles

You act:

Principle 1: in a way that upholds the constitutional principle of the rule of law, and the proper administration of justice;

Principle 2: in a way that upholds public trust and confidence in the solicitors' profession and in legal services provided by authorised persons;

Principle 3: with independence;

Principle 7: in the best interests of each client.

Code of Conduct for Solicitors, RELs and RFLs

Paragraph 1.4: You do not mislead or attempt to mislead your clients, the court or others, either by your own acts or omissions or allowing or being complicit in the acts or omissions of others (including your client).

Paragraph 2.2: You do not seek to influence the substance of evidence, including generating false evidence or persuading witnesses to change their evidence.

Paragraph 3.2: You ensure that the service you provide to clients is competent and delivered in a timely manner.

Paragraph 3.3: You maintain your competence to carry out your role and keep your professional knowledge and skills up to date.

Paragraph 6.3: You keep the affairs of current and former clients confidential unless disclosure is required or permitted by law or the client consents.

Paragraph 7.2: You are able to justify your decisions and actions in order to demonstrate compliance with your obligations under the SRA's regulatory arrangements.

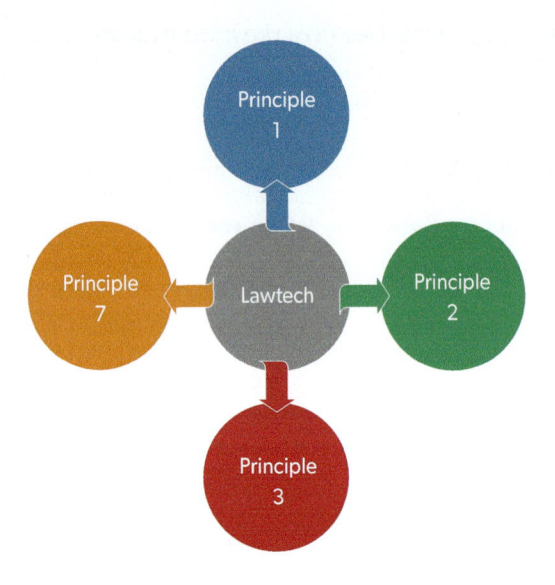

Fig 31: Lawtech and the regulatory Principles

The law of unintended consequences attaches itself strongly to lawtech. At law school you're encouraged to take care when using precedents, ensuring that you fully understand the legal mechanics behind the document. The same rings true for lawtech; if a solicitor uses technology to enhance their legal advice, and they don't fully understand the mechanics behind the information provided to them, how can they confidently say that they understand the foundations of the advice they are giving? This is particular the case in respect of lawtech that uses artificial intelligence and big data to predict trends in case law in order to determine a client's prospects of success before they issue proceedings.

Consider the following scenario:

Scenario: Precedent Generators

Facts

Imagine you are a trainee solicitor seconded to Quickie-Wills Limited, a very small SRA regulated firm. Only you and the Managing Partner (who is rarely around) work for Quickie-Wills Limited.

The Managing Partner of Quickie-Wills paid for a software house to develop a piece of software that automatically generates Wills based on client answers to a set questionnaire together with a brief explanatory note that is produced in your name. The clients complete this questionnaire online and then come into the office to sign the generated Will with you and their nominated second witness. The service costs £45 plus VAT which severely undercuts your local competitors.

Whilst you cast an eye over the Will when you print it, the Managing Partner assures you that the software "could never be wrong" so you have never really given it much thought. You found Wills and Probate very dull on the LPC and have no interest in pursuing it upon qualification; therefore you do not have a great deal of information about what makes a Will valid or not.

Whilst the Managing Partner is listed as the partner supervisor on each case file, after developing the software they left the country to live in Asia and live off the proceeds of their firm. You are listed as the fee earner and realistically handle the clients from first contact to when they sign their Wills.

Are there any issues for you or Quickie-Wills Limited?

Rules

The SRA principles likely to apply to this situation are that you act:

Principle 1: in a way that upholds the constitutional principle of the rule of law, and the proper administration of justice;

Principle 2: in a way that upholds public trust and confidence in the solicitors' profession and in legal services provided by authorised persons;

Principle 7: in the best interests of each client.

Code of Conduct for Solicitors

Paragraph 7.2: You are able to justify your decisions and actions in order to demonstrate compliance with your obligations under the SRA's regulatory arrangements.

Potential ethical issues/professional breaches

In this scenario it is unclear whether the Managing Partner is properly reviewing your handling of each client's matter, and most of the work appears to be generated automatically by the software without any solicitor intervention. Despite the Managing Partner's promise that the software could never be wrong, you have no way of verifying this as you do not have the requisite experience to review each Will produced. Given the Managing Partner didn't write the software themselves, you cannot even place any weight on the fact they have verified the statement.

It is therefore entirely possible that clients are being passed through without any detailed advice as to their position.

Possible Approaches

It is unlikely that you could confidently justify your decisions in asking the clients to sign their Wills without properly considering their legal position.

You could attempt to speak with the Managing Partner, asking for more training in order to enable you to consider the Wills in more detail and perhaps engage in a consultation with clients before signing them.

You could raise your concerns with the firm that you have been seconded from, raising concerns about the quality of your training and the level of oversight at Quickie-Wills Limited.

Ultimately both you and the Managing Partner may attract civil and regulatory liability if negligent advice is being given out as a result of the software.

As the production of Wills is not a regulated activity, in reality many Will writing companies are not law firms such as the one described in this scenario.

Consider also that some clients are not all that interested in how many flashing lights are attached to your delivery of legal services. Some prefer a face-to-face meeting than your firm's fancy video conferencing suite.

Lawtech can therefore be said to encourage the following:

(1) Very low standards of acceptable legal advice;

(2) The impression amongst the general public that legal services should demand lower fees;

(3) The making of dishonest or meritless claims by individuals who would otherwise not have considered doing so (precedent generators that clients don't really understand).

The biggest risk is that lawtech does something that you simply do not intend it to do. The implementation of lawtech is also not always necessarily legal. At the time of writing the SRA is currently engaged in a debate over the legality of the 'digital badge', which must be displayed on all websites of firms regulated by the SRA. There are doubts over whether this badge (which verifies the website associated with a particular firm is in fact associated with that firm) complies with data protection legislation when processing the data of consumers who click on it. This is a good example of lawtech having a beneficial purpose (verifying firms to consumers at the point of access) but having an unintended consequence (potentially unlawfully processing consumer data). We await an ICO decision on the validity of the badge.

In short it is very easy to breach any number of the Principles by using lawtech. In particular, complacency can result in solicitors not acting in a way that upholds public trust and confidence in the profession (Principle 2) or acting in each client's best interests (Principle 7).

9.8 Engaging with lawtech ethically

As with social media lawtech is both an asset and a potential compliance risk to both law firms and solicitors. What is so dangerous about lawtech? Well, as we have explored, the biggest danger lies solely within its complexity. One of the central tenets of our justice system has always been that the way in which it is achieved should be transparent. This can be difficult to achieve with lawtech as the technology can often be complex and difficult to understand, even by its creators. Solicitors using lawtech may find it more difficult to account to their clients, purely because they do not appreciate the mechanics of the decision being provided to them by lawtech.

To complicate things even further, when lawtech goes wrong it's not always easy to ascertain why or for what reason an error has occurred. Lawtech doesn't necessarily operate in isolation. Often, we see various forms of lawtech being used at the same time, or communicating with the internet. It therefore may become difficult to apportion blame on one party as a result of an error caused at one point during a complicated chain.

It is advisable to keep the following in mind when engaging with any form of lawtech.

Always ask questions

In Harry Potter and the Chamber of Secrets, Arthur Weasley counsels Harry Potter with the following advice: *"Never trust anything that can think for itself if you can't see where it keeps its brain."*[1] Whilst this related to a self-aware magical diary containing a fragment of Lord Voldemort's soul, it's a perfect analogy to attach to lawtech. If you are not sure how a piece of lawtech works, how can you confidently say that you can justify the weight of the information it is supplying you with? This of course applies mostly to lawtech that generates legal advice for forwarding to your client. However, the process applies to any piece of lawtech. Imagine you relied upon a piece of lawtech to generate and produce a bundle for a court hearing, and a malfunction in the software meant that several key witness statements were omitted. No amount of "but it was the computer what done it, your honour" is likely to save you from the wrath of an unamused judge.

If you are using a piece of lawtech for research purposes, how sure are you that the answer that the software has provided is correct? How certain are you that the research pool is enough for you to place weight on it when communicating it to a client? Particularly when using precedent generating pieces of lawtech, ensure you understand the clauses being presented to you. This will, of course, be easier for more experienced members of the profession, but less immediately obvious for more junior ones.

Again, to be clear, we do not suggest that you need to have a computer science degree to continue practising. You need only satisfy yourself that you are familiar enough with the operations of any lawtech you use that you can ask questions of it and determine the legitimacy of whatever it is providing you with.

---

[1] *J.K Rowling, Harry Potter and the Chamber of Secrets, (1988).*

Is it doing what it says on the tin?

As we may have said too many times already, buzzwords sometimes get the better of lawtech developers. Always ask, is the lawtech doing what it actually says it will? When it says, "we will compare all of the cases in existence", how can you be sure it actually is?

Consider the following:

Scenario: Trend predicting software

Facts

You are a junior personal injury solicitor in a large law firm that takes on hundreds of road traffic accidents every month. Your firm has just introduced a brand-new piece of ground-breaking legal software called Take-The-Claim-Away. Take-The-Claim-Away allows you to enter the characteristics of any new instruction and it will then search through a precedent bank held on Take-The-Claim-Away's server. Take-The-Claim-Away will then inform you what it believes the new instruction's prospects of success in court are likely to be. It boasts that it can mirror the prospects of success provided by any barrister, by using an algorithm that is based on artificial intelligence and blockchain technology.

You speak to a new prospect on the phone. They were involved in an RTA involving several cars and have sustained severe bruising to their back and whiplash. They advise you that they were not able to brake before hitting the car in front because they had a sudden outbreak of hiccups. They also tell you that they have a newly diagnosed illness named Hiccupitis, which causes unwelcome hiccups. After completing KYC checks you advise the prospect that you can act for them and they formally become your client.

When you put this information into Take-The-Claim-Away's server, it indicates that the existence of Hiccupitis is likely to mean the client's prospects of success are only 2.14% and that you should immediately take steps to settle the matter for a low quantum of compensation. Using this information, you offer to settle the client's claim for a few hundred pounds for minimal pain and suffering.

Several months later, on a separate matter, you come across several precedents of senior courts indicating that Hiccupitis does not disrupt the chain of causation. You realise that you probably could have sought a much more beneficial settlement for your client.

Rules

The SRA principles likely to apply to this situation are that you act:

Principle 1: in a way that upholds the constitutional principle of the rule of law, and the proper administration of justice;

Principle 2: in a way that upholds public trust and confidence in the solicitors' profession and in legal services provided by authorised persons;

Principle 3: with independence;

Principle 5: with integrity;

Principle 7: in the best interests of each client.

Code of Conduct for Solicitors

Paragraph 7.2: You are able to justify your decisions and actions in order to demonstrate compliance with your obligations under the SRA's regulatory arrangements.

Potential ethical issues/professional breaches

It is unlikely that many solicitors will be aware of how Take-The-Claim-Away's algorithm actually rifles through the precedent bank on its server. Before putting any advice to the client that is produced as a result of the information provided by Take-The-Claim-Away you should consider whether you are satisfied that its precedent bank is actually diverse enough for you to support the prediction of 2.14%.

Possible Approaches

You are ultimately responsible for the advice you give to your client, regardless of the way in which you arrive at such advice. This is because you have a duty under Paragraph 7.2 to justify your decisions and actions to demonstrate compliance with your regulatory obligations. You are unlikely to be acting in your client's best interest if you pass on advice based on information you do not fully understand.

You could consider and read into the cases that Take-The-Claim-Away has used to make its estimate in order to satisfy yourself whether you agree or disagree with the prospect of success generated. It is also questionable whether you should immediately take to heart the advice to settle the case for a low quantum; many other factors are likely to come into making this decision, including your negotiation skills and the client's wishes.

Lawtech policies and training

As we discussed in the social media chapter, for law firm management stringent and updated staff policies are an effective way of demonstrating that a firm has at least attempted to prevent any form of compliance breaches. The same is true of lawtech. However, as we know from this chapter, lawtech has a very wide definition. It is therefore difficult to have a 'lawtech' policy. Instead care should be taken to effectively communicate the risks of technology utilised in legal practice.

Where a particular piece of lawtech is installed that could create compliance risks (for example, precedent generators) care should be taken to ensure members of staff are properly trained to use these technologies. Leaving staff to '*train each other*' is unlikely to satisfy the practice competencies of the Standards and Regulations that you are running your practice in a competent way.

Do I even need to use this?

Certain branches of lawtech use a sledgehammer to crack a nut. It won't always be necessary for you to use "bleeding edge technology"[2] to solve

---

[2] *Wikipedia describes bleeding edge technology as 'a category of technologies so new that they could have a high risk of being unreliable and lead adopters to incur greater expense in order to make use of them'.*

legal issues, and using lawtech where it is not even needed gives rise to the potential complications we have set out above.

Guiding principles

The points from this section can effectively be summarised as follows:

> **Why?** – why do you need to use this lawtech? Is it necessary to achieve your end goal? Could you achieve your goal more effectively without it?
>
> **How?** – how has the lawtech arrived at this decision?
>
> **Justified?** – can you justify and transparently explain the outcome of the decision made by lawtech to both yourself and your client?

9.9 The future

Looking forwards, it is likely that lawtech will begin to become significantly more advanced and enmeshed within the legal profession. It is already on the radar of the law society and SRA, with the latter recently offering investment funds for lawtech that seeks to *promote increased access to justice and other prevalent issues within the legal profession*.

The scariest application of future lawtech is likely to be seen within the courts as they take further steps to digitalise their service where they can, but we are likely to also see innovative lawtech become much more prevalent in medium and large sized law firms with the deep pockets to fund the implementation of cutting-edge technology. But as new extremely advanced lawtech begins to permeate the legal profession the ethical risks increase significantly.

As the Ministry of Justice precariously attempts to replace a properly funded court system with making the courts more digital, consider the following application of future lawtech:

Ethics And The Rise Of Lawtech

Scenario: The future of lawtech

Facts

Imagine it is the year 2023. You have just obtained employment as a 'justice supervisor' in the criminal courts, a new initiative of HMCTS to tackle the workload of judges and magistrates. A justice supervisor is a qualified solicitor responsible for passing information about defendants who have pleaded guilty online into a computer system called 'LawNet'. LawNet balances the defendant's mitigating circumstances and then calculates the sentence against the sentencing guidelines for the particular offence. It then prints off a court order which you can choose to sanction or review and suggest alternatives. LawNet means guilty pleas are dealt with entirely without a court hearing.

LawNet deals mostly with low level offences from the magistrate's court, but it can implement custodial sentences provided they do not exceed six months (or twelve for multiple offences). You have been qualified for two years as a family lawyer and are not familiar with the criminal law; however a justice supervisor is considered a quasi-judicial role and has the potential to fast-track you to the bench.

During your training on LawNet, your trainer (who is not a lawyer) assures you that LawNet is more predictable and accurate than even a judge, so the possibility of it miscalculating a sentence is very slim. They tell you that most justice supervisors simply stamp the orders, particularly as there are so many to deal with in one day.

You spend your first day mostly signing the orders, assuming LawNet knows what it's doing. Several weeks into your role you review one case of drink driving. The defendant in this matter was four times over the limit when they hit and severely injured an elderly person. LawNet has recommended that the defendant be banned from driving for two years, complete 145 days of unpaid work, pay a £287 victim surcharge and pay the prosecution's minimal costs. After briefly considering the sentencing guidelines you think that this appears lenient, but you sign the order anyway because LawNet probably has a better knowledge of the sentencing guidelines than you.

Three months later you hear rumours that LawNet has never functioned properly, and as a result hasn't been balancing the sentencing guidelines properly. When you raise this with your supervisor, they tell you it's being looked into, but they can't risk this issue being leaked, and asks you to keep this to yourself.

What would you do?

Rules

The SRA principles likely to apply to this situation are that you act:

Principle 1: in a way that upholds the constitutional principle of the rule of law, and the proper administration of justice;

Principle 2: in a way that upholds public trust and confidence in the solicitors' profession and in legal services provided by authorised persons;

Principle 3: with independence;

Principle 5: with integrity;

Principle 7: in the best interests of each client.

Code of Conduct for Solicitors

Paragraph 7.2: You are able to justify your decisions and actions in order to demonstrate compliance with your obligations under the SRA's regulatory arrangements.

Potential ethical issues/professional breaches

This scenario moves away from the usual examples used within this book, which are typically based on scenarios that would occur in practice. The same ethical thought process must however be applied to this scenario.

There is a risk that serious miscarriages of justice are being sanctioned by you.

Possible Approaches

You should immediately raise your concerns with management above the level of your immediate supervisor that you do not believe that LawNet is properly applying the sentencing guidelines. It is likely to be unethical, and a breach of Principle 1, if you allow the potentially erroneous judgments to go unchallenged. Not doing so would almost certainly be seen to be acting without integrity and undermining the rule of law and proper administration of justice.

The fact that HMCTS would suffer bad publicity in this fictional scenario is unlikely to make a difference to your ethical approach. Your duty to the rule of law and administration of justice will take precedence.

Would it make a difference if?

You do not have the option to overrule LawNet, you are simply employed to affix the court stamp to the document to give it legal force.

The year 2023 may be an over optimistic estimation of such technology being implemented in the criminal courts. Systems are already being implemented in the criminal courts that enable defendants who wish to plead guilty to minor offences to do so online without the need to go to court. In the future it is entirely conceivable that automated systems could be used to analyse the correct sentence for those found guilty of a particular offence. To take this even further, in the (hopefully) far future we may even see "robot judges", which would weigh up the evidence submitted to them for both civil and criminal trials and produce a binding judgment with little to no human involvement at all. Would you ever be comfortable with a robot judge passing sentence over you? Or someone close to you?

And of course, we cannot leave out the fear of the legal press favourite, the truly artificial '*robot lawyer*'. In the far future it is not implausible to suggest there will be robots capable of providing tailored legal advice based on a client's individual circumstances. The difference between these robot lawyers and the lawyers of today is that they will be able to provide advice and prepare legal documents in mere minutes, making them not only incredibly efficient but also likely much cheaper than their fleshy counterparts. Despite robot lawyers and judges currently being purely hypothetical, whether or not this is ethical very much comes down to what this chapter has considered; can we be sure that the technology is balancing the evidence properly and doing exactly what it is being programmed to do? If we could not do this then it is difficult to suggest lawtech being used in this way would comply with the rule of law primarily due to a complete lack of transparency. More worryingly, what happens to the rule of law when our legislation is no longer interpreted and applied by human beings but instead by cold and calculating machines?

The SRA's Standards and Regulations already take a new approach of applying different sets of rules to different types of practitioner. It is arguably not long before we see some form of code of conduct that is aimed towards the creation of lawtech, and arguably this should be in place already to head off the lawtech revolution before its foundations become difficult to control. This has already been seen within the finance markets, with fintech (lawtech's financial counterpart) being bombarded with a myriad of updated regulation from the Financial Conduct Authority to stem off its rapid expansion. The legal profession is, arguably, not doing enough to curb a similar (albeit more nuanced) expansion within the legal profession. What kind of code of conduct would a robot lawyer follow?

9.10 Conclusion

The future of lawtech is bound to be extremely bold and exciting, but it arguably poses one of the biggest ethical and regulatory threats to both firms and solicitors alike. The lawtech market is currently less mature than its counterparts in the financial markets, and it would be hoped that the SRA will address the lawtech expansion with the same speed used by the Financial Conduct Authority to fintech. This of course remains to be seen.

As was floated in the conclusion of the social media chapter of this book, lawtech should of course be embraced, but carefully. And whilst you don't need to fear the rise of the robot lawyers just yet, if your firm installs anything that uses the description *"artificially intelligent blockchain equipped with big data enabled machine learning"*, you should raise your ethical eyebrow as far as it will go.

Lawtech risk overview

Lawtech	Regularly used by the legal profession?	Specific risks
Research enhancers	Yes	• Not always easy to know the extent of the database you are researching against. • Becomes easy to say there "is no answer" if the answer is not available on the database.

Ethics And The Rise Of Lawtech

Lawtech	Regularly used by the legal profession?	Specific risks
Precedent generators	Yes	• It can be easy to lapse into using a precedent without fully appreciating its legal workings.
Smart drafting software	More regularly in large firms.	• Easy for precedent clauses to be inserted that have unintended consequences for the client. • Easy to become led by the software without considering the legal nature of what you are trying to achieve.
Chatbots	More widely used outside of the legal sector, but they are gaining traction in medium-large firms.	• If client facing and giving out (basic) legal advice the information being provided to the end-user must be correct and clear (i.e. lawyer involvement is required).
DIY Law	No, largely used by companies providing non-regulated activities.	• As this is typically produced without lawyer involvement there may be a risk that the content is not legally correct.
Legal practice and risk management software	Yes	• Risks are slightly lower than other lawtech, depending on the CMS in question. • Some offer client facing 'portals' that allow clients to review the progress of their case. In this instance client confidentiality is key (for example, saving an email on the wrong file that a client can see). • CMSs are now expanding to incorporate lawtech like precedent generators and research enhancers, and the warnings attached above should be taken on board in this respect.

Chapter 10: Conclusion

It is now clearer than ever that the regulation of legal services will continue to emphasise outcome-focused principles with a strong requirement for solicitors to behave ethically. In modern legal practice ethics is becoming more paramount than ever.

Despite this paramountcy, this book has demonstrated that ethical concepts are often difficult to define, and differ from person to person and across generations and ethnic groups. Having read this book it is hoped that you will have gained a greater appreciation of the relationship between ethics and the law, and how this is connected to performing your regulated role as an officer of the court.

You should appreciate how your ethical obligations extend to your relationship with your clients, your regulators and the myriad of parties you will encounter throughout your legal career. You should understand that the diversity of ethical opinions, when combined with the regulatory framework of the legal profession, may mean that there may be more than one response to any given ethical conundrum. It is not necessarily the case that there will only be one right answer to any given issue.

It is also hoped that you will appreciate that ethical issues will present themselves in more subtle ways, be that in the consideration of often mandatory alternative dispute resolution media, the advertisement of a firm through social media or even the sending of emails to colleagues.

It was stated at the outset of this book that the authors intended it be used as a guidebook for practice, but it is only the starting point for developing yourself as "the ethical solicitor", or "the more ethical solicitor". As has been stated throughout, the intention of this book is to set out a decision-making methodology for use in practice, and instil a method of thinking in an ethical manner, with the intention of producing an ethical outcome. This should by now be very clear, and your ethical decision-making should now be at the implementation stage.

The next time an issue arises in your working day, your enhanced ethical mindset should be more alert to the potential ethical dimensions of the issue. As you think more about the ethical aspects of ordinary issues, both in and out of the work environment, the more you will realise how many decisions you will have to make in an ethical way. Self-reflection on your previous approach to ethical decision-making will allow some room for new decision making processes.

At a time where the legal profession and justice in general faces numerous threats, the need for ethics to remain strongly at the heart of what solicitors do is now more crucial than ever. If solicitors cannot be seen to act ethically then the principle of justice itself is at risk. The ethical solicitor, sitting on the Clapham omnibus, will know what the right thing to do is, act in order to achieve the right thing, and do so for the right reasons.

Know the right thing

Do the right thing

And do so for the right reason

Appendix

The following Principles and Codes of Conduct for Solicitors and Firms have been taken from the SRA website.

SRA Principles

You act:

1. in a way that upholds the constitutional principle of the rule of law, and the proper administration of justice.

2. in a way that upholds public trust and confidence in the solicitors' profession and in legal services provided by authorised persons.

3. with independence.

4. with honesty.

5. with integrity.

6. in a way that encourages equality, diversity and inclusion.

7. in the best interests of each client.

SRA Code of Conduct for Solicitors, RELs and RFLs

1: Maintaining trust and acting fairly

1.1 You do not unfairly discriminate by allowing your personal views to affect your professional relationships and the way in which you provide your services.

1.2 You do not abuse your position by taking unfair advantage of clients or others.

1.3 You perform all undertakings given by you, and do so within an agreed timescale or if no timescale has been agreed then within a reasonable amount of time.

1.4 You do not mislead or attempt to mislead your clients, the court or others, either by your own acts or omissions or allowing or being complicit in the acts or omissions of others (including your client).

2: Dispute resolution and proceedings before courts, tribunals and inquiries

2.1 You do not misuse or tamper with evidence or attempt to do so.

2.2 You do not seek to influence the substance of evidence, including generating false evidence or persuading witnesses to change their evidence.

2.3 You do not provide or offer to provide any benefit to witnesses dependent upon the nature of their evidence or the outcome of the case.

2.4 You only make assertions or put forward statements, representations or submissions to the court or others which are properly arguable.

2.5 You do not place yourself in contempt of court, and you comply with court orders which place obligations on you.

2.6 You do not waste the court's time.

2.7 You draw the court's attention to relevant cases and statutory provisions, or procedural irregularities of which you are aware, and which are likely to have a material effect on the outcome of the proceedings.

3: Service and competence

3.1 You only act for clients on instructions from the client, or from someone properly authorised to provide instructions on their behalf. If you have reason to suspect that the instructions do not represent your client's wishes, you do not act unless you have satisfied yourself that they do. However, in circumstances where you have legal authority to act notwithstanding that it is not possible to obtain or ascertain the instructions of your client, then you are subject to the overriding obligation to protect your client's best interests.

3.2 You ensure that the service you provide to clients is competent and delivered in a timely manner.

3.3 You maintain your competence to carry out your role and keep your professional knowledge and skills up to date.

3.4 You consider and take account of your client's attributes, needs and circumstances.

3.5 Where you supervise or manage others providing legal services:

(a) you remain accountable for the work carried out through them; and

(b) you effectively supervise work being done for clients.

3.6 You ensure that the individuals you manage are competent to carry out their role, and keep their professional knowledge and skills, as well as understanding of their legal, ethical and regulatory obligations, up to date.

4: Client money and assets

4.1 You properly account to clients for any financial benefit you receive as a result of their instructions, except where they have agreed otherwise.

4.2 You safeguard money and assets entrusted to you by clients and others.

4.3 You do not personally hold client money save as permitted under regulation 10.2(b)(vii) of the Authorisation of Individuals Regulations, unless you work in an authorised body, or in an organisation of a kind prescribed under this rule on any terms that may be prescribed accordingly.

5.1-5.3: Referrals, introductions and separate businesses

5.1 In respect of any referral of a client by you to another person, or of any third party who introduces business to you or with whom you share your fees, you ensure that:

(a) clients are informed of any financial or other interest which you or your business or employer has in referring the client to another person or which an introducer has in referring the client to you;

(b) clients are informed of any fee sharing arrangement that is relevant to their matter;

(c) the fee sharing agreement is in writing;

(d) you do not receive payments relating to a referral or make payments to an introducer in respect of clients who are the subject of criminal proceedings; and

(e) any client referred by an introducer has not been acquired in a way which would breach the SRA's regulatory arrangements if the person acquiring the client were regulated by the SRA.

5.2 Where it appears to the SRA that you have made or received a referral fee, the payment will be treated as a referral fee unless you show that the payment was not made as such.

5.3 You only:

(a) refer, recommend or introduce a client to a separate business; or

(b) divide, or allow to be divided, a client's matter between you and a separate business;

where the client has given informed consent to your doing so.

5.4-5.6: Other business requirements

5.4 You must not be a manager, employee, member or interest holder of a business that:

(a) has a name which includes the word "solicitors"; or

(b) describes its work in a way that suggests it is a solicitors' firm;

unless it is an authorised body.

5.5 If you are a solicitor who holds a practising certificate, an REL or RFL, you must complete and deliver to the SRA an annual return in the prescribed form.

5.6 If you are a solicitor or an REL carrying on reserved legal activities in a non-commercial body, you must ensure that:

(a) the body takes out and maintains indemnity insurance; and

(b) this insurance provides adequate and appropriate cover in respect of the services that you provide or have provided, whether or not they comprise reserved legal activities, taking into account any alternative arrangements the body or its clients may make.

Conflict, confidentiality and disclosure

6.1-6.2: Conflict of interests

6.1 You do not act if there is an own interest conflict or a significant risk of such a conflict.

6.2 You do not act in relation to a matter or particular aspect of it if you have a conflict of interest or a significant risk of such a conflict in relation to that matter or aspect of it, unless:

(a) the clients have a substantially common interest in relation to the matter or the aspect of it, as appropriate; or

(b) the clients are competing for the same objective,

and the conditions below are met, namely that:

(i) all the clients have given informed consent, given or evidenced in writing, to you acting;

(ii) where appropriate, you put in place effective safeguards to protect your clients' confidential information; and

(iii) you are satisfied it is reasonable for you to act for all the clients.

6.3-6.5: Confidentiality and disclosure

6.3 You keep the affairs of current and former clients confidential unless disclosure is required or permitted by law or the client consents.

6.4 Where you are acting for a client on a matter, you make the client aware of all information material to the matter of which you have knowledge, except when:

(a) the disclosure of the information is prohibited by legal restrictions imposed in the interests of national security or the prevention of crime;

(b) your client gives informed consent, given or evidenced in writing, to the information not being disclosed to them;

(c) you have reason to believe that serious physical or mental injury will be caused to your client or another if the information is disclosed; or

(d) the information is contained in a privileged document that you have knowledge of only because it has been mistakenly disclosed.

6.5 You do not act for a client in a matter where that client has an interest adverse to the interest of another current or former client of you or your business or employer, for whom you or your business or employer holds confidential information which is material to that matter, unless:

> (a) effective measures have been taken which result in there being no real risk of disclosure of the confidential information; or

> (b) the current or former client whose information you or your business or employer holds has given informed consent, given or evidenced in writing, to you acting, including to any measures taken to protect their information.

7: Cooperation and accountability

7.1 You keep up to date with and follow the law and regulation governing the way you work.

7.2 You are able to justify your decisions and actions in order to demonstrate compliance with your obligations under the SRA's regulatory arrangements.

7.3 You cooperate with the SRA, other regulators, ombudsmen, and those bodies with a role overseeing and supervising the delivery of, or investigating concerns in relation to, legal services.

7.4 You respond promptly to the SRA and:

> (a) provide full and accurate explanations, information and documents in response to any request or requirement; and

> (b) ensure that relevant information which is held by you, or by third parties carrying out functions on your behalf which are critical to the delivery of your legal services, is available for inspection by the SRA.

7.5 You do not attempt to prevent anyone from providing information to the SRA or any other body exercising regulatory, supervisory, investigatory or prosecutory functions in the public interest.

7.6 You notify the SRA promptly if:

> (a) you are subject to any criminal charge, conviction or caution, subject to the Rehabilitation of Offenders Act 1974;

(b) a relevant insolvency event occurs in relation to you; or

(c) if you become aware:

(i) of any material changes to information previously provided to the SRA, by you or on your behalf, about you or your practice, including any change to information recorded in the register; and

(ii) that information provided to the SRA, by you or on your behalf, about you or your practice is or may be false, misleading, incomplete or inaccurate.

7.7 You report promptly to the SRA or another approved regulator, as appropriate, any facts or matters that you reasonably believe are capable of amounting to a serious breach of their regulatory arrangements by any person regulated by them (including you).

7.8 Notwithstanding Paragraph 7.7, you inform the SRA promptly of any facts or matters that you reasonably believe should be brought to its attention in order that it may investigate whether a serious breach of its regulatory arrangements has occurred or otherwise exercise its regulatory powers.

7.9 You do not subject any person to detrimental treatment for making or proposing to make a report or providing or proposing to provide information based on a reasonably held belief under Paragraph 7.7 or 7.8 above, or Paragraph 3.9, 3.10, 9.1(d) or (e) or 9.2(b) or (c) of the SRA Code of Conduct for Firms, irrespective of whether the SRA or another approved regulator subsequently investigates or takes any action in relation to the facts or matters in question.

7.10 You act promptly to take any remedial action requested by the SRA. If requested to do so by the SRA you investigate whether there have been any serious breaches that should be reported to the SRA.

7.11 You are honest and open with clients if things go wrong, and if a client suffers loss or harm as a result you put matters right (if possible) and explain fully and promptly what has happened and the likely impact. If requested to do so by the SRA you investigate whether anyone may have a claim against you, provide the SRA with a report on the outcome of your investigation, and notify relevant persons that they may have such a claim, accordingly.

7.12 Any obligation under this section or otherwise to notify, or provide information to, the SRA will be satisfied if you provide information to your firm's COLP or COFA, as and where appropriate, on the understanding that they will do so.

When you are providing services to the public or a section of the public

8.1: Client identification

8.1 You identify who you are acting for in relation to any matter.

8.2-8.5: Complaints handling

8.2 You ensure that, as appropriate in the circumstances, you either establish and maintain, or participate in, a procedure for handling complaints in relation to the legal services you provide.

8.3 You ensure that clients are informed in writing at the time of engagement about:

(a) their right to complain to you about your services and your charges;

(b) how a complaint can be made and to whom; and

(c) any right they have to make a complaint to the Legal Ombudsman and when they can make any such complaint.

8.4 You ensure that when clients have made a complaint to you, if this has not been resolved to the client's satisfaction within 8 weeks following the making of a complaint they are informed, in writing:

(a) of any right they have to complain to the Legal Ombudsman, the time frame for doing so and full details of how to contact the Legal Ombudsman; and

(b) if a complaint has been brought and your complaints procedure has been exhausted:

(i) that you cannot settle the complaint;

(ii) of the name and website address of an alternative dispute resolution (ADR) approved body which would be competent to deal with the complaint; and

(iii) whether you agree to use the scheme operated by that body.

8.5 You ensure that complaints are dealt with promptly, fairly, and free of charge.

8.6-8.11: Client information and publicity

8.6 You give clients information in a way they can understand. You ensure they are in a position to make informed decisions about the services they need, how their matter will be handled and the options available to them.

8.7 You ensure that clients receive the best possible information about how their matter will be priced and, both at the time of engagement and when appropriate as their matter progresses, about the likely overall cost of the matter and any costs incurred.

8.8 You ensure that any publicity in relation to your practice is accurate and not misleading, including that relating to your charges and the circumstances in which interest is payable by or to clients.

8.9 You do not make unsolicited approaches to members of the public, with the exception of current or former clients, in order to advertise legal services provided by you, or your business or employer.

8.10 You ensure that clients understand whether and how the services you provide are regulated. This includes:

> (a) explaining which activities will be carried out by you, as an authorised person;
>
> (b) explaining which services provided by you, your business or employer, and any separate business are regulated by an approved regulator; and
>
> (c) ensuring that you do not represent any business or employer which is not authorised by the SRA, including any separate business, as being regulated by the SRA.

8.11 You ensure that clients understand the regulatory protections available to them.

SRA Code of Conduct for Firms

1: Maintaining trust and acting fairly

1.1 You do not unfairly discriminate by allowing your personal views to affect your professional relationships and the way in which you provide your services.

1.2 You do not abuse your position by taking unfair advantage of clients or others.

1.3 You perform all undertakings given by you and do so within an agreed timescale or if no timescale has been agreed then within a reasonable amount of time.

1.4 You do not mislead or attempt to mislead your clients, the court or others, either by your own acts or omissions or allowing or being complicit in the acts or omissions of others (including your client).

1.5 You monitor, report and publish workforce diversity data, as prescribed.

2: Compliance and business systems

2.1 You have effective governance structures, arrangements, systems and controls in place that ensure:

> (a) you comply with all the SRA's regulatory arrangements, as well as with other regulatory and legislative requirements, which apply to you;
>
> (b) your managers and employees comply with the SRA's regulatory arrangements which apply to them;
>
> (c) your managers and interest holders and those you employ or contract with do not cause or substantially contribute to a breach of the SRA's regulatory arrangements by you or your managers or employees;
>
> (d) your compliance officers are able to discharge their duties under Paragraphs 9.1 and 9.2 below.

2.2 You keep and maintain records to demonstrate compliance with your obligations under the SRA's regulatory arrangements.

2.3 You remain accountable for compliance with the SRA's regulatory arrangements where your work is carried out through others, including your managers and those you employ or contract with.

2.4 You actively monitor your financial stability and business viability. Once you are aware that you will cease to operate, you effect the orderly wind-down of your activities.

2.5 You identify, monitor and manage all material risks to your business, including those which may arise from your connected practices.

3: Cooperation and accountability

3.1 You keep up to date with and follow the law and regulation governing the way you work.

3.2 You cooperate with the SRA, other regulators, ombudsmen and those bodies with a role overseeing and supervising the delivery of, or investigating concerns in relation to, legal services.

3.3 You respond promptly to the SRA and:

(a) provide full and accurate explanations, information and documentation in response to any requests or requirements;

(b) ensure that relevant information which is held by you, or by third parties carrying out functions on your behalf which are critical to the delivery of your legal services, is available for inspection by the SRA.

3.4 You act promptly to take any remedial action requested by the SRA.

3.5 You are honest and open with clients if things go wrong, and if a client suffers loss or harm as a result you put matters right (if possible) and explain fully and promptly what has happened and the likely impact. If requested to do so by the SRA you investigate whether anyone may have a claim against you, provide the SRA with a report on the outcome of your investigation, and notify relevant persons that they may have such a claim, accordingly.

3.6 You notify the SRA promptly:

(a) of any indicators of serious financial difficulty relating to you;

(b) if a relevant insolvency event occurs in relation to you;

(c) if you intend to, or become aware that you will, cease operating as a legal business;

(d) of any change to information recorded in the register.

3.7 You provide to the SRA an information report on an annual basis or such other period as specified by the SRA in the prescribed form and by the prescribed date.

3.8 You notify the SRA promptly if you become aware:

(a) of any material changes to information previously provided to the SRA, by you or on your behalf, about you or your managers, owners or compliance officers; and

(b) that information provided to the SRA, by you or on your behalf, about you or your managers, owners or compliance officers is or may be false, misleading, incomplete or inaccurate.

3.9 You report promptly to the SRA, or another approved regulator, as appropriate, any facts or matters that you reasonably believe are capable of amounting to a serious breach of their regulatory arrangements by any person regulated by them (including you) of which you are aware. If requested to do so by the SRA, you investigate whether there have been any serious breaches that should be reported to the SRA.

3.10 Notwithstanding Paragraph 3.9, you inform the SRA promptly of any facts or matters that you reasonably believe should be brought to its attention in order that it may investigate whether a serious breach of its regulatory arrangements has occurred or otherwise exercise its regulatory powers.

3.11 You do not attempt to prevent anyone from providing information to the SRA or any other body exercising regulatory, supervisory, investigatory or prosecutory functions in the public interest.

3.12 You do not subject any person to detrimental treatment for making or proposing to make a report or providing, or proposing to provide, information based on a reasonably held belief under Paragraph 3.9 or 3.10 above or 9.1(d) or (e) or 9.2(b) or (c) below, or under Paragraph 7.7 or 7.8 of the SRA Code of Conduct for Solicitors, RELs and RFLs, irrespective of whether the SRA or another approved regulator subsequently investigates or takes any action in relation to the facts or matters in question.

Appendix

4: Service and competence

4.1 You only act for clients on instructions from the client, or from someone properly authorised to provide instructions on their behalf. If you have reason to suspect that the instructions do not represent your client's wishes, you do not act unless you have satisfied yourself that they do. However, in circumstances where you have legal authority to act notwithstanding that it is not possible to obtain or ascertain the instructions of your client, then you are subject to the overriding obligation to protect your client's best interests.

4.2 You ensure that the service you provide to clients is competent and delivered in a timely manner, and takes account of your client's attributes, needs and circumstances.

4.3 You ensure that your managers and employees are competent to carry out their role, and keep their professional knowledge and skills, as well as understanding of their legal, ethical and regulatory obligations, up to date.

4.4 You have an effective system for supervising clients' matters.

5: Client money and assets

5.1 You properly account to clients for any financial benefit you receive as a result of their instructions, except where they have agreed otherwise.

5.2 You safeguard money and assets entrusted to you by clients and others.

6.1-6.2: Conflict of interests

6.1 You do not act if there is an own interest conflict or a significant risk of such a conflict.

6.2 You do not act in relation to a matter or a particular aspect of it if you have a conflict of interest or a significant risk of such a conflict in relation to that matter or aspect of it, unless:

> (a) the clients have a substantially common interest in relation to the matter or the aspect of it, as appropriate; or
>
> (b) the clients are competing for the same objective,

and the conditions below are met, namely that:

(i) all the clients have given informed consent, given or evidenced in writing, to you acting;

(ii) where appropriate, you put in place effective safeguards to protect your clients' confidential information; and

(iii) you are satisfied it is reasonable for you to act for all the clients.

6.3-6.5: Confidentiality and disclosure

6.3 You keep the affairs of current and former clients confidential unless disclosure is required or permitted by law or the client consents.

6.4 Any individual who is acting for a client on a matter makes the client aware of all information material to the matter of which the individual has knowledge except when:

(a) the disclosure of the information is prohibited by legal restrictions imposed in the interests of national security or the prevention of crime;

(b) the client gives informed consent, given or evidenced in writing, to the information not being disclosed to them;

(c) the individual has reason to believe that serious physical or mental injury will be caused to the client or another if the information is disclosed; or

(d) the information is contained in a privileged document that the individual has knowledge of only because it has been mistakenly disclosed.

6.5 You do not act for a client in a matter where that client has an interest adverse to the interest of another current or former client for whom you hold confidential information which is material to that matter, unless:

(a) effective measures have been taken which result in there being no real risk of disclosure of the confidential information; or

(b) the current or former client whose information you hold has given informed consent, given or evidenced in writing, to you acting, including to any measures taken to protect their information.

Appendix

7: Applicable standards in the SRA Code of Conduct for Solicitors, RELs and RFLs

7.1 The following paragraphs in the SRA Code of Conduct for Solicitors, RELs and RFLs apply to you in their entirety as though references to "you" were references to you as a firm:

(a) dispute resolution and proceedings before courts, tribunals and inquiries (2.1 to 2.7);

(b) referrals, introductions and separate businesses (5.1 to 5.3); and

(c) standards which apply when providing services to the public or a section of the public, namely client identification (8.1), complaints handling (8.2 to 8.5), and client information and publicity (8.6 to 8.11).

8: Managers in SRA authorised firms

8.1 If you are a manager, you are responsible for compliance by your firm with this Code. This responsibility is joint and several if you share management responsibility with other managers of the firm.

9: Compliance officers

9.1 If you are a COLP you must take all reasonable steps to:

(a) ensure compliance with the terms and conditions of your firm's authorisation;

(b) ensure compliance by your firm and its managers, employees or interest holders with the SRA's regulatory arrangements which apply to them;

(c) ensure that your firm's managers and interest holders and those they employ or contract with do not cause or substantially contribute to a breach of the SRA's regulatory arrangements;

(d) ensure that a prompt report is made to the SRA of any facts or matters that you reasonably believe are capable of amounting to a serious breach of the terms and conditions of your firm's authorisation, or the SRA's regulatory arrangements which apply to your firm, managers or employees;

(e) notwithstanding sub-paragraph (d), you ensure that the SRA is informed promptly of any facts or matters that you reasonably believe should be brought to its attention in order that it may investigate whether a serious breach of its regulatory arrangements has occurred or otherwise exercise its regulatory powers,

save in relation to the matters which are the responsibility of the COFA as set out in Paragraph 9.2 below.

9.2 If you are a COFA you must take all reasonable steps to:

(a) ensure that your firm and its managers and employees comply with any obligations imposed upon them under the SRA Accounts Rules;

(b) ensure that a prompt report is made to the SRA of any facts or matters that you reasonably believe are capable of amounting to a serious breach of the SRA Accounts Rules which apply to them;

(c) notwithstanding sub-paragraph (b), you ensure that the SRA is informed promptly of any facts or matters that you reasonably believe should be brought to its attention in order that it may investigate whether a serious breach of its regulatory arrangements has occurred or otherwise exercise its regulatory powers.

SRA Assessment of Character and Suitability Rules

The SRA Assessment of Character and Suitability Rules can be found on the SRA website at https://www.sra.org.uk/solicitors/standards-regulations/assessment-character-suitability-rules/.

References

The authors have consulted, and sometimes cited, the following references during the writing of this book:

Solicitors' Professional Standards: Results from the Professional Standards Survey (*Cristina Godinho (UCL) and Richard Moorhead (UCL)*)

A Behavioural Theory of Legal Ethics (*Andrew Perlman, 2015*)

Designing Ethics Indicators for Legal Services Provision (*Richard Moorhead, Victoria Hinchly, Christine Parker, David Kershaw and Soren Holm, 2012*)

Legal Risk: Definition, Management and Ethics (*Professor Richard Moorhead and Dr Steven Vaughan*)

The 2015 Ethics and Compliance Effectiveness Report

Preparatory Ethics Training for Future Solicitors (*Kim Economides and Justine Rogers, 2009*)

Independence, Representation and Risk: An Empirical Exploration of the Management of Client Relationships by Large Law Firms (*Claire Coe and Dr Steven Vaughan, 2015*)

In Professions We Trust: Fostering Virtuous Practitioners in Teaching Law and Medicine (*Phillip Bond, Elena Antonacopoulou and Adrian Pabst*)

CISI Code of Conduct

Legal Ethics at the Initial Stage: A Model Curriculum (*Professor Andrew Boon, 2010*)

Lawyers as Professionals and as Citizens: Key Roles and Responsibilities in the 21st Century (*Ben W Heineman Jr, William F Lee and David B Wilkins*)

Virtuous Character for the Practice of Law Research Report (*James Arthur, Kristjan Kristjansson, Hywel Thomas, Michael Holdsworth, Luca Badini Confalonieri and Tian Qiu*)

Index

A

ACAS conciliation 225

Accounts Rules 25

Adjudication 226

Administration of oaths, affirmations or declarations 129

Adversarial system 201

Advertising 161

Advice of a barrister 158

Alternative Dispute Resolution (ADR) 199

    adjudication 226

    arbitration 221

    collaborative law 224

    collaborative lite process 225

    conciliation 225

    Dispute Review Board 226

    Early Neutral Evaluation (ENE) 226

    facilitative mediation 217

    forms of 211

    liti-mediation 217

    mediation 217

    negotiation 212

    no third party 212

    regulation of 211

Amoral solicitor 15

Anti-money laundering (AML) 43

A Question of Trust 4, 26

Arbitration 221

Arbitration Act 1996 221

Artificial Intelligence (AI) 231, 236

B

Bar Standards Board 31

Big Data 241

Bitcoin 239

Blockchains 231, 236, 237

Blogs 182, 197

Breach of contract 154

Breach of duty of care 155

    loss as a result of 155

Breach of integrity 39

C

Case Management Systems (CMS) 237

Character and Suitability Rules 2, 53

Chartered Institute for Securities & Investment (CISI) 12

Chartered Institute of Arbitrators (CIArb) 221

Chatbots 235, 241

CILEx 31

Client care 88

Code of Conduct for Firms 2, 25

Code of Conduct for Solicitors 2, 24

Codes of Conduct

    client's perspective 94

Collaborative law 224

Collaborative lite process 225

Compensation 144

Competence 27

Complaints 141

    complex cases 156

    failure to follow instructions 146

    from client 144

    handling 151

Compliance officers 103

    Compliance Officer for Finance and Administration (COFA) 2

    Compliance Officer for Legal Practice (COLP) 2

    role of COFA 42

    role of COLP 42

Conciliation 225

Conflict of interests 20

Contacting the opposing party 132

Corporate/commercial lawyers 104

Costs

    costs rules 202

    pricing information 145, 148

Criminal activity 21, 23, 27

D

Data protection 43, 133

Data Protection Act 2018 43

Digital Currencies 239

Dishonesty 24, 27

Dispute Review Board 226

Diversity training	40	solicitor	11, 16, 58, 72
DIY law	235	Ethically minimalist behaviour	48
Duty		Ethical/moral belief system	11
of care to third parties	107, 155	Ethics	
of due care and skill	112	and competence	25
to clients	108	and compliance	17, 32
to self-report	52	and morals	38

E

		and regulation	19
Early Neutral Evaluation	226	and social media	161, 167
Electronic communications	191	in financial services	42
Enforcement strategy	25	of ADR	206
Equality, diversity and inclusion (EDI)	39	training	11
		Executive tribunal	225
Ethical		Expert determinations	226

F

choices	10		
considerations of ADR	228	Facebook	161, 171, 172, 197
considerations of the CPR	203	Facilitative mediation	217
decision-making	32, 72	Fairness, definition of	94
dilemmas	63	Financial Conduct Authority (FCA)	42
minimalist	11		
motto	33	Firm culture	72
scenarios	6	Flickr	183

Foreseeability test (duty of care) 155

For-profit third party funding 131

Forums 171

Fraud 24

I

Immoral solicitor 15

Independence within the firm 74

Influence of other solicitors 74

Instagram 183

Integrity test (CISI) 12

Internal belief system 11

Internal hierarchy of a private firm 73

J

Justice and reasonableness test (duty of care) 155

Justice NOT Profit 130

K

Knowledge of the law (lack of) 156

L

Lawtech 231

   chatbots 235

   definition of 235

   DIY law 235

   fintech 260

   legal practice and risk management 235

   pitfalls of 246

   policies and training 255

   precedent artificial intelligence 235

   research enhancement 235

   risk overview 260

   smart contract drafting 235

Legal Ombudsman 2

   charges 153

Legal practice and risk management 235

Legal Practice Course 12

Legal rules v ethical rules 14

Legal Services Act 2007 19

Legal trends predictions precedent 242

LinkedIn 171, 177, 197

Litigants in Person 124, 125

   Law Society practice note 132

Litigation	199	Nuisance claims	159
Liti-mediation	217		

O

Lying to a client	146	Online forums	198

M

		Online identity	162
Machine Learning	236, 239	Outcomes-Focused Regulation (OFR)	3, 24
Managing client expectations	145		

P

Mandatory Principles (SRA Code of Conduct) *See* Principles		Personal integrity	87
Marketing	161, 163	Personal virtues	55
McKenzie Friends	132, 133	Power imbalance between a solicitor and client	100
Mediation	217	Practice Management Systems	237
Mediation Information & Assessment Meeting (MIAM)	207	Precedent artificial intelligence	235
Mistakes	123, 124	Precedent generators	242
correcting mistakes of third parties	120	Principles	3, 24, 30
		conflicting	31, 60
Misuse of client money	27	Principle 1	3, 34

N

		Principle 2	3, 35
National Crime Agency (NCA)	43	Principle 3	3, 35
Negligence	153	Principle 4	3, 36, 49
Negotiation	212	Principle 5	3, 37, 49
Networking	161	Principle 6	3, 39
New Standards and Regulations (STaRs)	19, 24	Principle 7	3, 40

287

Principles of negligence	154	backdated attendance note	152
Privacy settings 172, 178, 184,	186	confidentiality	71
Private emails	56	conflict of interests	20, 22
Proceeds of Crime Act 2002	23	conveyancing	121
Professional influence	140	criminal breaches	34
Professional Standards Survey	4	criminal legal aid applications	113
Proximity test (duty of care)	155	data protection	45

R

		deceiving clients	157
Registered European Lawyer (REL)	2	Declaration of Trust	114
Registered Foreign Lawyer (RFL)	2	derisory emails about client	191
Regulatory lawtech (regtech)	245	disbursements	104
Relationship between law and ethics	12	disclosing client information online	232
Research enhancement	235	double billing	69
Reserved legal services	133	drink driving	54
Risk index	25	encouraging settlement	158
Rules-based regulation	3, 24	fabricating documents	80

S

		Facebook post	174
Scenarios		forging signatures	129
abuse of process	127	fraudulent practice	7
anti-money laundering	44	helping someone to avoid arrest	96
arbitration	222		

inadequate pricing information	149	terms of a consent order	218
inappropriate dealings with the client	99	the future of lawtech	257
		third party funding	130
lawtech's flippant approach to the law	243	trend predicting software	253
		undercharged in a restaurant	59
LinkedIn post	180	undertakings	118

Self-reporting	52, 54
Service standards	145
Settlements	158
'Smart' Case/practice management systems	242
Smart contract drafting	235, 241
Snapchat	183

Social media

benefits of	164
blogs	182, 197
BSB guidelines	195
combining private and professional accounts	185
dealing with backlash	193
Facebook	172, 197
Flickr	183
forums	171, 179

LinkedIn request from client	188
litigant in person	125
lying in court	62
lying to cover oversight	146
lying to your client	208
omission on consent order	215
outline of a problem faced by a practitioner	6
part 36 offer	204
partnership agreement	111
precedent generators	249
pressure on junior solicitor	76
professional misconduct	53
recoverable costs	139
rude emails	57
stealing clients	134
tampering with forms	63

historical content/posts	186	Solicitors Practice Rules 1990 (SPR)	19
Instagram	183	Solicitors' Professional Standards	27
LinkedIn	171, 177, 197		
online forums	198	Specialist lawyers	156
personal accounts	164	Speculative claims	159
platforms	171	SRA Code of Conduct 2011	19
policies	190	SRA regulation: Current system	2
privacy settings	172	Statement of Legal Knowledge	123
professional accounts	164	Statement of Solicitor Competence	26
risks	166		

T

Snapchat	183	Tampering with documents	114
SRA guidelines	194	Terms of business	145
Twitter	161, 171, 175, 197	Third parties	
websites	171, 182, 197	external pressure by	73
WhatsApp	100, 179	influence by	81
WordPress	183	solicitors' duties	108
YouTube	171, 178, 197	Third party funding	130
Solicitor/client relationship	87	conflicts	132
Solicitors Code of Conduct 2007 (SCC)	19	Threshold criteria (SRA Statement of Competence)	123
Solicitors Disciplinary Tribunal (SDT)	5	Twitter	197

U

UCL Report of Professional Standards	67
Undergraduate Law Course	12
Undertakings	115
authority to give	116
breach of	117
enforcement of	118
interpretation of	119
recording of	120
sanction for breach of	117
Unethical types of behaviour	51
Uninsured entities	133
Unqualified/unregulated entities	133
McKenzie Friends	132
paralegal firms	132

V

Vexatious claims	159
Virtue ethics	17
Vulnerable clients	98

W

Wasted costs orders	158
Websites	171, 182, 197
WhatsApp	100, 179
WordPress	183

Y

YouTube	171, 178, 197